James W. Steele

Frontier army sketches

James W. Steele

Frontier army sketches

ISBN/EAN: 9783337147938

Printed in Europe, USA, Canada, Australia, Japan

Cover: Foto ©ninafisch / pixelio.de

More available books at **www.hansebooks.com**

FRONTIER

ARMY SKETCHES.

By JAMES W. STEELE.

* * * "Vulgar, again! everybody has a different sense for that word, I think. What is vulgar?"

Christie. "Voolgar folk sit on an chair, ane, twa, whiles three hours, eatin' an' abune a' drinkin', as still as hoegs, or gruntin' puir every-day clashes, goessip, rubbich; when ye are aside them, ye might as weel be aside a cuddy; they canna gie ye a sang, they canna gie ye a story, they canna think ye a thoucht, to save their useless lives; that's voolgar folk."—CHARLES READE.

CHICAGO:
JANSEN, McCLURG & COMPANY.
1883.

PREFACE.

THERE is an interesting phase of American life that has hitherto had its chief chronicler in the dime novel and its most frequent interpreter in the blood-and-terror drama. Only two or three authors, and among them the foremost humorists of their time, seem to have truly seen, and having seen, to have been able to make others see, the unwritten and unconscious poetry and the dramatic character of those isolated lives that, careless of themselves, pass away in the process of erecting an empire whose boundless horizon, whose toils and pains, whose untrodden loneliness, have all combined to form a class in which the characters of the desperado and the gentleman have strangely united their characteristics; where love, longing, and hope exist without any of their appropriate surroundings, and where grim humor and deep feeling, lacking all their usual forms, find expression not in words alone but in every act of life.

Beneath all the melancholy loneliness of wide plains, and the monotonous and oppressive sternness of mountains that lie changeless forever, there is a subtle something that cannot be described, or drawn, or clearly defined; a something that distinguishes everything from that which it most resembles; that makes a portrait to differ from the cold outlines of a photograph, and a face to differ from both. To capture this essence of description and cause it to appear in words upon the printed page, is the task of genius; and the author does not flatter himself that he has accomplished it. He is only certain that it is not enough to reproduce the impressions made upon the eye and ear, and that if there be something more than that between the lines of these sketches, the public will discover it.

These scenes are not inventions, and these men and women not mere figments of the brain. During years of association with them, they produced certain impressions that time has not dissipated, that have ripened with absence, and that, given in fragments imperfectly, and touched upon in transient articles, are now for the first time, but finally, given to the public in a form of some arrangement and compactness. They have been valuable as a private and personal possession. They have furnished food for pleasant thought amid the vicissitudes, labors, perplexities, and endless changes that come to every man. It may be a mistake to suppose that the aroma exhaled from such recollections may be conveyed to the reader's senses also; yet it is with something of that hope, that these legends of the campfire, and sketches of the soldier, the borderer, and the dumb denizens of the wilderness, are given to the reading world.

General Orders and the reports of district commanders are but dull reading, and there is no colder volume than the "Regulations." Officers of the army are not greatly given to the platform and the monthly magazine, and what they know and might so easily relate they seem purposely to be silent about. Yet they have had most to do with the development of Western civilization, have mingled with all the characters of the border, are themselves members of the unique community to which they do not seem to belong, and, leading lives apart, are yet intimate with all their surroundings. As a very unimportant member of the military brotherhood, the author gathered the impressions which, once written and arranged, seemed yet to lack the essential of a name. Many years of association with all classes, professions, and conditions have passed since then. All the impressions of the soldier have been modified, and have taken the form of conviction. And that conviction is, that, with all his little and great failings, the American regular officer is the most accomplished of his calling among all the varied uniforms of the world, and that he remains, through all vicissitudes, the most self-sacrificing and uncomplaining of all the life-long servants of the Republic. He is a frontiersman in the best sense of that word, and, unspoiled by association, he remains true to his untarnished record of a hundred years — a gentleman. He has been always respected, and not seldom loved, by the turbulent and impatient characters who have constantly surrounded him. As all the incidents and characters that go to make up these chapters have been seen and understood from the military standpoint and gathered from the inexhaustible fund of military narrative, while they are not stories of "battles, sieges, fortunes," they are yet what they are called — "Frontier Army Sketches."

I may add, finally, that it seems impossible to explain the interest that clings about lives that are the poorest and humblest that this world knows, except upon the hypothesis that poverty and hope have ever an unconscious pathos of their own. If it be true that men and women are ever and always the same — the helpless victims of circumstance that seems intention and of a fatality that seems a plan — still everything that this whirling cinder bears upon her wrinkled surface fades into insignificance when compared with the myriad-minded being whose loves and hopes, whose toils and disappointments, make up the sum of life. These are all of that class whom the world might well spare, if by the world we mean only those who fill the largest places in life, but who at last do but take their places with all the rest, in the commingled dust of beggars and of heroes. It was humble life as the author knew it, in that *terra incognita* of the far Southwest. That land of dreams and shadows and disappointing realities has changed its superficial character by having been opened to the world by railways that stretch their iron length through valleys that were voiceless when the material of these sketches was acquired, and beside reluctant streams that have crawled slowly over their leagues of sand since the soldier and the priest came together and encamped beside them. Yet not advancing civilization, nor anything, can materially change that realm of rainless years; of rivers without verdure; of brown mountains; of wide and silent deserts; of thorns, and cactus, and wind-blown sands; of indolence, idleness, and peace; of cloud shadows and the brightness of a sky forever blue; of the hopeless sadness of perishing races stranded at last upon those tideless shores. As reminiscences born in such a land, touched here and there with the recollections wrought by a faded uniform and a rusty sword, this little volume is offered to the reader.

CONTENTS.

I.	Captain Jinks	9
II.	Jornada Del Muerto	24
III.	Men of the Border	43
IV.	Brown's Revenge	58
V.	Copper Distilled	80
VI.	Joe's Pocket	105
VII.	New Mexican Common Life	143
VIII.	"Peg,"—The Story of a Dog	163
IX.	A Good Indian	183
X.	Jack's Divorce	198
XI.	Coyotes	210
XII.	A Guard-House Gentleman	220
XIII.	Woman Under Difficulties	240
XIV.	The Priest of El Paso	254
XV.	A Fight Between Buffaloes	272
XVI.	Chicquita	282
XVII.	Army Mules	301
XVIII.	A Lonesome Christian	314

FRONTIER ARMY SKETCHES.

I.

CAPTAIN JINKS.

IT is necessary to caution the reader against misapprehension at the beginning. This chapter does not contemplate a discussion of the merits or peculiarities of that ancient gem in the repertory of *opera bouffe*, which has sometime since been sung and acted to its death, but which may still linger in the recollections of some of the elders. But there is a great deal of truth told in broad burlesque; if it makes a palpable impression upon the public there must always be truth as a basis. The genius, whoever he was, who wrote "Captain Jinks," had in his mind a portrait, more or less truthful, when he concocted the atrocious jingle and called it a song. Very few of those who have heard it, and still fewer of those who have sung it, ever saw anything in it beyond a little fun, and an opportunity for some stalwart actress, with startling physical development and a wonderful yellow wig, to mince before the footlights, and display her misconception of him who, even more than the lamented Dundreary, is the ideal of gentlemanly snobbery.

As hinted, Captain Jinks is not entirely a myth; but there may have been many portraits of the professional soldier in more lasting literature that were scarcely nearer the truth. Thackeray must have watched him as he sauntered down the street, and gone home and made a sketch of him. Dickens had an inkling of him, though he, too, knew him only from afar. It is more than probable that the large class of men who are apparently idle, careless, dressy, nonchalant, in time of peace, and brave, enduring and self-sacrificing in time of war, are much the same the world over. There has ever been among mankind a weakness for the sound of the drum, the strains of martial music, and the rustle of a banner that represented a common cause, whatever that cause might be; for the glint of bullion and the measured tread of battalions, and the touch of that slender glittering thing that in all time has stood for justice and honor, and not infrequently for that right which, with a change of its initial letter, means a very different thing. It is this common passion which makes the varied uniforms of the world cover hearts very nearly alike in what they love and hate.

But there is one individual of this type who is especially the present subject of discourse. Of all the soldiers of the world, he is least known on fashionable streets, and most seldom seen at select parties and in the choice seats at the opera. With civilization and its pleasures and occupations he has little to do. There are few gay seasons or long leaves-of-absence for him. Of all the homes along the far border of a growing republic, his is farthest and most isolated. He is the soldier of a country that has the brightest and newest banner of all, dyed though it has been with the stains of many a desperate field; and those silken folds represent to him all there is of abstract devotion and love. It is that of a country which in its supreme struggle raised and sent to the field the most intelligent, enduring, undaunted and brilliant armies the world has ever seen; which in a single year, in the midst of divided sentiment, could rouse in her sons all the traditional skill, courage, valor and patriotism which lurked in the hearts of a long-peaceful but fighting and glory-loving race. But at the end they sank again into the office, the shop, and the furrow, as mysteriously as sank the targe and plaid of the followers of Roderick Dhu upon the mountain side; and he, the last remainder of the host, thinks, not without cause, that his cold-shouldered country has almost forgotten him.

Under all these disadvantages, the United States army officer claims intimate kinship with his brethren of the buttons the world over. There are none who wear with more jauntiness a modest blue coat and the very nattiest trousers and boots, or whose caps are more perilously perched upon the forward right-hand corners of ambrosial heads. In the matter of mustaches he excels the German, and in vivacity of movement he is beyond the Frenchman. He is a rattling shot at billiards, and very cool and silent at whist. He has an eye to the points of horses, an acute judgment as to the qualities of liquors, and really and truly adores womankind with a devotion and strength that cavils at nothing they may do, think, or say, and which, had he no other virtue, is sufficient to keep him forever in the great brotherhood of gentlemen. He is isolated and utterly cut off from that world which is all there is to most of us, and his world comprises as its chiefest features only arms, orders, and duty, and the apt surroundings he has contrived for himself in the midst of a thousand difficulties and disadvantages.

But here, in mountain fastnesses and the dreary isolation of the wilderness, you strangely come upon the only genuine chivalry extant in American life. I may be taken to task for this wholesale statement; for the over-busy, nervous, money-getting citizens of this great country claim all good qualities as their own. Therefore I will explain: Chivalry, in its essence, means not a careless but a careful regard for the opinions, feelings, and personal comfort of others, but more especially of women. Besides that, it means entire but polite candor, and no tricks in trade or anything else. It means that the affairs of life are conducted "on honor." Captain Jinks in the wilderness practises this code, and has done so for so long that while staid and respectable citizens might smile at his punctiliousness, they, together with their wives and daughters, would find him a very pleasant companion, and might do well to try to find time to imitate some of his very foolish airs.

Do the gentlemen who sit a-row at attractive loitering-places rise up *en masse* when one poor little woman passes by? And if they do not, and are excused from that, are they ever careful lest some masculine phrase should reach her ear, or the cigar smoke should blow in her face? Is a woman's request a binding law if it be a possible thing? Most of these questions must be answered in the negative. Very often the American gentleman accosts his lady friend in the street with his hat over his eyes, his hands in his pockets, and with a lazy politeness which indicates that he is anxious she should not make the mistake of imagining she is any better than he.

We may go further, and, leaving out women, inquire how Captain Jinks possibly excels us. He takes off his hat in his own office or room, and does likewise when he comes into yours. He expects to be requested to seat himself, and if you allow him to stand he goes away and does not come back so long as he can avoid it. He does not often back-bite and insinuate, and you cannot always know upon your first acquaintance with him what and whom he especially dislikes and hates. Such things, with him, lead to rapid settlements of difficulties; and Jinks is therefore, as we should all be, careful. There is no need of any action for slander where Jinks and his companions live, for words and opinions are supposed to be valuable, and are cautiously used. He will endeavor to lend or give you anything you ask,— but you must not ask. There are other things he will do upon proper invitation, which are not so much to his credit. A little sip of something out of a mahogany case is seldom offered at the wrong time o' day. A little shuffling of a clean deck, and an unimportant transfer of currency, is generally agreeable when he is not busy,— and he never is. Jinks is somewhat frivolous, over-polite, and nonchalant, and carries a very high nose ; but he will fight. Any intimation that he would not, would hasten matters very fast in that direction. And the ugliest antagonist in the world is this same tender-handed fop, because it is in his line of business. He stands in the same relation to other men in this respect that the terrier does to other dogs ; he spends no time in carefully considering the size of his antagonist. Only of late years has the duello come to be looked upon as wrong and foolish by the great majority of army officers. Elderly gentlemen, long since retired to office-chairs, have recollections of that sort which they sometimes mention ; and it appears that even in these instances death was more often bargained for than achieved.

Captain Jinks is a strictly professional man, and after some years of military life knows more of his specialty — which is a good deal to know — than he generally gets fair credit for. There is a common impression that to own a commission signed by the President, and to wear a uniform, is to be a soldier. Many an inchoate hero has had this impression dissipated by a few months' association with the old ones. The traditional routine, the customs, the business, and the exact drill, require years in their mastery. The army is almost wholly governed by an unwritten code, which has, in its place, as much binding force as the common law. You would not suspect that Jinks was ever a business man; yet the complicated system of accountability for public property requires something very little short of business talent for its proper comprehension. It is the most endless and intricate bundle of red tape imaginable, at least to the beginner; but, if not clear, it is at least accurate, to the practised quartermaster. The government is an uncompromising creditor, and will stop Jinks's pay for an old camp-kettle, ten years after the loss occurred, if things come to the worst. He is accountable for all the houses, fuel, forage, animals, tools, wagons, and scattered odds and ends of a post as large as a respectable village, the residence of some hundreds of people. They are all on his "papers," and must be cared for and kept straight. Every company commander must of necessity be a business man, and has a running account with a hundred men. Military efficiency means money, in the sense that there can be no efficiency without it; and the first qualification of an officer of any grade or station is economy and good judgment in the care of property and the expenditure of funds.

Nor is this all. Like an editor, Jinks must have a very varied and extensive fund of general information. He is alike autocrat and justice of the peace. He is the head and leader of a hundred careless, irresponsible men, who in time become human automatons, obeying orders and doing nothing more. He learns, through his intercourse with them, to know intimately each one, though at a distance.

He is often called upon to exercise the functions of physician, priest, and executor, to the same man. He must know how to exercise at once kindness and firmness, and to command the fullest respect with some degree of love. If there is a foible, a weakness, a want of courage or capacity, on the part of the commander, be sure the ranks will find it out. Jinks is a tyrant as well, and the fact need not be disguised from a thousand who know at least that much of him. So are railroad managers, the heads of manufacturing establishments, and "bosses" the world over. But the even tenor of his tyranny is assured by those "regulations" under which the common soldier's rights and privileges are as fully guaranteed to him as are those of his commander. Jinks and his companions have made some of the most daring and careful explorations of modern times. They traversed the mountain passes of an unknown world more than fifty years ago, and mapped and described the routes of travel and immigration long before railways and immigration were thought of. They did it faithfully and skilfully, and without any reward. There is even at this late day a more accurate knowledge of the climates, characteristics, geography, and natural history of the world west of the Missouri, among the officers of the army, than among all the *savans*.

Perhaps it may not be uninteresting to know how Captain Jinks lives. The changeless empire of monotony and silence hedges him in. Nowhere within reaching distance are any of those things that the majority of mankind value most. He has but to go a little way from the flag-staff to be utterly alone. Yet, so far as his little acre of actual occupancy goes, he has transformed the desert. Here is a quadrangular space, as neatly kept as a parlor floor. In the centre floats always the sheeny representative of that for which the soldier lives. On every hand are the oddly-shaped houses, sometimes handsome and costly, often only log cabins or adobes. But you will find nothing like squalor within. There is comfort and neatness always, and not infrequently elegance, and a very successful attempt at luxury. As a rule, Jinks and his wife care little for the house itself, if only the furnishing reaches the proper standard of luxury and taste. There are books, music, curtains, carpets, a very well-furnished table, and a very fair display of china and silver. Jinks is something of an epicure, and frequently dines upon dainties which an alderman could not procure. He saves himself from an hour of inanity every afternoon by thinking what he will have for dinner, and then asks every disengaged person he can find to come and help him eat it. You wonder, as you watch this hospitable soldier in his wanderings, where he obtains the spice of content. In these houses are to be found elegant and well-dressed women, though peradventure their gowns may not be in the latest fashion, and their social gossip not of the latest sensation.

Around this nucleus cluster the thousand belongings of military civilization. Horses neigh in populous stables, and mules perform their characteristic antics in the corral. The sound of hammer and file is heard, and the woodyard and warehouse are open. There is the trader's store—an immensely attractive spot, which may be called the club-room of the border. There the loafing instinct which Jinks has in common with the rest of mankind is gratified by the clatter of ivory balls and the aroma of tobacco. These are the only features of Jinks's life which make that life like that of the world to which he no longer pertains, and which, with all its enjoyable things, he has by no means forgotten, although it seems to have almost forgotten him. There is no danger that he will ever degenerate. The discipline of his daily life would keep him from that. His military ceremonies are performed in full dress, and midnight on the lonely guard-beat sees the untimely ceremony of "grand rounds" performed with as much punctiliousness as though in view of the commander-in-chief.

But the incorrigible Captain Jinks will swagger, will insist on regarding all professions below par in comparison with his, and will so persist in carrying an air of careless superiority with him wherever he goes that the more sombre-clad and fogyish portions of mankind will look slightly askance at him, and in some instances conceive quite a dislike to him. But we must be allowed to remark that he would be rather a poor soldier if he were not more or less guilty of these things. It is only when he is placed among civilians that they are noticeable; and they are the direct result of an isolated professional training. Is not the sailor known of all men at sight? And did anyone ever think of it as strange that he was not in all particulars like themselves? A man who has spent years in the acquirement of certain unconscious personal traits and ways cannot be expected to divest himself of them as he would put off a garment. He is no soldier who is not proud of his uniform, and in nine cases in ten the American officer will be found to be an honest man, and in the strictest sense a gentleman. His life in peace is one long preparation for that hour of his country's need when he shall lead up to the battery the blue ranks he has so often drilled, and follow into the jaws of death the starry emblem he has so often gathered in his arms as it came down at the sunset gun. Every year he endures hardships at the camp-fire and upon the march, of which he gives no sign as you see him passing by. We cannot blame him if he be, or seem, a little proud of the slender blade which, after all, is not his but his country's. Let us not be too much mistaken in our Captain Jinks. Of such as he — just such foppish, careless fellows — have ere now been made great generals, lamented heroes, statesmen, and presidents. Useless ornament though he might be if the millennium were only come, and reminder of the strength of monarchies rather than of peaceful republics, the time has been when a few more available Jinkses would have saved the country many a life and many a million of treasure, when, in impending peril, we scarcely knew the equipment of a camp or the duties of a picket-guard.

It would be easy to discourse upon the lights and shadows of Jinks's life in a manner that, while it would do no harm, and might even be considered flattering to him, he would resent as an unwarrantable intrusion into his private affairs; for one of his characteristics is, that he has never seemed anxious to have himself and his belongings — his tastes, traits, loves, hates, and the details of his private life — inquired into and discussed by mankind. He has, I think, seldom been heard to complain that people do not understand him. If it is because he has long ceased to expect that they should, the conclusion has given him little pain, for he has also ceased to care. The army is, indeed, a little world by itself, that is unaffected by stocks and trade, by flood, fire, or disaster, by changes in politics or revivals of religion. In it the lines are drawn very straight, and are not often crossed. It has its own news, its own gossip, its own penalties, and its especial pleasures. One would not suppose that the element of domesticity had much place there; yet under singular difficulties this is one of its strongest features. Jinks, as a family man, seems capable of mingling with great skill the characters of *pater familias* and the occasional roisterer. He has a vivid conception and a keen appreciation of home for its own sake — a home that he never made and cannot own, that does not suit him and cannot be altered, and that he leaves, in his innumerable pilgrimages from post to post, without a sigh, cheered by the hope of a better. Yet one may recall, among his recollections of that frontier that is a thousand miles beyond the crudest civilization, homes that were bright with the refinements of the highest type of our social life, that were filled with cheerfulness and warmed by the indescribable felicities that made the place restful and luxuriant with that rest and luxury that do not depend upon the price of the furniture. Jinks has absorbed all the good there is in the peculiar form of aristocracy he affects. His dining-table possesses a social and material charm quite irresistible to all who are so fortunate as to get their legs under it. One goes away and asks himself where all these things came from, and ever after remembers that spot in the coyote-haunted desert which offered him so restful a glimpse of the beauty of woman and home, and a taste of the clean hospitality of a gentleman about whom there was neither effort nor pretence.

Aladdin is a character of childish fable. There are no fairies; alchemy was a dream; men are only men. From whence does Jinks derive the mysterious quality that enables him to survive the crudest associations, the wildest surroundings, the hardest fare upon the weariest marches, the slenderest resources, the most thankless services, and still remain the inimitable Jinks — clean, quiet, nonchalant, transforming the spot where he is bidden to abide, changing all the sensations of the place where he has pitched his tents? It seems a marked peculiarity of the American soldier. He is Jinks unconsciously. That celebrated charge of "conduct unbecoming an officer and a gentleman," upon which the plumed and buttoned and intensely official court-martial assembles, hints at the deepest infamy of military life; and that is a most damning specification, if proven, which asserts that "in this the said

Lieutenant So-and-so wilfully lied." It is so arranged that Captain Jinks may be guilty of a thousand peccadilloes; may spend his nights at poker, and his leisure hours at any gallantry that may be at hand; but he must do his whole duty in camp and field, and privately and officially must keep himself clear of any possible entanglement in sly deception or private crookedness. He does not always succeed in this; *errare est humanum*. But then he gets himself cashiered.

If Jinks were better known, he might travel long and far upon his character as "a good fellow." He may if he will, and often does, acquire an inexhaustible fund of anecdote and personal reminiscence. He knows well the by-ways and corners, not of cities, but of the wide domain of the republic. The dews and damps of innumerable midnights, the grays of a thousand mornings, the shadows of mountain pines, the wide loneliness of trackless wastes, the vicissitudes of the camp and the march, the familiar touch of earth and the companionship of nature, have all combined in his education, and allied themselves with that imaginativeness of his without which he would be but a mere frontiersman like the rest. There are few reminiscences more charming than those he can call up when he will, and it seems to please him to clothe the most doleful and disappointing of his experiences in the garb of the ridiculous, and to burlesque the tragic element of all his adventures by flood and field.

There seems to be, in Jinks's case, neither adequate incentive nor sufficient reward for the desperate bravery in behalf of country and cause which he often displays. There are no spectators, no press bulletins, no medals or stars, not even promotion, as his reward. Plain and mountain-pass have witnessed many a heroic death that was never mentioned in the newspapers, and that no one cared for but a wife, a mother, or a far-away sweetheart. Many a pallid face amid the grasses of the prairie, and many a bloody blue coat, have the stars looked down upon after a day of thirst and hopelessness and desperate defence. Unknown amid the eternal silences that are his battle-fields, there is many a mound unmarked by so much as an inscription, washed by the rains and digged by the wolves, where some hero of the republic sleeps. He at least does his first and last great duty unhesitatingly and always. So long as there was a cartridge or a man, there is no instance of vacillation or surrender in the annals of far western warfare. As Custer died, with all his men around him, so are all the Jinkses expected to go when the occasion calls. The universal civilian should remember, and be no more than just, that his fair record of courage has never had a stain, that his life challenges the admiration of every man whose heart swells at the story of dauntless valor, and that he is, after all, as fair an example as our civilization can show of what, for want of a better name, we call a Gentleman.

II.

JORNADA DEL MUERTO.

ONE evening, about sunset, the vehicle which is by courtesy called a coach, drawn by four little mules, with its driver and expressman, and four passengers inside, started out of the obscure village of Peralta on that southward journey which few who have made it will ever forget, and which afterwards seems a strange adventure, undertaken under cover of darkness, and for some purpose that was itself a dream.

Peralta is the very dogsburg of a land of squalid towns. It is as though it had been gently shaken in a blanket, and indiscriminately dropped in the midst of a few acres of sand. Sand is there an element. It blows through every chink and cranny, and lies ankle deep in the street. It pervades all that is eaten and drunk and breathed, and lies in windrows and heaps in the meandering street. This is all in accordance with the Mexican idea; for a few hundred yards away the ground is grass-grown and hard, and that which stands in the changing sand from chance might easily have been placed upon solid ground by purpose. Worse than all, it stands at the hither end of that ninety miles of treeless and waterless wilderness that to many has been in fact all that its name implies: *jornada del muerto*— "the journey of death."

Of the four passengers, one was a medical officer of the army, one was a trader, one a man who was anything and had no characteristics save that he wore a blue blouse and had a gold bar on his shoulder. The fourth, a large man in middle life, who sat with his back to the front and his long limbs thrown across the middle seat, was as evidently a genuine borderer as though that fact had been placarded upon him. His great beard was plentifully sprinkled with gray, and the soles of his huge boots, upright before his audience, seemed as though they might serve as tombstones should he chance to follow an old-time fashion of his kind and be buried in them. His slouch hat was pulled low over a pair of gray eyes and a kindly and honest face, and he held his Winchester gun across his knee with that constant yet careless grasp which is one of the small signs betokening the man accustomed to danger and to the vigilance which in these regions becomes a habit.

The gold and purple and amber faded, and the far snow grew pink and gray, then whiter than before in the starlight, and soon there was nothing of earth in the scene save the tall cactuses that took fantastic shapes as they nodded against the glow of the horizon, and the vague and misty undulations of a wilderness that, clothed in night and silence, seemed a part of some other and unreal world.

Four women together, strange to each other, and without some slight counterpoise of masculinity, would either have kept silence for a long time at first, or have politely and distantly chatted. But men do not so; and each of our travellers had in a short time given his fellows some vague idea of who he was, where he was born, and what he liked best in men, horses, climates, and cookery;—not specifically and in order, but as men are sure to talk of such things. Then comes a little modest bragging on the part of each; and he who goes too far in that is straightway snubbed into ill-humor or docility, as the case may be, either of which conditions answers the purpose equally well. After this comes silence, yawning, and finally sleep. Only part of this programme could be carried out here. Sociability was a necessity; for if four men sleep on the Jornada, popular tradition would make it seem probable that they might not awake again. No man in those days became absorbed in his neighbor's story or his own, to the extent that his ear was not also open to the far-away galloping or the sudden shout that proclaims that ubiquitous Apache who is so much dreaded and talked about and so seldom seen.

The desire for something outside of one's own ever-revolving thoughts is as common as humanity. To this end is all that immense literature that is born in a night and dies in the morning. For the gratification of the appetite which is insatiable, are the remotest corners of the earth ransacked, and all that is done and suffered in all climes and races condensed into paragraphs and laid at even the day-laborer's door. But where this is impossible and unknown, its place is taken by an art the oldest and most graceful in the world — the art of story-telling. To the dweller in remote and unfrequented corners of the earth the ability to wander easily through the past of his life, to talk of the eternal *ego* without egoism, to cause his limited audience to see his situations as plainly as he remembers them, and to call out the laugh or the curse which is his applause and reward, is considered as a matter of course. The silent man is looked upon with general suspicion, and has few friends. But no man is asked formally or in turn to tell a story. He begins as soon as he can get an audience by cutting in upon his neighbor's fast-waning discourse, and he continues through a running fire of comments, jokes, and minor adventures. This, with the addition of some show of form, is the much-vaunted Indian oratory. This is that art of talking in which rough men sometimes attain a smoothness and proficiency that might well be envied in the politest circles of the great world in which it is popularly supposed everything is done that is ever done, everything known that is within the bounds of human attainment and endeavor. It is the art that is simplest and most attractive where form is absent, and where humor and pathos lack egoism and consciousness.

For the most part, the large man was silent. His companions seemed none of them to be of the class with which he was most at home. The trader told of events which had occurred in a country neighborhood in some Eastern state, and duly mentioned the names and relationships of all his characters, with other important and interesting details. The medical man told of college adventures and flirtations, and touched a little upon science. The man who was nothing and had no particular character, sat silent, only occasionally throwing in an interjection or an exclamation of mild astonishment. He was not yet acclimated, and his course of action undoubtedly tended to make him popular with the doctor and the trader.

Finally, that waning blood-red morning moon — that ghost of brightness so seldom seen by a sleepy world, and which seems to steal around the verge of the universe at late hours to avoid observation and remark — began to show her gibbous face above the horizon and add a little light. The dreary undulations of the landscape began to grow more distinct. Thirty miles of the journey lay behind; and the lonely backward track, and the still lonelier route to come, oppressed the party with that vague and weary uneasiness that one at least of them had never felt before.

But now a change seemed to have come over the big and silent frontiersman. As his companions grew silent he grew active and uneasy. He peered curiously out upon the road, and seemed intent upon the outlines of the hills. He arose and stood with his foot upon the step, and looked ahead and behind, and close beside the track. He excited the curiosity of his companions, who had long since set him down as stupid; and they improved the opportunity presented for new amusement.

"Ever been here before?" said the doctor.

"You bet."

"Oh!" said the trader; "lived here?"

"I rec'n I spent ten thousand dollars not a mile from this 'ere spot."

"Looking for it?"

The big man bent his head, and doubled his huge figure beneath the curtain, lounged back into his seat, drew a long breath, pushed back his hat, and remarked:

"I'll tell ye all about it."

There was the general and impressive silence of consent and waiting.

"I've heerd you boys talk for about six hours. Now I'm a goin' to talk myself, but I wouldn't 'nless this 'ere place didn't remind me of it. Fust of all, there aint nothin'— nary thing — in this 'ere that people calls grit, an' pluck, an' sense, an' all that. There's nothin' but luck — jest luck.

"I come out from Missouri to Californy in them times they calls '49.— I'm a forty-niner myself. They was flush times then, an' money was as plenty as water, an' plentier. But still a man couldn't save nothin', an' after a year or two I hadn't much more money than I've got now, wich the same aint much. But wile I stayed there I spent more, an' had more fun an' more fights, an' cared less, than any man in all Californy. An' then, as was nat'ral in sech cases, things got to goin' bad with me, an' times to git close, an' in '54 I come down through Arizony an' them parts. In Tooson, in two weeks, I won ten thousan' dollars at poker,— jest luck ag'in. Then I stopped short. I laid low for three or four days, till I got a chance, an' then come on to this 'ere infernal country with my money. I had a mind to stop gamblin' an' try an' make a livin' like some folks I've heerd of—honestly. I knowed a man's luck didn't do him a good turn more'n once, an' I concluded to go back on it in time. I got down there to Cruces, an' some fellers pusuaded me to come out here to this infernal hornado an' dig fur water. A passel of us come out here, an' found a swale."

Here the speaker painfully extricated himself from the combinations of the vehicle, crowded himself out again, and for some moments was engaged in looking for some feature of the landscape.

"I thought I seed the place," he said, as he resumed his seat.

"Where you left the money?" said the doctor.

"This thing I'm a tellin' ain't no joke to *me*," he quietly said. "Both of you young fellers has said somethin' smart now about the on'y pile I ever had, an' the next smart thing I sh'd like to say myself ef possible. As I was sayin', we found a swale where it looked damp. Me an' my party we dug, an' dug. There ain't no man knows any better'n me how to make a hole in the groun'. I larnt that in Californy. But we didn't find no water. Afore we wus through, we dug all over this —— desert, an' finally I tumbled to the fact that there wa'nt no water, an' w'at's wus, no more money."

"Is that so?" chirped the medical man.

"Wait till I tell ye. D—n it, it riles me to think of it!" bellowed the speaker. "That wan't the wust of it. Afore that missable fool diggin', I had gone an'—an' married. She wus the puttiest thing in all this diggins. I tell ye I ain't never seed no woman to suit me sence, an' she's—gentle*men*, she's been dead this fourteen year, an' that's the wust luck I *ever* had."

The story-teller cleared his throat and went on: "Well, arter that I went down to the settlements ag'in, an' then the guv'ment sent some people here, an' *they* dug, an' dug, an' didn't find no water—nary drop. The hull thing looked like a bad job, an' folks made up their minds to go without water. Plenty of 'em did. This 'ere road 's been the death of many a mule, to say nothin' of other folks. An' now w'at do ye think they tell me in Santy Fee? W'y, they say a man named suthin', I forgit w'at,—a feller that never had no luck, an' hadn't orter had,—come out here 'cos he kinder hadn't nowhere else to go, an' commenced a diggin', an' struck water in forty foot. He has a ranch now, an' a guv'ment contract. Congress give him all the wuthless land in sight, an' he's sometimes sober, an' makes lots o' money. Ain't that luck?"

The speaker seemed irritable, and brought his great fist down with a thump upon the seat beside him.

"Why, yes," said the doctor, "everybody knows that; we'll reach there about five o'clock. I wish I was there now."

Silent men sometimes make up for lost time when once they are started; and the speaker continued:

"An' do ye know w'at I come down here for? Don't? Then I'll perceed to tell ye. 'Cause I'm a fool. There's people as visits graveyards an' things w'ere ther friends is. I'm a goin' to visit *my* cimetry. I've tried everythin' else sence I was there last, an' sometimes I've concluded I'd nigh forgot all about it. 'Pears to me I'm a gittin' old now, an' the hankerin' comes stronger. I don't know purcisely where the grave is I'm a huntin'. P'raps there ain't none; but I want to see the place where I lost — lost my woman I hadn't had a year."

The big man seemed not so strong as he appeared. He was silent a moment, and nervously fanned himself with his hat. Then he sat for a few minutes looking dreamily out upon the vast plain, and in the midst of his reverie muttered disconnected anathemas upon the Apaches. After being left alone by the rest for awhile, he began again:

"Ye see, I went back to the settlements frum here, an' jined a party goin' back to Californy. I tuk one more chance, an' owned one team out'n the twenty-odd there wus in the train,— me an' my wife. I wan't broke any then. I wus big an' strong, an' didn't mind my luck much, it seemed like. We got a start early in September, an' wus a goin' back by way of Arizony, naterally. Thar is a place about a hundred mile from here on t'other trail, called somebody's cañon — the allfiredest place fur Injuns in the world. We camped at a spring at this eend all night, an' airly in the mornin' started through. Arter we got along a little ways, at a suddint turn in the road, the fust team come chuck up ag'in a barricade o' rocks, an' a swarm o' 'Paches come down on us frum all sides. We'd passed a passel o' soldiers on the road, but as luck ud hev it, of course they wa'n't there. That ere, gentlemen, wus the wust massacre that ever I've knowed of. There wa'nt no help, an' they jest hed the drop on us. I 'member at the first, seein' some o' the women jump out'n the wagons, an' run a screamin' down amongst the chapparal, a tryin' to hide. I wus up in the lead, an' started back to where my outfit wus, fust thing. I never got there. Suthin' or somebody struck me over the head from behind."

Here the speaker added greatly to the delineation of his narrative by leaning forward and bidding his auditors place their fingers in a deep and ugly scar upon his head.

"I fell down, an' I rec'lect gittin' up ag'in an' runnin' on an' on. It seemed as though I never got to where I wanted to, an' I turned dizzy, an' commenced a gittin' blind. But I kep' a goin', till all of a suddint I forgot everythin'. When I come to my senses it must 'a been a week arterwards. I never edzackly knowed, but it wus on a narrer bed in a orspital. Ye see, them soldiers kem along arter us — arter everybody wus killed. But they found me somewhere, and toted me along wi' 'em, an' one day I kinder woke up, a lyin' on this 'ere bed, an' a feller in a uniform wus a holdin' of my wrist, an' a lookin' down at me, an' a smilin' as ef he war nigh tickled to death. I tell you," with a glance toward the doctor, "*he* wus a doctor as knowed his bizness. I crawled roun' that place till I was middlin' strong agin', and kep' a thinkin' it all over. From all I could hear, I concluded I was the only man left. I wus riled, an' I went an' 'listed in the Third Cav'lry a purpus for to kill Injuns. I didn't keer fur nuthin' else fur a long time, an' I sarved out five years 'listment. Then I went back to Californy. But I ain't had no luck. I ain't done no good fur years. I'm a thinkin' now contin'ally o' that day in the cañon. I tell ye, sometimes I think maybe some o' them women got away. 'Tain't so; I know 'tain't so, an' it's no use to speccrlate. But she wus sech a purty thing, an' sly, an' smart. But what makes me think o' her is beyant that. Ye see she wa'n't very well, an' wus ailin' a little, an'—"

He did not finish the sentence, but leaned forward and placed his face between his great hands and was silent. But after awhile he resumed the tale, to which thus far there had been no replies or questions.

"Gentlemen, 'twouldn't be no use fur any of ye to tell me I'm a fool. I've been a thinkin' o' this fur fourteen year, an' now it's got to be thet I ain't good fur nothin' else. Other men has ther youngsters, an' never thinks of it; but I can't hear a little 'un cry — wich I hain't often — 'thout gittin' kind o' weak. But ther's one thing I kin do: I kin go back an' find that place in the cañon. I've as good a right to visit my fam'ly cimetry as any man a livin', an' I'm a goin' to do it." But his voice grew tremulous as he added, in a milder tone. "But I'd give all that ten thousan' an' all the water on the hornado, ef I cud on'y see, jest once, that baby that never wus born."

None of the men to whom he had spoken were

dull, but all had evidently been mistaken in their conception of this man's character. He was now invested with a degree of interest that had not at first attached to him. So far as they knew, he was the sole survivor of one of the historic massacres of the country. They silently respected the story, and the feelings of one to whom it seemed to have been a brooding memory for so many years. The medical man, at least, was a gentleman of some learning, culture, and delicacy of feeling. He divined the vulnerable and very tender spot upon this coarse giant, and now perhaps felt the peculiar leaning toward him which all his cloth experience in regard to what bids fair to prove a special case.

"See here, my friend," said he, "who told you that your — ah, your wife — was certainly killed? I wouldn't raise your hopes, you know; but then there's no telling about such things unless they have been actually proven. Now, I have heard that there were survivors of that massacre still living somewhere in the country. *You* are alive, you see, and — ah, well, you can't 'most always tell." He had thought he would say something comforting, and had broken down and ended with an expression that, critically considered, was little short of ordinary slang. But presently he continued : "Now, you see, the chances are that if things were as you state, that — ah, in view of the scare and the excitement, the little one would come into the world without any great delay, and if the mother was very strong, you know, why, such a thing is not impossible as that you might yet see the ——"

He suddenly stopped, for the frontiersman was leaning forward in his seat, and with quick breath was drinking every fateful word. "My God!" he said, "do ye think so? Air you in yearnest? Nobody told me she was dead — and everybody . . . . But she is — she is; an' ef she wa'nt, it wouldn't know sech as me."

For a few moments, everybody sat silent. The doctor seemed trying to look, as closely as the darkness would permit, into the countenance of the man in whose mind hope very dim and far, and despair very imminent and immediate, seemed struggling for the mastery. But at last he seemed to have come to a conclusion, and beginning very cautiously, remarked:

"I have travelled this road many times. I know of such a case as this would seem to be, not far from here. Everybody knows of it, in fact. I am satisfied, my friend, that your journey may not be for nothing — I say *may* not be. I am very cer—" He stopped again, for the big man seemed to be getting into a dazed condition, rubbing his eyes, and pulling himself together, as one who believes he has been dreaming. The doctor placed his hand upon his arm. "Be calm," he said; "I will tell you all I know, now that I have begun."

"All what?" thundered the frontiersman. "Say it quick an' fast, an' be done with it. How am I to live thisaway? An' here, you, there wus one o' you doctors as saved my wuthless life a long ago. Fur God's sake, don't another of ye kill me."

"I'll tell you all I know," said the doctor, "after breakfast. Meantime, my friend, if you don't wish another of my tribe to take charge of you, you must be calm. You are no child; you should be able to restrain yourself if you wish to be considered a man."

Thereupon the medical man tried to divert the channels of conversation. He was not successful. The party was constrained and silent, and the big man looked out upon a landscape to which the growing light added no charm, with an expression upon his face that made more than one of the party pity him.

The short summer night had faded, and that rare first touch of sunlight upon mountain snow, which more than anything in nature bears the similitude of a kiss, began to appear. The tired beasts seemed to take new life, and pushed eagerly on. Far in the distance could be faintly heard the first crowing of the cocks, the bleating of goats, and the cry of asses, while the thin blue breakfast-smoke could be seen curling from the chimney of the little adobe castle which was the lucky man's ranch.

All that the frontiersman had heard of him was true. He had a well of unfailing water, that was better than all the gold mines of the surrounding mountains, and a government contract, and was happy in his first luck. He ushered the four travellers into the house as though he had known them for years. He had a *protégée*, the child of a Mexican woman who was a dependent of the establishment, whom he considered one of the attractions of the place, and of whom he never ceased to talk. For he was of that class commonly known as "good-hearted," and was capable of a generous appreciation of things not always and entirely his own. When the child came into the room at these early breakfasts provided for passengers in the stage, he always dilated upon the girl and her peculiar history. The facts bore him out. She was a creature of fourteen, who looked eighteen. She had an enormous quantity of that red hair which is crimson in the sunshine, and eyes of the variety which, for want of some better term, are called brown, being in reality both brown and black. She was round, lithe, graceful, and, in fact, a very favorable specimen of the being who is sometimes the result of the admixture of the blood of two dissimilar races

"Do you see that garl, gentlemen?" said he. "That's the loveliest little thing in Mexico, and differs from them all in her birthplace and her nussin'. Her mother's my cook, an' nothin' to me more 'n that; an' I've plenty of my own, but they was born in a house." And therewith the garrulous good fellow hurried away to attend to some necessary affair, intending to hasten back and finish his proud tale.

The four travellers sat and watched, with some pardonable impatience, the preparations for breakfast. The doctor stealthily kept his eye upon the big frontiersman, to whom the sight of the pretty child did not seem to be in any way interesting.

From time to time the mother entered and busied herself with the affairs of breakfast. She seemed an almost middle-aged Mexican woman of the better class, care-worn and wrinkled with the world and its struggle, as all her kind are when youth fades. She was accustomed to strangers, and did not perceive that the frontiersman had regarded her from her first entrance with a dreamy stare. The *frijoles* and the *chile-con-carne* had occupied her attention, and she started when the big man rose up in her way, his gray eyes glittering and his lips white, and faintly spoke a word in Spanish — so faintly that none understood.

She did not let fall the brown dish she held in her hand; she was ignorant of all nerves and proper sensations. But she placed it upon the table, and looked steadily at him. Her face began to pale a little with fear and horror. As slow recognition dawned upon her, she sank down upon the floor and turned away her head, praying rapidly after the fashion of her race. "*Ave Maria!*" she muttered. "*Soy la desdicha de este mundo. Soy tu hija abandonada; me socerras en tu merced, y me salvas de las visitas de los aparecidos; ah, Madre de Cristo, me salvas!*"

"But I am no ghost," he said. "Don't you know me? W'y, now look here,—say, don't go 'way. I'm drunk, or crazy, or dreamin', or else you are *my wife*."

She rose while he spoke, and the look of terror changed to one of anxiety and consternation. "Oh, go away," she said, in her lisping English. "It is very long. *Tengo otro hombre, y mochos muchachos.*" And mingling her Spanish and English, horrified and distressed, she passed backward through the door. What wonder? Dead husbands are not wanted to return and interrupt the arrangements that have come about through their deaths. This poor woman had a second living husband, even then in the door-yard, and acted as many another would have done in a situation so strange and so improbable.

Then the proprietor returned, and attempted to finish his interesting remarks upon the child. He had at last got to the curious manner of her birth in the chapparal, when she came in again. The frontiersman listened as one who dreams. His eyes rested lovingly upon the child, who knew and cared as little for him as though he were indeed dead in the cañon.

"Chicquita," said he, as he advanced and held out to her a trembling hand, "do ye know who I am? Yer mother does. W'y, now, come,—can't ye?" His fond and confident expression changed to one of pitiable suffering, as the girl ran from him with a scared and wondering look and took refuge beside the proprietor.

"Look here, Mister," said that person. "I don't know you, but ye're actin' like a fool. What are ye a skeerin' this one for? Now stop yer foolin' an' eat yer breakfast ef ye want to, an' ef not, be done with yer nonsense in my house."

"She's my own little one,". gasped the other.

"I'm her father. Go call her mother to tell ye,— an' mind yer jaw, or I'll—"

Then the woman, with red eyes and a face in which the evidence of a strange contest was visible, again entered the room.

"No, Señor," she said, "I not know you,—go." And she sank into the uttermost corner of the room, and covering her face with her dingy shawl, rocked herself to and fro.

The proprietor seemed reassured, and advanced upon his antagonist. "Who are ye?" he said. "The man you claim to be is as dead as Moses. He wus dead w'en this garl wus born. Ye can't play no sich stuff as that. *She* won't look at ye. Chuck, who is this feller, anyhow?"

The spoiled beauty looked at the frontiersman disdainfully, contemplated him for a moment, and broke into a careless laugh. The victim sank into a seat like one stricken. The actions of the child were but natural, for the instinctive recognition of relationships is but a fable. The broken man, denied by his wife, and derided by the child of whose dear existence he had dreamed for so many years, insulted and defied by an officious stranger, crept away and hid himself in the coach, and was there when it passed out upon its onward journey.

The remaining miles were passed in the glow and cheerfulness of day; but the party was now a silent and constrained one. There sat with them a man who seemed very old, and who was seemingly crushed by that century of suffering which it is possible to concentrate into a single hour.

There came an autumn afternoon in that same year, when the yellowing leaves beside the ashen stream trembled in a wind that bore the slightest breath of cold. The imperturbable mountains still lay about the scene, casting long shadows across the low valley. He had gone to the bad, and had gone very quickly. But his stage-journey friend stuck to him while the colossal strength gradually became childish weakness, and the pillow upon which the white head lay was softer than any it had ever felt before. It was he who held the big, emaciated hand on that afternoon, and smiled sadly as his patient talked. "Ye can't save me this time," he said. "Ye're good ones, but there's no use in it now."

It were fitting if that mother and daughter could have been near then, while, as the shadows lengthened, he said good-bye. There was no hope of glory, no illumined path stretching out before him and across the river. "Good-bye. I'm glad to go. I couldn't help it. I never had no luck. It's all right *now*."

And for the last time—lonely now, indeed, but as he had lived, without fear—the frontiersman started out upon *la jornada del muerto*.

III.

MEN OF THE BORDER.

NO one would ever learn from innumerable volumes that our country had developed anything characteristic, save that which, as Americans, we are bound to consider as abstract greatness. Of course not; America is yet too young to have developed classes whose peculiarities serve to separate them from the great mass of their countrymen, or to give them a place of their own in the annals of change and progress. In this supposition, if it be as common as it would seem, there is a mistake.

There is a life where habits, prejudices and tastes which have been bred in the bone are forgotten; where the grooves are turned a-wry and broken, and in whose strongly defined yet fleeting characteristics are to be seen the most wonderful of all the changes that peculiar surroundings are capable of working upon personal character.

The borderer is a man, not born, but unconsciously developed by his associations, surroundings, and necessities. He may have seen the light first on the Chesapeake or the banks of the Juniata; he may hail from Lincolnshire or Cork. Far Western life will clothe him with a new individuality, make him forget the tastes and habits of early life, and transform him into one of that restless horde of cosmopolites who are the foam of that slow wave of humanity which creeps toward the setting sun, and subsides at last in that green and abiding peace which has changed the wilderness into homes and farms, built railways and cities, and in a quarter of a century added one-third to the wealth of a people in comparison with whose greatness the Roman Empire was a mimic show.

The life of the border is necessarily a transitory one, and is fast passing away. The peculiarities of existence and men there will disappear before fast-advancing civilization, and leave no record of themselves, even as the backwoodsman has left none. And yet the frontier may be said to have a language, a religion, and a social life of its own. It has a habit of thought and action unique, vigorous, and not wanting in the elements of that which everywhere expresses religion, honor, and pathos. The people whose tastes or whose fates lead them hither have a world to themselves alone: a world of loneliness and lost comforts, where cities, banks, railroads, theatres, churches, and scandals have not yet come; a world where births and weddings are few, funeral ceremonies are short, and tears are almost unknown. There is here so close an affinity between nature and man that nature is an hourly teacher in a land that is as solemn as the sea, and where, as upon the sea, the mists of the horizon bound the world. The days, unchanged by the ceremonies and observances of civilization, are all alike, each one as melancholy as a Puritan Sabbath. Nature is herself, and spreads her feasts and acts her orderly caprices at her own pleasure. Acres of flowers, leagues of beauty, bloom and fade and come again, unseen by man, who does not as yet understand his own dominion. Solitary birds fly silently by. The animals stare at the new animal — the passing man — almost unscared; and silence is a power.

And yet the borderer is not a "child of nature." Men never are. It is a fiction of the poets. He is, in his wildest state and his nearest approach to simplicity, a creature of education, but of an education so peculiar that the term scarcely expresses it. He is undoubtedly a very different character from the backwoodsman who has been called his prototype, and in all respects a much more modern one of that large class who are the unconscious victims of circumstance. He who a generation ago was engaged in hewing out openings in the vast forests of Ohio and Indiana was clad in buckskin and moccasins, and practised in a homely manner, but conscientiously, the virtues of hospitality, uncouth but disinterested kindness, and general and strict personal honesty. If he was ignorant of the graces of civilization, he also knew few of its vices. He had not been in cities and had not carried their characteristic vices with him into the wilderness. The weapon of his day was an honest rifle, and he had not an arsenal of death slung about his waist. In all these things the modern frontiersman sets at naught the idealisms of Cooper, the time-honored traditions of the middle states, and the well-established ideas of novel-reading mankind.

The ideal borderer, the type of his class from eastern Kansas to the Rio Grande, you are apt to find in calf-skin boots, with wide-brimmed hat worn askew, and nether limbs encased in fancy cassimeres. There are often rings upon his fingers and blazing jewels upon his breast. He is inclined to be loud and defiant in dress, manners, and general deportment. He clings with the tenacity of second nature to the language of the dance-house and the brothel, and uses in his discourse the picturesque phraseology of draw-poker. The unhappy thought of Colonel Colt, which has filled more unmarked graves than the plague and eternally settled more disputes than all juries, is his constant and valued companion, and he wears his rakish hat a-wry upon his oily locks with the air of the king of all the loafers.

But he is not a loafer. He is quarrelsome, jealous of honor, and still very much of a man and a friend to those who understand him. He scorns to conceal actual impressions and thoughts, but in this he is only very unnecessarily sincere and independent. He will take a stranger's last dollar at a game which he does not understand, but he will likewise lend and share to the last cent and the last morsel. He hates what he is pleased to consider "airs," cannot abide to be patronized, and is intolerant toward all who chance to disagree with him. His great fault is a disposition to bluster, to assert himself, to deny to the rest of mankind the privilege of being ever or by any chance in the right. But he is brave, sincere, and faithful, when once enlisted in any cause.

This kind of man, with the many variations which exist among classes always, is the frontiersman. California has seen him these twenty years. He is here and there in all the villages of Colorado and New Mexico, and his habitation is in every sheltered nook in many thousands of miles of plains-country. With all his faults, it may be justly said of him that he is a man who depends upon his courage, who has chosen his life and will never leave it, and who is the fit and capable vedette who stands upon the verge of the mighty civilization which is destined to follow him when he and his unconscious work shall have passed into that dim limbo that has no historian, and leaves no record, monument, nor representative. It is not necessarily a startling announcement, that the borderer does not feel called upon to live entirely without the solace and comfort of woman. We may be saddened, but hardly astonished, to know that the bold-faced curse of the by-streets of the most populous and enlightened of the cities of the world is also here, bolder, gaudier, and more shameless than ever. Ministering to every baseness, inciting to every crime, worse than her male associates by so much as woman fallen is always worse than man, the tipsy queen of the demi-monde flaunts her finery among the shanties of every border town.

But there is another class who, in a feminine way, are like unto their husbands and brothers. They are indeed few, and it will be long before there will be complaints of a surplus of maiden ladies on the border. How or why any of them ever came there, is something of a mystery. But they live in the ranche and the adobe, and are wives and mothers, and are content—and, it is hardly superlative to say, as happy as their more elegant sisters of the East. Their nearest neighbor may be twenty miles away, their chances for gossip few and far between, and all their amusements and occupations masculine and homely. They know more of the economy of the camp-fire, the qualities of oxen, and the habits of the coyote, than they do of the prevailing fashions, or of cunning variations in the style of bonnets and the color of hosiery. But the neat bed in the corner, the clean hearth, the neatness of dingy adobe or sod walls, and the trailing vine over the low roof, in many a frontier house, proclaim the touch, the taste, the love and care, with which, in loneliness, poverty, and isolation, a woman still adorns the spot which is her home.

There are children too. You need not think to escape the cry of infancy by going westward. They never heard the sound of the school-house bell, and are ignorant of the functions of a Sunday-school superintendent. They are even deprived of the ordinary amusements of children. They ride no gates, slide upon no cellar doors, and make no small escapades, to be found and carried home by the police. But the mud-pie proprietorship of a hundred leagues is theirs. All their lives they have heard the bark of the coyote, and watched for the coming and going of the bison, and in the majority of instances are the tow-headed, boggle-eyed urchins that children of the English blood the world over are ever apt to be.

Partly to circumstances attending trade, particularly freighting, but mainly to what may be called the migratory instinct, most of the people of the far frontier owe the fact of their residence there. So far east as western Kansas, there is yet a more natural motive — the desire to obtain a home and land. There is no more natural illustration than is here apparent of how the human mind goes back in its desires to the original source of all wealth, and to the first meaning of the word *home* — a home that is ours because we have made it. In the search for this, there is no danger that can daunt, no difficulty that can discourage. The pertinacity with which the pre-emptors and squatters have clung to the idea of home-getting, amid surroundings in which there seems so little present happiness and so little future hope, is not the least surprising feature of their hard lives. But with regard to a large class with which this article has mainly to do, the question as to why they are there, and what they find to do, is harder to answer. The plains ranch proper is always a small store, in which is sold bacon, flour, and a very bad article of whiskey. The travel is mainly confined to certain roads, and, notwithstanding the trans-continental lines of railway, is at certain seasons of the year by no means inconsiderable. By this travel the rancher lives. The brown walls of his hovel, seen from afar, are hailed with delight by men who have not drunk nor smoked since the night at the last stopping-place. To pass without moistening his clay, would be to the average plains-man an act strongly indicating mental decay.

But the proportion of people who manage to live on the border without any visible means of support is larger than it is anywhere else outside of the great cities. The hangers-on of the ranches go and come unquestioned. Their dark and bearded faces disappear, and they are gone, perhaps only for a day,—though if forever, it leads to no inquiry and excites no alarm. It is certain that the Anglo-Saxon can become anything. He can be Indianized and Mexicanized, and upon the frontier he becomes an Arab—not a weak imitation or intentional pattern, but of his own kind, and after his own fancies and necessities. Taciturn, suspicious, and courageous, hospitable in peace and unscrupulous in enmity, the Bedouin of the border is a man who wears clothes of a familiar pattern, and speaks English; and there his resemblance to the race from which he sprung almost ends.

Yet the verge of civilization is a field for the gathering together of all kinds and classes. Here is the patient, plodding, phlegmatic German, fast forgetting every tradition of his fatherland in the absorbing wildness that makes all men alike. Here is the Irishman, with the rich brogue of Tipperary still upon his tongue, but changed in all else which tells of the green isle of peat, potatoes, and blarney. Here is the down-east Yankee, oblivious of all the ideas of the land of baked beans and hard cider, turning his native cunning to account at poker and California jack. Here is the characteristic son of the South, still speaking the mincing dialect that has been borrowed in the name of gentility from the thick tongue of the negro, but, for a wonder, forgetting to insert "Sir" at the ending of every sentence. But all are changed, at least in name. The German has become "Dutch Bill," or "Dutch" something, no matter what; the Irishman is always "Pat." The New Englander often answers to the name of "Yank," and the Southerner is willing and proud to be called "Kaintuck," or "Tennessee," or even "Cracker." Thus is true democracy made manifest. The real names of individuals are often unknown to acquaintances of years. Any peculiarity of person or history brings about its apt cognomen of recognition. The man who squints is "Cockeye" for all time. The lame man is "Limpy," and the slender and attenuated one is "Slim" Dick, or Tom, or whatever the name that was once his may be. The surprising thing is that these names are accepted and gloried in. Indeed, those that are born of some peculiarity of personal history are proudly borne. To be Buffalo Bill, or Fighting Joe, is to be famous. "Mister" is the designation of a stranger; but if a borderer calls an individual "Mister" after he has known him a week, it means that he does not particularly like him, to say the least.

Brusque and rude as all this seems, there is no country where the established forms are more rigidly observed. If you are invited to "take suthin'," it is offensive to refuse. If you are asked to "set up and eat," it is not a mere form; you are not only really welcome, but expected to return the compliment should your host ever come your way. In the immense expanse of country, men who live a hundred miles apart are often near neighbors and intimate friends. The necessities of the frontier produce a freemasonry in comparison with which the actual brotherhood is a tame and meaningless thing. If a ranchman lends his neighbor a mule and tells him to leave it at Sims's or Slocum's, a hundred miles away, he is certain of finding the animal there when wanted. Honesty and punctuality are the current exchange of the country, and a short shrift and a sudden ending is the meed of absolute necessity to him who habitually wrongs his neighbor.

Another bond of union among all white men on the border is common enmity to the Indian. Hatred of the Apache and the Kiowa will be the uppermost feeling in the borderer's mind so long as there is a disputed territory claimed alike by him and his enemy. Year by year the ranks are thinned in many an encounter that is never heard of in the world of newspapers, and year by year the frontiersman counts fresh accessions to his ranks. While right and justice and policy are discussed elsewhere, the contest proceeds without any abatement between the parties interested. The sentence of doom that is written against the red man, while it is slow in its operation, seems utterly irrevocable. The horde of adventurers who invade his hunting-grounds are hardy, bold, and cunning as he. Within a century one of the great divisions of a common family will have passed away, and its only history will be a history of decadence and death, preserved in the meagre annals of its first and last enemy, the borderer.

So much isolation and habitual loneliness has been the cause of curious relationships, and of these the fashion of partnerships is a remarkable one. Two men, often very unlike, will associate themselves, not so much as sharers in the gains of business or adventure — though that is also included — but simply as "pards," adopted brethren. Each one's quarrel is also the quarrel of the other. They are always encountered together, and hold all troubles in common, together with all pleasures. In most cases, a genuine affection seems to exist between them. There is rather an opinion that whoever has no "pard" is, until cause be shown, a rather "mean cuss," "who can't live with nobody." A separation of two partners, and a dissolution of the mysterious tie, causes as great a scandal as a divorce case in other regions.

But there is yet another side to the frontiersman's friendship. His neighborly obligations are all outside the obligations imposed by the sixth commandment. The revolver is not always carried about for nothing, and its owner is quick of hand and eye, and generally sure of his weapon and his aim. There is no man upon whom a reckless code of honor is so fatally and foolishly binding. An insult, fancied or real, is settled then and there with a life, and the bystanders are the judges of the fairness of the transaction. To maul and pummel is childish, and leads to no adequate result; to murder is gentlemanly and proper, and, withal, the fashion. The old code of the duello was a tame and insipid thing compared with a row in a "saloon" in a border town. There is no code, no law, no jury. Each man, in the heat of passion, is the judge of the gravity of the foolish word, the drunken insult, the hastily-spoken taunt, or the ancient grudge, and therefore gives his own life or takes another for it, as depends upon his soberness, his quickness, or his courage. We talk of the fashions which rule society, where there is society; of hoops, panniers, chignons, and bustles, with all their accompanying bonnets and trains. On the border, men willingly die to be in the fashion.

Human nature becomes accustomed to all surroundings that are forced upon it, and to solitude easiest of all. The frontiersman would smile if you told him that his life was a monotonous one. Wanting even the newspaper, he is more gregarious than other men are, and makes a companion of something, and even an animal is made to serve in that capacity when there is no one else. The dog, dear as he is to many men everywhere, is doubly a friend in the wilderness. His master sleeps and eats and talks with him. He may be the mangiest cur that ever barked. No matter; it is not a country in which to be too particular. There is another animal that commonly leads a persecuted life and dies a violent death among Christian people, that here finds a better lot and more appreciation. Our friend will search long and far for a surplus and unnecessary cat, and name him comically, and teach him innumerable tricks, and make him altogether an important member of his household. Sometimes, in the Southwest, a long-eared and solemn-countenanced little ass will be found making himself very much at home upon the premises, clumping clumsily about the shanty, investigating the cookery, climbing upon the bed, and going in and out with an irresistibly comic air of proprietorship. But the opportunity for companionship with his own kind never passes unused with the hermit of the wilderness. There are nightly gatherings at every ranch, and the resource for amusement is usually the pastime that is as old as Babel: that of story-telling. Each man has something to say, mostly upon the interesting subject of his own adventures and past life, and palms his narratives off for very truth, and, as every listener knows, usually makes them as he goes, out of whole cloth. Some of the most outrageous travesties upon truth ever said or sung have beguiled the dull hours in the frontier cabin. The next resource is the card-table, and in mining districts the sums that sometimes change hands would startle the visitors at Saratoga. With most frontiersmen gambling is a passion, and some of them are most accomplished members of the card-dealing fraternity.

It should not be imagined that this man is impatiently waiting the coming of a higher civilization, or that he even wishes it to come. It suits him as it is, and when the change comes he will go. It is better not to need a thing than to have it. The unknown life of every man is more or less a protest against law, refinement, obedience, and the odious "duty." Habit has accustomed these men to freedom from the restraints of civilization; from a bondage that all men sometimes feel, and which these, at least, will never renew. They have discovered that the refinements of life may be purchased at too high a price. For them the veneer and the varnish have cracked, and the original man shows through, the savage that each one of us really is. In these, the unconquerable impulses of eternal nature have found permanent expression. They are those who will tolerate never again the monotony of society. They have abandoned forever the daily paper, polished boots, books, insincere conversation, politics, intrigue, and the treadmill endlessness of that routine which we call domestic life.

Our frontiersman has his excitements and his pleasures, ferocious and deep, and for which he refuses to be called to account by society or any earthly authority. The man who shall transfer to canvas some one of the scenes which each midnight brings to the inner room of the trader's store in a New Mexican mining camp, and shall do it well, will preserve for all time the most striking feature of American frontier life. We shall see the dead silence and the rapt attention, as the guttering candles or smoking lamps flare upon each sun-browned and grizzled face; the hard hands and hairy arms; the look of covert exultation, as the winner draws toward him the coin and the bags of yellow dust. We shall read the quick glance that suspects a cheat, and the deep curse that records a mistake. And standing there, almost as intent as the players, will be those who watch the fascinating passion in its varying record of gain or loss. The dim light will throw the rough beams along the roof into shadows and lights with grotesque alternations, and blackness will lurk among the lounging figures in nooks and corners. But pervading all — the essence of the picture — will be that suggestion of folly and ruin which mere words cannot paint: that look upon faces that tells of the homelessness of years, the days of toil and sacrifice, the months of delving and hoping, all gone in a single night; and also of that bewitching hope that ever waits upon the devotees of the god of chance, and the end of which is despair, broken hearts, and death.

IV

BROWN'S REVENGE.

OJO CALIENTE was of itself a prominent feature in a landscape bare and brown, and stretching in rocky monotony and silence for leagues on every hand. Even to those wise ones who find among the "ologies" a sufficient explanation for all the strange things this old world did when she was very young and soft, the decided eccentricities of nature are always invested with something of the terror of mystery and the charm of strangeness. As for this particular spot, many thoughtful eyes had looked upon it; many wise heads had speculated at its brink. A conical mound, very symmetrical in shape, and some thirty feet in height, rose from the surrounding plain. Its top was a circular basin, about fifteen feet in diameter and of unknown depth, always full of limpid, sparkling, bubbling water. There alone in all the thirsty land the delicious element abounded, rejoiced, and ran over. Clear, pure, and — cold, of course? No, it was scalding hot. There was the wonder. It was one of the mysterious openings into our common mother's fervid heart. Through a notch in the rocky basin's edge the stream ran over, as large as a man's body,— a volume that might have supplied a town with hot baths, and almost have cleansed the grimy denizens of Constantinople itself. But it did not seethe and rage, and then compose itself in intervals of fitful and deceptive slumber. Through all seasons and all times, through heat and cold, the stream was as constant as woman's love, or wickedness. Where the torrent spread itself out and cooled in the plain below, the tall grass and coarse weeds, and some hardy ferns, grew rank and luxuriant, with their roots constantly bathed in a frost-defying warmth. And the terrapins and wart-grown lizards and long-legged mottled toads gathered there and lived a fortunate life. Amid the dense growth and balmy vapors the rattlesnake forgot to stiffen his odious coils in a half-year's slumber, and lay content and stupid, but still venomous, all the season through. The rough bowlders gathered a green coat of slimy moss as they lay in the ooze; and in winter, when the hoar-frost or the light snow lay on all the hills, that bit of verdure was like a flowery acre strayed from the tropics.

Such a place, lying as it did on the main road from the low country to the hills, had not failed to attract attention and suggest a use. And that use was, of course, in accord with the ideas of the country. Ojo Caliente was a ranch; and while to a certainty the ranch idea could not be left out, there was also connected with it a new idea in the wilderness: it was a watering-place. The scalding flood was supposed to possess medicinal properties, and an enterprising man occupied the slope of the hill with a rambling adobe, the front of which, standing next the travelled road, was the "store," while an array of rude chambers straggled up the slope toward the spring. Each room was furnished with a long wooden tub, into which the water was conducted by a trough. Some tall cottonwoods flourished beside the wall, and, gaining vigorous growth from the warm stream that touched their roots, gave an oasis charm to this one spot in the treeless landscape.

The place was likewise a hotel, and the smoke of some camp-fire arose each night from the trampled and dusty spot beside the garden, and mules brayed within the square enclosure which was supposed to be a sufficient protection against the Apache. Here and there a limping rheumatic sat and chafed his limbs, and talked of his complaint, and waited for health. Other than the waters, there was no physician there. Neither was there any pretence of infirmity as an excuse for idleness and pleasure. There was no need of pretended illness in this region as an excuse for dissipation.

The proprietor of the place — the inventor and maker of all save the scalding spring itself — was a man whom every denizen of the country knew, and none knew well. He had come from no one knew or ever found out where, and had improved his possessions with a lavish hand and no small expenditure of money. He was called wealthy, and daily added to his store. His cattle grazed upon the surrounding hills, and with rare skill and vigilance he kept them safe from the universal enemy. His place was known as a good place, and his meals were "square" meals. As neighbors go in that country, he was a good neighbor; and many a mule was lent, many a broken wheel mended, and many a meal given away, for men whom he had never seen before. Personally, he had failed to take upon him the likeness of the border. Middle-aged and grave, he dressed in a civilized garb, and his oddly-shaven face had in it a look of settled melancholy. By a stranger, all these things were seen and forgotten. "Odd feller," they said, as they passed on; "wonder where he come from?" and that was all.

But those who had known him longer had studied these peculiarities to better purpose. There was a rumor in the country that his name was not really Denham, and in many a camp-fire talk it had been remarked that no man had ever heard him mention the place of his nativity or speak of his family. Yet the unconquerable dialect of his youth betrayed him as an Englishman; and this was the only circumstance they could absolutely claim as knowledge. Yet he was never questioned; for, liking him well, there was still something about him that forbade familiarity.

He was proverbially quiet, and even timid. He carried not the accustomed arsenal upon his belt, and was never known to take up a gun. In these things his servants acted for him; and while he had been known to stand calmly at his door and watch an Indian running-fight for the possession of his herds, the idea of actual participation in the defence seemed never to have entered his mind. So they sometimes called him "the preacher," and the irreverent nicknamed him "padre;" and when by chance he heard them, he turned and walked away with a peculiar and unwonted look upon his melancholy face.

Once when a miner died at his house, and was filled with that late repentance that usually comes to torment the closing hours of a hard life, Denham stood with others in the room. They told afterward how "the preacher" seemed to restrain himself in the desire to say or do something at the dying sinner's bedside. He came, hesitated, went away again. He again returned, bringing with him a small worn volume, which he opened and tried to read. His lips were dry and his face grew pale, as he read: "I am the resurrection and the life; he that believeth in me——." His voice choked in the utterance of the words that take in all there is of hope; and he closed the book and left the place. There were those who were ready thereafter to declare, in their rough fashion, that if he were not a preacher he ought to be.

Frontiersmen are not inclined to love men who are not of their kind. But in this case, after four years of divided opinion, the larger portion of that scattered population who had aught to do with the proprietor of Ojo Caliente were ready to fight for him. He did not swear, he refused to drink, he avoided slang. His language was such as some few of them could hardly understand; and with every temptation that the reckless and devil-may-care spirit of the country offered, there was no suspicion of a single slip in his conduct. He counselled peace in the midst of strife. He gave advice to those who asked it, but meddled with the affairs of none. Each man believed himself to be his chief friend. He was accounted acute and far-sighted, and a crowd of men, ever ready to act more from impulse than reason, made discovery of that fact. He was the depository of the confidence of every bearded fellow in a radius of a hundred miles, and he kept the secrets like a priest. But none could divest him of his strangeness. He read books — or, rather, a book. For a long time they thought it must be one some of them had heard of, mayhap seen: the Bible. But when one of their number once slyly looked at the open page, he discovered that other scarcely less wonderful volume, Shakspeare. Once, on a frosty night, he read to the story-tellers around the fire a tale that had in it rather more of that wonderful "touch of nature" than they were accustomed to in theirs, and they clamored for more, and listened until the moon went down. And each rough son of the wilderness carried ever after a bright imagining of her who would have borne the logs for Ferdinand, and fancied he could sometimes hear Ariel sing among the pines.

Men who lead a strange life are generally unconscious of that life's strong peculiarities. Had his friends been critical, they would have questioned the motives of a man who, while so unlike them, yet chose to live among them. With all his kindness he was still a man apart. You could tell, as he sat with thoughtful face at his door in the shimmering summer afternoon, that his heart was not in this country. He started at the slightest sound. He scrutinized strange faces with a kind of covert interest, and seemed ever ready to fly, abandoning all. The long-looked-for mail that brought letters — evidently precious things even to the coarse and apparently hardened men around him — brought nothing to him. If Ojo Caliente and its lonesome landscape was not his home, then where could it be, since he had no interest in any other?

It is well known that the lonely graves of the border sometimes hide strange histories — strange and untold. The boundless waste of plain and mountain is the great refuge of those who would hide from themselves. It is not the man doomed to spend the days of his years between granite walls, not he who sees his last goods go down under the sheriff's hammer, not even he to whom law is interpreted as the grim code which puts a halter upon his neck and his coffin before him, who knows most of remorse, most of fear, or most of despair. Of all suffering men, he suffers most who, burdened with unpunished crimes, hides from the world. There is a punishment that comes at midnight, that no man may avoid. This is hell. There is need of none more fiery. You think faces will tell the tale; but there is no such incomparable liar as the human countenance. The man who scowls and frowns at the fit of his collar or the quality of his dinner may live long and carry a gnawing devil in his heart, and give no sign.

Thus Denham ate and slept well, and looked after his affairs, and had only a melancholy face. But he was ever watching. As he sat at his door, and the evening shadows crept downward from the mountain-tops, he could see the dim specks upon the brown road grow larger and larger, and they were never out of his sight or thoughts until nearness demonstrated their character and showed him their faces. This watchfulness was the man's characteristic; a sign of long-past trouble or crime, whatever that trouble or crime was. Not that his friends thought so. Uneasy watchfulness might have a thousand causes, and is oftenest not regarded at all. Once convict, once even suspect, and all signs are easily read and exaggerated by those whose function it is to suspect expertly. And yet there is ever more than natural oddity in the man who walks with bent head and locked hands, and upon whose ordinary occupation creeps ever in the absent action, the muttered word, the startled look, and the sudden change of countenance. The man Denham had these characteristics. "I reckon he's the feardest of Injins of any man in these parts," his neighbors sometimes remarked. He was afraid, but not of Indians. There was but one man of whom Denham stood in mortal fear, and he knew not if that one terrible creature were alive or dead.

And in the long and tedious hours that wait upon an order of events that men may never control lest they should interrupt retribution, it occurred that Denham's ghost came at last and sat himself down like Banquo at the feast. Even his far home in the wilderness was doomed to be the lure of fate and the cause of his discomfiture. For with grim pertinacity men's crimes, even their mistakes, do often hunt them out. One evening, business, or a not uncommon desire to be alone, took him over the hill and far down by the sedgy garden. It may have been that his brooding mind had that anticipation of evil which we imagine our inner consciousness sometimes has. But in an hour he returned slowly toward the house, his hands behind him, and his bent and prematurely gray head regarding only his own slow footsteps. Entering at the rear, he passed slowly through the low rooms, pushing aside the canvas that hung as a door before the entrance to each apartment. The frost of the late autumn of a prosperous year had come, and upon rude benches a half dozen frontiersmen sat before the blazing fire in the public room, engaged in the old business of storytelling. He approached the strip of soiled canvas which hung between him and them, slowly, as was his wont; and as he came a voice, that was not a familiar one fell upon his ear. It was not familiar, for the man was a stranger; and yet that coarse and strident laugh was like a knell to George Denham, and his face flushed and paled as he sank upon a seat. Then, as he cautiously peered through upon the group, he saw the stranger, lately arrived, full of talk, and the only man whose coming had ever escaped those watchful eyes. He was not a creature to be frightened at, only a bearded fellow of forty, red-faced and brawny-handed,— as evidently a man whose best years had been spent upon the border as though the fact had been placarded upon him. Already he was on familiar terms with the men around him, and had begun the narration of his adventures. As Denham waited and listened behind the curtain for confirmation of his fears, he knew the stranger did not lie as he talked.

"Gentlemen," said he, "I never were here before, but I'm usen to this kind o' thing. I kim to Californy when I were kind o' young, about '50, an' kinder struck a lead, an' made money mity fast. I stayed 'round thar fur twelve year,—yes, I reckon it wus twelve year,—an' all the time, gentlemen, I had a woman back in Injiany whar I come frum. I don't know how's this might strike some o' you; but I had, an' it were a long time to wait, you bet ye. An' so finally I concluded I'd go back an' see my old gal, awaitin' so long, ye know. Well (any gent as has a chaw o' terbacker kin accommodate me), as I was a sayin' (thank ye, boss), I started fur to go back agin, an' when I got down to Saccermento, thinks I, what ud I be doin' to be a carryin' around about ten thousan' dollars an' suthin' more? 'Buy a draft,' sez they. 'A draft?' sez I; 'we ain't usen to ño sich in my part o' the country.' But the war wuz broke out, ye know, an' I see some mity purty bills — they called 'em treas'ry notes — as they said wuz as good's the old gold. Sez I, 'Mister, them'll do,' an' I chucked my dust inter ten o' the biggest. 'Twar a mighty small roll, I tell ye, for to be wuth ten thousan', an' I jest folded 'em into a slip o' paper an' chucked 'em into my jacket pocket, an' started. It war careless, I know, but I 'lowed I needn't tell of 'em bein' thar. Well, I come clear across, an' war a'most home, 'till I got on a road in the state of Missoury. We wuz a hoopin' it up one night, scootin' over the perary at about forty mile a hour, an' I went to sleep. In the mornin', gentlemen, when I felt fur my money, it war gone. It's been long ago now, an' all past an' done; but I tell you it mighty nigh got me. I wuz a thinkin' of the old gal — dreamin' of her, in fact, — an' to wake in the mornin' a sittin' in a seat a rattlin' to'ards home arter twelve year o' hard work, an' busted — teetotal busted, — it war too bad. Gentlemen, I ain't much on the weakness, but I could a' cried. I tackled the conductor. Sez he, 'There ain't no man got off this 'ere train sence two o'clock, an' you got on at one.' Then he ask 'em, sez he, 'Will any man objec' to bein' sarched?' An' they sez no. Ther wuz no crack or chink o' that car we didn't sarch. Ther wuz no wimmin on, an' hadn't been, an' no man cud naterally objec'. Finally, sez the conductor, sez he, 'You ain't never had it.' I jest knocked him inter a cocked hat. I wuz riled, an' it wuz a comfort for to do it. An' then I jest clim' down off'n that train an' started back. I hain't seen my old woman — shan't never see her — she's dead. Gentlemen, I'm a busted man. I don't claim to be nuthin' else. . . . . Kin you accommodate me, pard? — thank ye."

As the speaker, with indescribable gusto, placed another quid in his mouth, there was a perceptible feeling around the circle of listeners. It is mistaken philosophy, and mistaken religion, to speak of the hardness of the human heart. It is careless and selfish, but there is no more responsive thing when awakened by that unstudied strain which is like the harmony we may hear when the chords of a harp are touched by a baby's fingers or by a passing robe. It was not intended, and a thousand attempts might not reproduce it. It was music, nevertheless.

"But," said one, who was younger than the rest, "why did you not go home? What did ye act that-a-way for?"

Then the stranger turned his head slightly to one side, and closed his opposite eye, and regarded the speaker for a brief moment. It was the pantomime which means, "What ails *you?*"

"Air ye aware, young feller, that a man can't go home arter twelve year, poor an' ragged an' ornery, an' tell 'em he had a lot o' money stole from him night afore last? Do ye think a man's mother-in-law 'd b'lieve any sich thin stuff?" Then, as the younger one retired into the shade of contempt, the speaker turned again toward the circle of silent listeners, and continued: "Ye see, under sich circumstances, a feller keeps his ragged britches on a purpose. He thinks he's a goin' for to hug his wife, an' kiss his babies, an' be independenter'n a mule, an' play it low down on 'em all fur about a week, an' then tell 'em all about it, so's to 'stonish 'em, and finally buy a farm. A feller kind o' wants to make it as *creamy* as possible, ye know. An' then to be tee total busted. Them's hard lines, gentlemen; I say them's hard lines."

And all this time Denham sat unseen behind the narrow curtain, and watched and listened. It was dark there, and only one lance of yellow light from the bright fire lay across his face. At first his countenance had a look of consternation, as he glanced at his new guest, and felt his pockets, and looked into a far dark corner where lay an expressman's portable safe, probably purchased at some quartermaster's auction sale. Then, as the conversation went on, his look changed, his mood melted, and the dim shadow of a strong resolve came into his eyes. But no one can describe the emotional panorama a man's face is supposed to present under such circumstances; because, if these changes occur at all, it is only when the restraint of other eyes is taken away. I have already said, with the man Denham as an example, that men's faces are great liars. But a change came over him as he listened, whether perceptible or not. He arose quietly and went to the safe that lay in the corner. He took a key from his pocket, and very silently and cautiously took from the safe a packet, seemingly a folded written document of some length. Then he went quietly back, and seated himself again, listening intently to the stranger's story.

They were hard lines, he had said; and almost as he uttered the words, Denham came among the group. He did not sit down, but where the light fell full upon his face, stood regarding the stranger.

"Do you know me?" said he.

"W'y — well, no — not adzactly. How'd do?" and the good fellow rose and proffered his hand with a look of inquiry and anticipation.

Denham feigned not to see the hand, which it seemed he dare not take; and when the stranger had seated himself again he stood looking at the fire in forced calmness, but his eyes were anxious, and his voice was hoarse. Presently, as by a mighty effort, he said :

"Friends, I have something to say to this man, William Brown,"—the stranger started,—"and to you all. Please listen to me, and understand that I do appoint you all to be my judges and my jury. Some of you tried and hanged the horse-thief at Pinos Altos, and two of you captured and brought back the man who killed Tom Hicks, and he was tried and condemned. I am ready to stand by your verdict. God knows, I want no better men."

The bronzed and bearded group upon whom the firelight glanced as this man seemed to place his life in their hands, sat silent. It may not have seemed as strange to them as it does to the reader. They were the law-makers, as well as the executives, of the country in which they lived; good men and true. No cringing prayers, no promises, no tears, availed with them. Yet the American history which is yet to be written will not deny justice to the grim law-makers of the border. Every man's life was in his brother's hands. They dealt justly, not as under the abstract obligations of an oath, but as every man himself hoped for justice.

Perhaps they did not quite understand the speaker's words; but they sat unmoved, and waited. It was not a hasty court,—they would see it all clearly by and by. The speaker continued :

"William Brown, I have heard your story, and I declare to these men that it is true. See here," and he held up in his hand a small square volume;

"this is a Bible. I believe this book to be God's book, and on it I solemnly swear that *I am the man that robbed William Brown.*"

A look passed from one to the other round the circle, but no man spoke. Only the stranger rose up. Some who read this may imagine the ease with which a man comes at last to handle a long-accustomed tool. The soldier and his musket are almost one, and there is a flash-like celerity with which the Lascar slips his crooked knife from its greasy scabbard into the bowels of his antagonist. Such as this is the intimacy of the borderer with his weapon. Ere Denham could speak again, or scarcely look round, the slender muzzle of Brown's pistol was in his face.

But there were other eyes and hands equally quick, and as the avenger hesitated a moment to say something, old Joe Maxwell's hand was upon his arm. "Sit down, stranger," he said; "we're a tryin' this case, an' don't want no interferin'," and his gray eye had a look which meant more than his words.

Borne up by the sense of his lofty purpose, Denham stood calm, and in the silence which ensued took from his pocket the packet, which he unfolded, and handed it to old Maxwell.

"Can you read it?" said he.

The old frontiersman looked doubtfully at it, handed it back, and remarked, "Read it yerself, an' I reckon we'll git the sense on it."

"Gentlemen," said Denham. "this is my will and my story together. I wrote it more than a year ago, for a man may die, and though I never thought to divulge its contents during my life, yet the time is come when it is best that it should be known. I can remedy my offence, die happier, and be thought better of when I am dead. As between this man and me, I have suffered most, and justly. I could tell my story, but it is already written here."

His auditors were probably not conscious of it, but as he stood there, close by the guttering candle, with a peculiar and glorifying light upon his face, he greatly impressed them. His manner was that of a man who has overcome—who has conquered himself. He opened the paper and solemnly read what is here set down:

"IN THE NAME OF GOD, AMEN. I, James Dodd, clergyman of the Church of England, of Witham, in the county of Essex, and now of the United States of America, do herein write my last WILL and TESTAMENT, and do hereby enjoin upon all that it shall be duly executed, though wanting legal form, and without witnesses, for I would that I might die without shame, and that none should read until I am dead.

"I give unto William Brown, once of the state of Indiana and now of parts unknown, and unto his heirs and assigns, my property of Ojo Caliente, and all lands, houses, appurtenances, and fixtures thereto belonging. And I give unto him my strong-box and all therein, namely, twenty-three thousand dollars in coin and dust. I give unto him and them all my cattle and goods, and all property of all kinds, to have, hold, and use the same forever.

"And I hereby enjoin upon all to whom this shall come when I am dead, that they by no means hinder the injunctions of this my Testament; for I do most solemnly declare that what I give to the said William Brown is already his, and to the doubting I commend the following, my confession:

"I am fifty-four years of age. I was born in the county of Essex, in England, and came to America in the year 1848. I was a clergyman, and all my life, until the time whereof I speak, I have feared God, and, praying always, walked in His law. If they yet live, I have a wife and two daughters, whereof the eldest must now be twenty years old. More of them I will not speak, for since my fall they have not seen my face, and I would that they and I should suffer all manner of apprehension and sorrow, and that they should mourn me as dead, rather than know of my sin and crime.

"I was poor; and though I urge not that as any excuse, God knows the longing of a man for his family's sake. I thought often of how I should improve my condition, and dreamed of wealth. Yet I could not attain it. I dare not abandon a calling for which God and not my flock knew how little I was fitted, for it secured at least my bread. Thinking these thoughts, I was on a railway train in the state of Missouri, on the night of December 22, 1862. On the car were only eleven persons—males; for it was a bitter night. I arose and stood near the stove, where a lamp burned dimly above my head. And as I stood there, there came a man, and standing beneath the light, and seemingly careless of my presence, he took from the pocket of his vest a small flat package, folded in a slip of yellow paper, upon which was a name. He unfolded the package, and as I looked he counted certain notes, called, as I know, treasury notes. I perceived that there were ten of them, and that each was of the denomination of one thousand dollars.

"I went again to my seat, and the man to his. But I pondered what I had seen. In my heart I thought that God had not been just to me. The man I saw was a rough and uneducated man, and he, I thought, will spend all this in the pleasures of his kind, while I, knowing so much more of the good that money may be made to do, am deprived of all.

"And I thought further. How, said I, might a man obtain this money and go happy and unpunished? I knew that mere criminals were fools, easily detected, and betraying guilt that any skill would enable them to hide; but I thought I could do better than a common thief. Where should I hide it, that I might calmly defy search? I arose and went near the man, and I saw that one small corner of the package was above his pocket. My face burned; I could feel the blood rushing through my veins. So near it seemed, so easy. I went again and looked into my small and poorly-furnished travelling-bag. There was no hiding-place there, for men look keenly into linings and corners wherever they may be, and there is where mere thieves make mistakes. But I unconsciously took into my hand the commonest article in life: a piece of soap—only a small square, new and unused. I carried this with me to the platform, a place where I remember the wind howled and the fine snow drifted and cut my face. I cut from the end a small mortise and carefully saved the piece. Then I hollowed out the interior, not too much, and threw away the crumbs. I remember the simple and childish piece of work as vividly as though with the same knife I had cut a throat. I again approached the sleeping man, snoring heavily upright in his seat. I looked about me; there was not a wakeful person in the car. As I gently drew from his pocket the packet, and knew that I held ten thousand dollars in my hand, my hair seemed to rise upon my head, and all my life, with everything good in it, went backward. But it seemed too late to retreat. It was done, and I sealed the money in the soap-cake, bruised the end that had been cut, as though by falling, and placed the whole in my bag.

"Very soon, it seemed to me, the man awoke and called out that he had been robbed. The doors were locked, the train stopped, and every one offered himself for search. Every nook was investigated. I offered myself and all my belongings with avidity, for having yielded to crime, I became hardened. The cake of soap fell upon the floor; a man picked it up, smelled of it, and finally it was tossed upon a seat and lay there for many minutes.

"Finally it became apparent that the money could not be found, and there was a general impression that the man had lost none. But when he was told as much, the speaker was stricken a blow that might almost have killed him, and the cruelly wronged man left the train and went away, raving and cursing, into the bitter night.

"But as the train sped on its way, there was one even more wretched than he. I was afraid of my shadow. I dared not return to my innocent wife and prattling children, and attempt to account for my wealth. Since then, I have not seen them,— no, nor any creature who could remind me of the days of my innocence and happiness. I have been punished, for I would give my life to see those toward whom I may never again turn."

The reader ceased, and turning from his manuscript, said: "And now may God, through Christ, forgive all my sins, and restore this man his own, and let me die."

There was a deep silence. The stranger had changed from red to pale, and sat gazing at the fire, his fingers twitching nervously, and an indescribable look in his eyes. Perhaps years had quenched the bitterness of his wrong; and as he heard the story of the man who had suffered more than he, he seemed to forget vengeance. Finally, old Maxwell rose, hitched up his waist-band, and desired to hear the opinion of his compeers, adding, "It are bad, an' sneakin, an' a d——d low-down game all through; but 'tain't no killin' 'fence, in my opinion." But when he sat down, there was no response. The groups sat silent, looking into the dying fire, their heads bent, and each man evidently thinking more of the strangeness of the story than of his function as juryman. Finally the stranger arose slowly, buttoned his ragged coat, looked around upon the group, and advanced slowly toward Denham.

"Parson," said he, "I told ye all I wuz busted. I ain't got no luck. My gal's dead years ago, an' my friends is forsook me. It's been so long sence I had a raise I don't know how sech a thing 'ud feel. You done it,—done it sneakin'ly on a sleepin' man. I don't want nothin' now,—I don't want yer bilin' spring, nor yer orspital, nor yer money, notuthstandin' it's more than I ever had. Ye kin burn yer will,—ye kin keep yer curse; an' I'd even scorn to kill ye. Let me tell you suthin that, with all yer smartness, ye ain't learned yit. Ye can't blarst a man's life, an' cure it all by givin' back. I hain't no children, no wife, no home, no character, no nuthin'; an' ye can't give them things to me. I tell ye I'm busted, an' you done it. I want none of yer trumpery ; keep it,—an' be damned eternally to ye!"

And hurling this frightful anathema behind him, he strode through the open door and out into the night, and his footsteps died away upon the road.

One by one the men arose, and silently, with no glance aside, went away, leaving James Dodd, clergyman and thief, alone in his stolen house and with his stolen wealth. They spent no time in parleying; they passed no sentence, and it may be that they even pitied him; but at least he was forsaken and despised in the midst of disgrace and crime.

Some passing traveller found him there; for when the frosty sunlight streamed through the dusty panes in the early morning, the face it shone upon was a dead man's waxen mask. The suicide had ended all with one ghastly gash from ear to ear.

It was long ago. The spring murmurs on, and the tall cottonwoods grow green and beautiful in the desert. Nature and truth alone are triumphant. With all the characters of its little tragedy dead and forgotten, Ojo Caliente is still a green oasis in the brown landscape, in no way more remarkable for having been the scene of Brown's Revenge.

V.

COPPER DISTILLED.

THE most extraordinary of all the efforts of American romance are those which, without any foundation in truth, have created the widely-accepted picture of the American Indian. When confronted with the actual hero, the beautiful characters of Cooper cease to attract, and, indeed, become in a sense ridiculous. Lordly, reticent, content, eloquent, brave, faithful, magnanimous, and truthful, he made those sons of the forest seem, whose scattered descendants now linger upon coveted reservations, and, in unhappy squalor, seem patiently, if not lazily, to await final oblivion. Filthy, brutal, cunning, and very treacherous and thievish, are their descendants and relatives who still wander in a condition of marauding independence west of us. Every tradition repeating the story of Indian bravery, generosity, and hospitality, fades like mist before the actual man. The quality of moral degradation, inborn and unmitigated, runs through the whole kindred, from King Philip and Red Jacket down to Sa-tan-te, Sitting Bull, Kicking Bird, and Spotted Tail. The common instincts of savagery, as illustrated in all the tribes and kindreds of the world, are intensified in these. Brave only in superior numbers or in ambush, honest only in being a consummate hypocrite, merry only at the sight of suffering inflicted by his own hand, friendly only through cunning, and hospitable never, and, above all, sublimely mendacious and a liar always, the Indian, as he really is to those who unfortunately know him, seems poor material out of which to manufacture a hero or frame a romance. All missionary and philanthropic efforts made in his behalf have thus far failed to amend his life or change his morals. Always prominent in the history of the country, ever to the fore in philanthropic literature and high-plane oratory, always the impediment to be removed, and afterward the dependant to be supported, mollified by semi-annual gifts, and oiled and pacified by periodical talks about the Great Father and blarney about " brothers," through campaigns, councils, treaties, and tribal relations, he has finally come to almost the last years of his career, with only the one redeeming fact upon his record, that he has never been tamed and never been a servant. Neither has the hyena.

The ordinary reservation Indian is not a curiosity. The greasy red blanket, the variegated shirt, the extraordinary hat, the shanky legs, the brass jewelry, the shuffling gait and inturned toes, the encrusted rancidity, are seen every circus-day, and give such other evidences of nearness as even a blind man need not mistake. He sometimes indulges himself with a change of scene, and travels for his health, and threads the usual one long street of the Western town with his motley cavalcade of lean ponies, rawhide paniers, squaws, young ones, and colts. But the details of an unsought and irksome acquaintance with the wilder tribes of the plains and mountains may more probably contain here and there an item of interest.

And if one knows the Indian of eastern Kansas one need have no difficulty in recognizing on sight his brother of the plains. The family resemblance is complete. Stolidity, and a surly indifference that passes for dignity, are noticeable traits of first acquaintance. To sit around, to loaf, to be always present where not wanted, to go and come as though all hours and seasons and all enclosures were his own, are some of the endearing amiabilities that he practises when not on the war-path, and while he is on speaking terms with that other power, the government of the United States. When not offended by some dereliction in etiquette undiscoverable by any but himself, he is, contrary to the general opinion, garrulous as a magpie and inquisitive as a coyote. He does not go home when he can find any other place, and will make a long sitting on the agent's door-step, without much apparent anxiety about the welfare of his family. I have written the word "home" with a knowledge of its great inappropriateness to anything that may be an Indian's. If he has any, it is the lodge, erected in the open prairie, and apparently as far as possible from any water. It is the "tepee" from which was taken the idea of that cumbersome and elaborate tent familiar to all during the first year or two of the great war. The clean and carefully-sewed skins which form the cover represent many weeks of hard squaw labor. The poles were brought from the mountains, perhaps hundreds of miles away, and are worn smooth with constant dragging. Within this lodge is gathered all there is of Indian comfort. Around the walls lie piles of skins — the beds and clothing of a numerous family indeed, if both Indians and insects are to be counted. In the intervals of occupation by the first-named, they are usurped by a horde of dogs, who are less to be blamed than pitied. If there be a fire, it is of that curious fuel called "buffalo chips." It is kindled in the centre, and the fuel is left to burn, or merely to smoke, as shall happen on that particular day, and the smoke is left to find its way out on the supposition that the interior must finally become too full to hold any more.

Between the straggling lodges loiter the population who by chance find themselves there in the intervals of looking after the agent, and the soldiers' and officers' quarters; children, young men, and the variety known under the disrespectful heading of "bucks." Dangling from saddles, tied to poles, and hung to every available projection, are ragged pieces and bloody lumps of buffalo-meat, the whole sum of the ordinary commissariat, in all stages of odorous decay.

Everywhere and always the men are idle and the squaws at work. The hideous and toothless crone, the picture of unpitied age and misery, is never too old to toil, never old enough to rest. To her and her daughters fall all the endless tasks of a nomadic life. Her place is that of a slave; a slave born and predestined, to whom rest and liberty shall never come. She is beaten, abused, reviled, driven like any other beast of burden. She is bought and sold; wife, mother, and pack-animal, joined in one hideous and hopeless whole — a squaw. She must know but one lesson: to toil and be silent. Nevertheless, in all that is peculiarly Indianesque, she excels her master. In cunning, hatred, and revenge, in the specialties of cruelty and the refinements of torture, she has no equal on earth or in Hades. The saddest fate that can befall the captive is to be given over to the squaws.

There is really no more beauty to be found among Indian "maidens" than there is among gorillas. Never were the features that pertain to the unmixed race modified for beauty's sake. More false than even Cooper's wonderful tales, are the poems which descant upon the charms of dusky love and the romance of wilderness affection. Poetic license is a wanton and wayward thing, and has been made to caper nimbly to strange tunes ere now. But the man who invented those charming but phenomenally false Indian ideals, and first crowned the universal squaw — squat, angular, pig-eyed, ragged, wretched, and insect-haunted — with the roses of love, ought to see the woman once, and, as a punishment, to be subjected for a season to her indescribable blandishments.

It is an experience probably not to be objected to for once, but a repetition of which is not desirable, to watch for an hour the operations in progress among this assemblage of heroes and nymphs.

There is a young squaw, who has become the possessor of a little flour, and therewith she is up to her elbows in the process of making bread. She has a small fire, a battered iron pan, and sits by a little pool of muddy water in which the young ones have been wading, and out of which the dogs have lapped. She pours in *quantum sufficit* of water, and stirs the pasty and streaked mass into proper congruity with one unwashed fore-finger. Presently she wipes this upon her encrusted piece of a blanket, and places the mass in the ashes. Near by sits an old woman preparing a freshly-killed carcass for that process after which it becomes jerked beef. Her task it is to cut the whole of the animal into long thin strips for drying. But the ancient operator is the curiosity, not the beef or the process. Grey-haired, wrinkled, and haggard, her dried limbs scarcely concealed by sodden rags, she is the picture of hopeless and toiling wretchedness. You may stand an hour by these two; you may talk, laugh, pity, or question, and they will never betray by sign or look the least knowledge of your presence.

Yet, if you would see the very pink of hauteur and personal pride, you have but to observe yon gaunt and greasy son of the wilderness, who believes himself to be the glass of fashion and the mould of form. He is as unconscious of his odors as though redolent of patchouly and white rose. He is truly unwashed, and nearly naked save in the respect of paint, and, if the impolite truth must be told, swarming with that enterprising insect to which the Scottish poet wrote an apostrophe. He regards you with folded arms and defiant face, and desires to impress you with the idea that he is indeed "heap."

I am not discussing the digger, celebrated in California annals; nor any of the bug-eating pieces of tribes that are regarded with so much contempt until they begin to fight, like the Modocs. These, philanthropic reader, are those plains Apaches who have made us wish we were somewhere else with the baggage so many times, and who stand unexcelled in all the qualities so unpleasantly admirable in Indian character—endurance, cunning, ferocity, and vindictiveness.

In Indian society, each family is the producer of all the articles required in daily life. Clothing, food, and weapons are all manufactured from the raw material. Barter and exchange were introduced by the white men, and even yet there is little wanted in exchange by the Indian that he is not much better without. It is true that so many ponies and robes were necessary always in that very particular negotiation, the purchase of a wife. But each family is self-supporting, and comprises within itself the whole theory of patriarchal government. Resources are few, and actual wants as well; and in this or any encampment may be seen in an hour the whole Indian economy. There are squaws who bring fuel and water, and others who are engaged in the tedious and laborious process of stretching and scraping that finally results in the white, pliable, and elaborately-ornamented "robe," which is the representative of Indian comfort, wealth, and art. There is the crudely-awful process of savage cookery constantly going on, and the ponies to watch, catch, and saddle. There is the endless packing and unpacking of a nomadic life. There are lodges to build and to take down again, and a hideous master to wait upon and please. The squaw does it all. Early in life she becomes old, and adds innumerable wrinkles, that attain to the dimensions of cracks, to a face that was repulsive even in babyhood. She is stoop-shouldered, bow-legged, flat-hipped, shambling, and when at last she dies, nobody cares or cries, and she is even denied a soul and a hereafter. Through all her tasks and toils, she carries, strapped to a board and slung upon her back, the little, winking, brown-faced, silent babe, who seems never to laugh and never to cry She loves it, too, with a love that is the one human trait in her character.

I once had for some months the indirect charge of three Apache children. During that time, and until they ran away, they were in malice, cruelty, filth, ill-temper, and general hatefulness, the nearest approach to little fiends I have ever encountered. It was necessary to watch them to keep them from killing each other. But they never cried, and were quiet, sly, and predatory, as so many weasels; and while there was plenty of beef and bread, it was found impossible to keep them from eating out of the waste barrel.

In the manufacturing processes of the Indian, nothing is wasted. His hunting is not pleasure-seeking slaughter, as ours is, but a means of livelihood. He is, or was, as cautious to prevent waste of numbers among the shaggy herds of the plains as the white man is of the thrift and well-being of his tame kine; and for the same economical reasons. For from the buffalo, aided by a little wood, all his life's necessities may be supplied.

Indian life is full of tawdry pomp and barbarous ceremonial, and in every camp, while the women steadily toil, the men are engaged in some noisy rite necessary to the proper celebration of some late feat, or to propitiate success in some contemplated exploit. He is a tremendous braggart, our red friend, and he who boasts longest and loudest is generally taken at his word, as is usual everywhere. It is to obtain opportunity for this advertisement of personal prowess, that a "dance" of some kind is always going on. Their names and purposes are nearly innumerable, and the candid uninitiated is not able to perceive any great difference in the screams, leapings, and horrible hootings, which characterize them all. Some of these noisy ceremonials are said to be religious, but all there is of religious sentiment is condensed into the one word "medicine." Everything in life has its place in one or the other of two classes: it is either "good" or "bad" medicine. Camping-places where some evil has befallen are ever after bad medicine; and all days and places where some defeat, sickness, or loss was suffered, are classed in the same category. All things that were fortunate are placed on the opposite side. In this book-keeping and running account with fate, I do not know if there is a column for things indifferent and belonging nowhere, to finally balance with. The high-priest of this religion is the celebrated "medicine-man." The precise qualifications of this dread person are somewhat indefinite. I am forced to confess, after knowing him personally, that the only perceptible difference between him and his fellows seems to be that he is, if possible, idler, raggeder, and lazier than they are. But, dance or no dance, the buck usually wears the scalps he has taken, dangling from the greasy waistband of the unique article in pantaloons known as his breech-clout. This sketch may seem to the Eastern reader somewhat one-sided, though it is not so. What soft and twilight picture of She-mah-ga, the white dove, and We-up-mukh, the swift one, could be expected from one who has so often seen dangling from the waist of some loud heathen the long brown hair of his countrywomen?

One would naturally infer that begging would be incompatible with the Indian character. By no means; he is the most persistent and importunate beggar on this continent. Governmental management of him seems to have produced the impression upon his mind that there are constantly large arrears due him which he ought to have, and that every white man owes him something. Failing in his demands, he immediately proposes to "swap." He is apparently surprised at the white man's inability to always see the advantages accruing from these business operations, since one of the articles frequently offered in exchange is his squaw. One of the strongest evidences of idiocy to him is the fact that he can get more for a robe, a pony, or even for a paltry bow-and-arrows, than he could for a whole family of squaws.

The language of all Indians is peculiar. The comparatively few words used are coarse and guttural, and so useful a part of it is action and gesture that any man may talk Indian — not speak it — who is at all skilful in the use of pantomime. The mellifluous names of mountains, lakes, and rivers must not be taken as examples, as they were probably never pronounced by the aboriginals as we spell them. In lieu of a complete vocabulary they use many signs, even in conversation among themselves. A class of deaf mutes are scarcely more skilful than they in communicating ideas without words. I have seen long conversations carried on between very communicative specimens of copper-color and officers of the army, only prefaced by the word "how" and a most demonstrative and cordial shaking of hands. A circular movement of the hand over the head aptly indicates a day, a jog-trot movement describes a horse, and the two together express that prominent idea of a wide and desolate region, a day's journey. A yet different movement of the hand indicates a buffalo — showing, in a way not to be mistaken, the peculiar gait of that animal. Numbers are indicated by rapidly throwing up the hands, displaying as many fingers as answer to the number to be indicated. Of course there are words enough to definitely specify all things common to Indian life, and in a great many dialects. I have the idea, without any pretensions to aboriginal scholarship, that these savage tongues comprise but little beyond the ordinary forms of speech not capable of being written.

There are many ideas of Indian skill and cunning that, while they are correct to some extent, are overdrawn and extravagant. The curious fact is that the trapper and miner and the hunter of the border, the *voyageur*, and, indeed, most of those whose strange tastes have led them to follow and find pleasure in a frontier life, are capable of outwitting him in almost every instance. They understand what he is sure to do in a given case, and so either do it themselves or take measures to render his manœuvre harmless. The trade they have learned from him they excel him in. By nature the Indian is possessed of a genius for stealth, like the cats, gaining his livelihood by still-hunting. He has an instinct of cunning that has sometimes been dignified by the name of strategy, but in his operations against an enemy he exercises but little strategy that is nobler than lying. He can cover his head with brown earth and lie among the coarse grass at the roadside, and, having thus concealed his sinister visage, speed an arrow after the traveller. He can occupy thirty-six hours in crawling a few rods to steal a mule he must have wanted very much, as I have known him to do, and finally succeed in his purpose. He will smoke the pipe which is the universally recognized sign of amity and peace, with many signs of good-will and much pacific grunting, and the same day lance you in the back, if there be fitting opportunity. He will be at great pains to make a false trail, and will imitate the sounds of nature, and by a thousand devices attempt to mislead. But he has not a fraud in his repertory in which the white man has not long since learned to outwit him.

The few white men who have abandoned civilization and race for Indian society, aiding their adopted friends by a superior knowledge of civilized modes, are leaders, not followers. It is quite superfluous to add that they are the worse of the two, and have just humanity enough left to cause them to desire rather to reign in hell than serve in heaven.

The art of reading the face of nature, so common in frontier life, is one so strange that we are apt to regard it as an instinct. To the Indian the track of the antelope is as plain as the path of a tornado. He tells the number and kind of his enemies, and the hours since they passed. He invented a system of signals before the days of Morse, and the smoke upon the distant hill, or the brief fire upon the mountain-side, convey to him tales he never misunderstands. He traverses the vast surface of the monotonous wilderness, and, with an instinct as unerring as that of the bison, reaches his destination. He hovers for days upon the path of his enemy, always near and always watching, yet never seen or heard save by those who have learned his art. All these things the white man has stolen from him. There are many men on the border who earn a livelihood by outwitting the Indian at his own game.

It is a misapprehension to regard the weapons of the Indian as inefficient, and to wonder how he managed to live and perpetually fight before he became acquainted with fire-arms. These he uses, and very efficiently, in warfare; but he has never discarded his own. The ancient bow-and-arrow, probably the first efficient weapon made by men, and used in all climes and races, is yet, in the hands of a Comanche, one of the most effective of weapons. A great American philosopher was ridiculed for recommending that the colonial troops should be furnished with this arm — for this among other things; and yet the great genius of common sense was right, for it is infinitely more effective than that flint-cocked blunderbuss, the Queen Anne musket. Our Indian uses it in its simplest and rudest form — merely a piece of elastic wood, with a string made of sinew. The arrow is often an elaborate specimen of savage handicraft, being about twenty-eight inches in length, and elaborately feathered and ornamented. The ornamentation is peculiar to the tribe that made it, and the head is of iron, sometimes of flint, and is fastened in a cleft of the stick in a very neat and effective way by a wrapping of fine sinew. This slight and fragile shaft will transfix the huge body of the buffalo, coming out on the opposite side, and penetrates where the huge modern bullet is flattened or turned aside. It is almost noiseless,* and at thirty yards seldom misses its mark. Once wounded, there is small chance of recovery, for the dried sinew relaxes in moisture, and the wood comes away and leaves an inextricable triangle of iron behind.

* He who has heard the *swish* of an Apache arrow is no more likely to forget it than he is the shriek of a shell.

Indian fighting is not the placid and time-killing amusement it is sometimes imagined to be. Unless taken in mid-winter and by surprise, we have been passably well castigated at least half the time in all our little, cruel, revengeful and doubly costly wars with them. And taking him by surprise is very much like catching a weasel asleep. The plains Indian is a master of horsemanship, and his brother of the mountains knows every tepid water-hole and every pass, and climbs like a goat. He of the prairies has a trick of being always upon that side of the horse that is opposite his enemy, and almost entirely concealed. Rapidly riding in a circle, he discharges his arrows under his horse's neck or over his back. He is here and there like a flash, and his great endeavor is to invest his enemy on every side, and offer him every possible inducement to exhaust his ammunition. I have no advice to offer that gallant handful of skilful men known as the army of the United States. They are acquainted fully with all there is of the Indian, and have reason to be. The modern soldier, trained in the mysteries of the skirmish drill, lies quietly in his place and speeds after his foe the messenger that weighs four hundred grains, and that, singing as it flies, tumbles many a savage rider six hundred yards away. To fire deliberately, to waste no bullets, and to have a sufficiency of cartridges and of water, means generally drawn battle, or, rarely, absolute victory. How very easy it is to write recipes!

This is plains fighting. There is a slightly varying system among the mountains of New Mexico,

There, all is concealment. The Indian of that region never meets the soldier, and the latter very rarely gets within hailing distance of the Indian. There is no noise, and from behind the rocks in the cañon, or concealed by the sage and cacti, the arrow is sped that cuts short many an unsuspecting life. Indian dead are seldom left on the field. A prudence that is natural enough makes it desirable that losses should not be counted, and scalps should not be taken to be danced and exulted over.

The name of the Great Spirit figures largely in all reports of Indian eloquence, just as the name of the Deity does in the fervid eloquence of the common politician. It seems probable that the great Idea is as much a myth to the one as to the other. The theology of the Indian is simply a superstitious fear of something he does not understand. What kind of a heaven or hell he has imagined for himself, no man can precisely tell. There are no strictly religious forms, and certainly no idea of worship as we understand the term, and nothing that is regarded as especially sacred. The religious idea is not prominent, and seems almost entirely included in the "medicine" business before referred to. Of that which we call superstition, there is plenty; and, as with ourselves, luck is extensively propitiated.

Of course, in speaking of the Indian, the common class is the just criterion. Yet, as is well known, the red race, and every other, is not wanting in examples of force, dignity, and comparative greatness. King Philip, Tecumseh, Red Jacket,

Billy Bowlegs, are historic characters. Sa-tan-te, Kicking-Bird, Sitting Bull, and a grotesque category of their like, have been very extensively mentioned in later times. In some of them, the common farce of Indian dignity has been condensed into something like the genuine article. The Indian has never been humble, and is unlikely to be much abashed in the presence of dignitaries, unless some one of them has become known to him to his great cost; his firm conviction being that the meanest of his race stands at the head of all created intelligences. His is a race egoism, like that of the Chinese. When he goes to Washington, and attracts attention, and is interviewed and stared at, he believes it is because he is great and envied. In his mental constitution there is prominently wanting the faculty of appreciation. He knows that the wires that are stretched across the great country that once was his, "whisper" mysterious messages in the ear of the white man, and that insensate paper "talks." But the knowledge produces in his mind no respect for the people to whom the strange communings come. He does them the honor to accept them as facts, without further care or inquiry about them; and the idea that they are any evidence of knowledge superior to his never enters his mind.

With the old story of barbarity, cruelty, and rapine, the world is long since familiar. Nor is the conclusion just, that is so often prompted by philanthropy and by pity for the poor Indian, that the terrible story has been exaggerated. Indian atrocities that have come directly under the notice of hundreds of law-abiding, charitable, and truthful men, would, truthfully delineated, be unfit for the ears of any but those whose business it might be to investigate them. It would be almost impossible for any man personally cognizant of the doings in portions of the Southwest for the last few years, to look his neighbor in the face and calmly tell what he has seen. The burnings, the ravishings, the impalements upon charred stakes, the cutting off of eyelids, the chewing of finger-joints, the knocking out of teeth and drawing of nails, and nameless mutilations of the dead;—are these things told in daily newspapers? They have occurred in hundreds of instances that the reader has never heard of, and, I trust, will never hear of. But the frontiersman has not only heard—he has seen; and hardy and accustomed as he may be, his dreams are made hideous by the remembrance of indescribable scenes.

The man who is there, and who cannot go away, understands that last and chiefest trait of the Indian character which is either unknown or disregarded by all the divines and all the philanthropists: the inborn love of killing. There are animals whose strongest instinct is a thirst for slaughter that cannot be permanently assuaged. We know this, and accept the fact, but many of us do not understand and will not believe that there are men of the same kind, and whole tribes of them; that the Indian, in his natural condition, and before he has been fenced about by those surroundings of civilization which he cannot break, has this as his strongest trait, and that he has never, under any circumstances, entirely changed his character. This is why each tribe is, compared with the territory it occupies, a mere handful in the desert. A great incentive to war is the pleasure of torturing the captives. The whole history of the Indian is a history of blood. We have only glimpses of it, gory and incarnadine, lurid with devastating flame and ghastly with agony. Tribes and races have been utterly exterminated by other tribes, leaving only rude tumuli and broken pottery to tell of them and all their works. They are in unknown regions fighting now. They live and fight and die alone, their great victories celebrated by a midnight orgy, with shouts and groans alike dying among echoes that never speak again. It is contrary to Indian nature to desire to be at peace when war is possible. The tribal glory that he loves comes from war, and it is his only passion. If offended, even causelessly, he does not seek redress save sometimes as an excuse, and does not ask to have his wrongs righted with any desire that they should be. He begins to kill — and complains afterward. His massacres are sudden and unexpected in the midst of apparent harmony. The hunger for murder and torture is sated for a time, and all the tedious explanations and theories come afterward.

And yet this chapter is but the ultra-Missouri view of the case — conclusions gathered from actual contact. By a strange inversion of logic and the meaning of words, I have heard such views of the

Indian called prejudices; which must mean, if anything, that they are conclusions formed without knowledge — pre-judgments. Yet it is quite apparent that a good deal that is said on the other side, and in support of the directly opposite view, is said by those who have many of them never seen an Indian in his native and unconverted state. They have attained to a high plane of right, justice, and truth. They measure the Indian question by general rules, that, though enlightened and just beyond dispute, yet do not suit the hard facts of the case. They have had no adequate experience with the noble red man, who, if they could see him and know him well, would be found to possess a vast capacity for astonishing his best friends, by a yawning gulf of want in every noble trait. I believe I understand something of the philanthropists, and, instead of reviling them, I honor their views upon a subject of which they seem to stand upon one verge and I and my fellows upon the other. There is another side to the story, and these I conceive to be some of the items of it:

The Indian is a ward of the government, and yet, in his tribal capacity, a sovereign power capable of making treaties and ceding his vast and unused possessions.

He is a man independent in his own nationality, governed by his own laws, and neither knowing nor bound to know anything of ours, and who must yet be held amenable to trial and punishment in our courts, under laws of which he knows no more than he does of logarithms and the Greek particle.

He is the victim of a complicated system of compensations for his various surrenders, which he does not understand, and which seem to have been specially framed for the benefit of unscrupulous commerce and the fostering of trading schemes, and the formation of rings stronger than the government itself.

With phenomenal short-sightedness and unwisdom, he has been located upon new reservations where in the course of a few years he would be precisely in the way again; and what is more, he has an absolute right to stay there which no reasonable man can deny him.

He is the ancient and time-worn subject of political experiments, that are adopted and then lost sight of at once. Notable among these is that which seems to be based upon the idea that the piety of an agent would inoculate a tribe and chemically change an atmosphere in which everybody was supposed to be bent upon doing everything that was wrong and avoiding everything that was right, and to be spoiling for a fight always.

He has been fed, coaxed, and fought at the same time. He has consequently become a vicious boy, bad enough by nature and spoiled by management that would demoralize an angel. He has drawn rations in Arizona, in the midst of hostilities vigorously conducted by him in New Mexico; and has consequently been occupied during his intervals of rest and refreshment in laughing at his enemies, and reviling those two antipodal officials, the Secretary of War and the Secretary of the Interior.

It has been seemingly forgotten that he is rather a quarrelsome person, to whom revenge is religion. Consequently those in whose hands it entirely rested to bring him to terms, and rectify his somewhat savage notions of right and wrong, have been left without any jurisdiction over or control of the causes of his numerous complaints; and this, while his revenges are always directed against his readiest victims, the defenceless. A woman's long scalp-lock is as valuable and honorable to him as a warrior's. He has never been made to understand that the dispensers of his rations are able also to fight him, and willing. If he were given to know that the ability to feed was combined with the power to control, he would, were he but an animal — which he is not — be careful of his behavior.

In addition to this, it is time that it should be understood that there is no human power that can stop the migration from east to west. That situation must be accepted not only because it *must*, but because civilization is of more consequence than barbarism, and homes of greater importance than the preservation of vast hunting-grounds — a million acres to each hunter. After years of vacillation and costly experiment, it is time that some rational attempt were made to meet and improve a situation that is unavoidable. There is one man who can do it, understanding, as he does, more of the frontier, more of the immigrant and of the Indian, than statesmen and secretaries have either leisure or opportunity for. It is Captain Jinks, the careless and jaunty one, whose qualities and capacities not one in a thousand understands. He is the hardiest frontiersman of his times, and over countless leagues of dreary marching, and beside innumerable camp-fires, he has done what it would seem no other man who had aught to do with the Indian business has done: he has kept his honor and his uniform clean. He is court-martialed and dismissed sometimes, for petty offences not criminal save to "an officer and a gentleman," or for a human disobedience of petty orders. But have you lately heard of him as speculating in Indian supplies, or as a member of any "ring?" He is not good, and could seldom be accurately described by the somewhat worn phrase, "a Christian gentleman." He takes cocktails, and plays at cards sometimes, and is guilty of many a peccadillo. But his environment is peculiar. Nine times in ten he believes that death is better than dishonor. He does not want the Indian management, because he says he believes it to be demoralizing. It is no more than one of Jinks's peculiar reasons. It is his business to obey orders; and when he must he will take it. Then, by degrees, the "young men," whom the chief is always saying he cannot control, will find themselves restrained by the relentless doors of the post guard-house, in company with the man who has been selling them whiskey, until reflection shall have cooled their ardor. The preparations for a raid or an escapade will be observed, and the parties thereto required to give bail. Every ration and every dollar will go to those entitled to them, and to no others. He does not take sides; he does not argue the case; he obeys orders, and is interested in having others do precisely the same thing. A few dozen of him will keep a thousand citizens out of the Indian Territory, where they say they are determined to go, and yet have no especial love for either Creeks, Choctaws, or Seminoles, whose rights he is protecting. He is in a fight every summer — a fight that is never of his own making; and we do not object *then* to his methods of persuasion, or to the fact that he represents the power of the sword, and not that of the hymn-book and the gospel of peace.

It is time that we should cease to indulge in theories and hopes. It is getting to be a very old question to be still unsolved; and undoubtedly we have made a failure thus far in our management of it — a failure that is as ridiculous as anything we have ever done as a nation, and that has resulted in infinite wrong. Our Indian is bad, and we insist that he is good. Our management is equally bad, and we practically insist that that is also good. The management of her colonies by England has always been a reproach to her. She did not persuade when they were determined not to be persuaded. But she has managed them, and also her Indians. There is no more ineffective treatment for savages than the recipes of philanthropy. These are not the days of cruelty, conquest, and extermination, with which Christian philanthropy has contended so long. There seems to be no cause for the application of the rule of submissive quiet and gentle persuasiveness under all circumstances. If we wish to prevent sudden raids, reprisals, massacres, the burning of homes and the violation of women, and wide-spread horror and dismay, we must find a way not only to be just, but also to be strong. If we feed and clothe, we must also govern and prevent.

VI.

JOE'S POCKET.

"DRUNK ag'in! I swar, Joe Biggs, you air the orneryest human as lives. Don't say nuthin' to me, fur I can't stand it. Thar's the bed!" And the maligned Joe Biggs blindly flung himself upon the creaking cords of a not very luxurious couch, aided thereto by a movement on the part of the speaker that was too vigorous to be regarded, even by a person in Mr. Joseph Biggs's condition, as a caress.

The people outside laughed a little at their comrade's reception, though in all likelihood expecting something of the kind as they escorted him home from the sutler's store, and began an irregular retreat as the tumbled flaxen head of the woman appeared at the door. Moonlight is kind to anything at all resembling beauty; but homeliness, as embodied in a chalky face, untidy hair, a scowl which bodes no kindness, and over all a shabby night-dress, has no friend in the beams that seem to cover all homeliness save such as this. The woman turned away again, and retired into the darkness of the cabin; the retreating footsteps of the roisterers died away in the distance, and soon, under the placid beams, it was as though there were no drunken men or cross women in all the mountain world.

It was a cabin beside a rock-littered path. The pine logs of which it was constructed had been cut from the stumps that dotted the hill-side hard by, and, so far as rude skill could make it so, the place was comfortable enough. It was the ancient model of the frontier cabin, strangely placed in a country of adobes and earthen roofs. There was one door, one window, a chimney of mud and stones, and a small yard, enclosed by a homely and crooked apology for a fence. It was such a house as one might easily find at this day in the Green River region of Kentucky or in southern Indiana, and looked as though it might have been taken up bodily and brought thither as an architectural curiosity. The surroundings were pines, verdure, and general mountain coolness, in strong contrast with the tiresome adobe villages and low fields which lay in the valley below. Nor was the cabin entirely alone. A quarter of a mile away was the quadrangle of green grass, in the centre of which arose a slender flag-staff, surrounded by houses but little better than Joe's, but in which dwelt men and women so different that he saw them only from afar, and never heard their names. There were glimpses of white canvas, horses neighed in long sheds, and, as if to guard the bare standard of authority, a sentinel paced back and forth before the flag-staff, and two brass guns stood open-mouthed and glittering on either side. In a word, it was that universal condition of settlement and safety throughout the land — a military post. A spot than which it would have been hard to find one more green and brilliant, was enlivened all the year by the parade of arms, and the incense of military devotion arose each morning and evening in the sullen growl and lingering blue smoke of a gun at whose echoes the deer started and listened and the rabbit bounded away to his cover in the copse.

But if you followed the road that struggled indistinctly past Joe's cabin, you would soon find yourself among balsamic odors in glades and dells, rocks which had been rolled from their original beds and tumbled down the hill, and hill-sides whose brown earth showed signs of curious work. It was a land of wild scenes and wilder men, protected only by force from the Apache, and where the dwellers, even in their worst estate, could dream of nothing better. But it was also the land of gold. Where the stream ran through the valley, a mile away, the little mule drew, in an endless path, the shaft of the primitive *arrastra;* the Mexican patiently rocked his cradle with dirt carried thither upon a donkey's back; and over all the scene brooded the restless spirit of American enterprise, keeping ill-assorted company with ancient peace, wandering, prospecting, speculating, and gambling, — rough, vindictive, generous, and ever athirst for wild adventure and possible wealth.

Joe Biggs was that sort of person who needs no particular description to those acquainted with his species in a mining country. He was, or had once been, a Tennessean, though so long absent from his native country as almost to have forgotten the fact. Though still a robust and middle-aged man, he had been for many years a mountaineer, and a constant victim of all the vicissitudes which here, as elsewhere, befall a man whose principal characteristic is recklessness. It would seem to be an unfavorable soil for the growth of domestic infelicities, and that any kind of prudence ought to enable a man to leave them out of his category of sorrows. But Joe had not that prudence, and in the appearance and temper of his last wife he was the most unfortunate man in these diggings. He was the kind of man that is always married — married without regard to place, circumstances, or compatibility. There are many men like Joe. The world could easily be deluged with narratives of domestic sorrow; only the afflicted parties seem to agree at least upon the point of successful concealment.

Years before, when the mountaineer's tall figure was very straight and his tawny beard knew no thread of gray, in his saunterings in and about the village he one day came upon a maid of the nut-brown variety, whose eyes were very black and whose brown shoulders were very shapely; and as she milked goats in the little corral, he leaned upon the adobe wall and tried to twist his Tennessean dialect into something like Spanish. It is useless to tell the rest. The dead-and-gone beauty who was his wife for a few years had long been among the memories and regrets that men everywhere carry about with them. We cannot tell what thoughts were at work in Joe's heart, as he delved in the mountain side, while the daughter she had left him sat near and watched the work, or how sweet the water tasted that the little one brought him from the spring, or what weighty and important affairs were discussed as her lively chatter went continuously on through all the work, and Joe's kindly bass came in between. Fathers and daughters are an exclusive company; all the world knows their proverbial intimacy, and how in this perfect equality of June and December, June is generally conceded to be, if not the bigger, at least the wiser of the two.

But Joe's last matrimonial venture was of a different kind. He sadly knew it was so, and made no especial concealment of the fact among his numerous and very festive acquaintances. She was an attenuated and awkward Texan belle when he first saw her — one of the kind that is constantly wandering westward, and is ever ready to be married upon a day's acquaintance, and to almost anyone. A man is a man; and their tastes have not been highly educated by their surroundings. Joe must have been demented. He often thought of the circumstance as one that might have that extenuating possibility as an excuse; for he came, saw, conquered, and led his angular bride away from the cottonwood beneath which the ceremony had been performed, all within three days from his first sight of her "folks's" camp. Then the imprudent man's troubles began; and for about a year he staggered home from the trader's store, in manner and form, and meeting with the same deserved reception, as set forth in the beginning of this history.

So, as the woman comforted her wakefulness

with muttered words that were only a compromise with profanity, and her man Joe snored in fortunate unconsciousness of the storm, there was still another person in the cabin, who, more than any of the three, was the sufferer through habitual drunkenness and domestic strife. The daughter was fifteen years old; an age which, with such as she, means all the softness, tenderness, and beauty of youth, with the almost mature attractiveness of womanhood. That her training had thus far been peculiar and imperfect was not her fault, nor that of her uncouth tutor. He was rough and coarse, as his kind ever are; but years of roughness and coarseness sometimes fail to blot out in a man's heart the time when he himself was young and untouched by the iron that sears and hardens. As he went daily to delve in the hill-sides, ever searching for the yellow dust and ever finding only enough to feed desire, the child went with him, grasping his big finger with her tender childish clasp. As she lay asleep on his ragged coat in the pine-shadows, while the noon heats baked the bare brown hills that were dotted with pine stumps like huge nails half-driven, the long lashes trailing her flushed cheek and the withering mountain flowers in her little tired pudgy hand, old Joe's heart warmed toward her with a feeling that brought back everything that was good in the early youth of a wild life. The mountaineer was not utterly bad, nor entirely weak; and day by day her fingers twined in his beard, and her immeasurable love crept into his heart, and a consciousness of his trust grew upon him. And then the little one had the virtue of a generation of East Tennessee mountain virtue in her veins. But Joe never thought of that. The rough miners sometimes saw their neighbor engaged in strange occupations, as they passed by. Leaning on his pick, the child's bright eyes fixed upon his face, and forgetful in his earnestness that not only walls but mountains and trees have ears, he told her of the country and the people where he was born; of coon-hunts and log-rollings; of the few months during which he had learned all he ever knew of the hardness of the benches of a primitive school-house; and, more than all, of his mother. He tried to make the wondering infant understand that such as he could have a mother, and he tried to teach her some of the things that mother had taught him. Perhaps there were other listeners than the passing miners or the wondering child, as, in his blundering way, he told her of those mysteries we all do but dream of and hope for, but with dreams and hopes that are not as the visions of the night. But Joe told his daughter of that Maker of all things, whose presence seemed to rest like a shadow upon these primeval silences, and of the Christmas of so many hundred years ago, and, indefinitely and with many blunders, of right, wrong, love, kindness, and duty. But in the end he always came back to the beginning of his story; to what he "used to was" and "had orter be now," and to his mother. He seemed to fancy that she might be living yet. "When your daddy finds a pocket, we'll go back there, little 'un," he often said.

Joe's bad ways had begun but lately; and his daughter, still his companion, but no longer a child, began to have the dawn of trouble upon her fair childish face. Now, when the woman's tongue had abated its vigor, and she too seemed to have at last forgotten her husband's offence in slumber, the girl arose and glided through the open door into the brilliant night. The conventionalities of the world had little place in her life, and as she leaned upon the broken fence and looked down the mountain road, her feet bare in the dew and her round arms lying listlessly upon the topmost rail, she was not conscious of herself, or that the beautiful light, so unkind to her step-mother's features, transformed hers into those of a Madonna, as she looked up into the blue depths with the tears upon her lashes. By and by, in the vague unhappiness she could hardly define, and for which she knew no remedy, she laid her head upon her arms and did what the woman of all times and races is apt to do: she cried. It was past midnight. She heard faintly the sentinel's challenge, as the nightly pomp of the "grand rounds" came and passed; the faint clink of arms and the small commotion at the guard-house, as the surly crew of prisoners fell into line to be counted; and, lastly, the retreating footsteps and settled silence that proclaimed the untimely ceremony done. She had heard these sounds a hundred times; they were not curious, and she straightway forgot them in her girlish tears.

Presently the sound of a quick footstep came nearer and nearer up the road. It was a jaunty figure that came rapidly toward her, as she raised her sorrowful head to look. The crimson scarf upon his shoulder proclaimed him only officer-of-the-day, but it was worn like the baldric of an earl. The moonlight played upon button and epaulet, and kissed the sombre plume in his hat, and flashed up and down the bright scabbard he carried upon his arm. But all this was not so much the fault of Lieutenant Thurston, U.S.A., as of the moonlight. He was only a soldier, but he was young, and had about him a certain *élan* that should distinguish every man that follows the flag for love of arms. As he came he timed his footsteps to the tune he whistled — something that had in it a suggestion of life-let-us-cherish and devil-may-caredness that was strangely at variance with the sleepy hour at which he marched.

This blithesome son of Mars had finished his rounds as required in regulations, and under the influence of wakefulness, and stimulated by the night's balmy splendor, had continued his walk up the mountain road. Was that all? Young men's actions sometimes find unconscious excuses in what they are pleased to call their hearts. He had often been here before; so often, that every gaunt cactus and every gray stone in the rugged road was a familiar thing. As he came blithely, so he always returned thoughtfully. About the hardest thinking the lieutenant did was when he was returning from Joe's house. Then the remembrance of a home three thousand miles away used to come unsatisfactorily into his mind. He thought of the starchy respectability, the gold-spectacled and precise propriety, of the middle-aged gentleman whom he designated as "the governor." Then, there was a fair sister or two, and a circle of acquaintances. But the crowning reflection was, "What would mother think?" This lady the lieutenant knew very well, and all her prominent characteristics were long since so well memorized that he thought with a compunctive pang of the pain he might inflict by an alliance with anything that lacked the grand essential of "respectable connections." That there was another side to the question was also true. He was far away from anything that touched family respectability. He was literally owned, and all his hours and movements were governed, by the great republic whose uniform he wore. His home was his quarters, his profession his sword. Long years would probably pass before he would even see the home or the people who, little as they suspected it, had almost passed out of his life.

Joe's daughter was not in the habit of waiting for this young man beside the fence — not by any means; and if you had questioned her, she would have deliberately, not to say indignantly, denied it. But the young soldier had reached that stage of his experience when he often came so far merely to see the homely house in which lived and slept the creature who was most in his mind. He had often seen her, and spent a half-hour in listening to her lisping English, watching the flushes come and go upon her cheek, weighing her tact and evident intelligence, and, after a careless fashion, falling more deeply in love. But it had always been upon seemingly casual occasions, and by daylight.

As he espied her, he stopped suddenly in his tune, and said, as usual, "By Jove!"

She, after hesitating a moment between inclination and a natural sense of propriety, stayed where she was, and the flush on her cheek was strangely at variance with the tear-marks that were also there.

This rash young man could not have felt more intense pleasure at meeting any of the queens of society than he did then. It was reason enough to him, as it would have been to most of us under similar circumstances; and he came near and held out his hand. Then he also leaned carelessly upon the fence, and looked at the sweet oval face, red and brown, glorified by the moonlight and stained with tears.

"You've been crying," said he.

"*Si, Señor;*—yes," and then, grateful for the listening ear, she began to tell the cause of her unhappiness. In the attempt, her sorrows overcame her, and she laid her head down upon her arms again, and cried harder than ever.

There was, indeed, little use for her to do aught but cry. Her friend already knew, or guessed, the story. But the effect was such as might have been expected under the circumstances. The pretence of comforting, combined with a secret desire to have the pretty trouble go on as long as possible, came to the lieutenant on this occasion as naturally as it does to all men.

"Don't cry," he said. "It will all come right in the morning."

Such miserable platitudes are not expected to amount to much in any case; and they did not in this.

"The—the woman b-b-eats me," she said, and the sobs became more violent.

Then the usual remarks were at an end. "Beats you!—do you mean to say that the miserable old—ah,—that she has ever struck you?" and his face grew to an unseemly red at once.

"Look here!" he continued, as she made no reply; "why don't you and the old—and your father—cut loose from this sort of thing? *You* and he can live together, can't you? Go somewhere; do something; but," he added, "don't go very far."

Then he came a little nearer—so near that a tress of the girl's long black hair lay beneath his hand. "You must not imagine that because your disr——that because your father gets drunk every night, and the—the other creature strikes you, that you have no friends. If this kind of thing occurs again, we'll make it *warm* for them;" and the lieutenant placed his hand caressingly upon her shoulder.

Perhaps he meant well—we will suppose he could hardly help it; but it was a mistake. The girl arose from her bent posture, and turning toward him a haughty and indignant face, and eyes that showed a remarkable capacity for the expression of anger, without a word, went into the house.

As Lieutenant Thurston walked slowly homeward, he was not thinking so much of respectable connections as of something else. His mind was very much occupied with a new idea of the woman he had just left. Our military friend was learning that womanliness, and the indescribable and invisible virtue that clothes it, are, regardless of associations and education, an instinct and inheritance. Old Joe's beautiful child was not a mere half-Spanish girl. On this night at least, if never again, her Saxon blood and her father's homely teachings had come to her aid. The soldier pondered these things. He was deeply stung, and his face burned with mortification. But he was not ignoble, and the unspoiled honor of his fresh manhood asserted itself. "If that is the kind of woman she is going to be," he mused, "then, by Jove! I can't see what family respectability has to do with it all." And he was more deeply in love than ever.

. . . . . .

In the morning, Joe's spouse awoke sullen and sour, and berated him more than ever. The girl went about with a sad face, over which came at intervals a red flush, possibly caused by recollections of last night. The miner went away silent and sad, and the girl stood in the morning sunshine again by the broken fence, and watched the guard-mount afar off, and thought she discerned a tall figure there, and almost wished he would come again. How small her world was, and how large a figure one man could make in it, she never reflected. It is ever so. A woman's world may be filled by a very tiny dot, so she but loves it.

When Joe Biggs came again, at noon, he talked aside to his daughter:

"We can't stand this much longer, kin we, Sis?" and as she only answered by a look, he continued:

"I've done made up my mind. We'll quit. It was a mistake o' mine"—pointing with his thumb over his shoulder toward the house—"but I meant it well. Do ye 'member the place over the mountain I showed you once when we wus thar? Well, there's suthin' thar that's wuth goin' after. How do I know? Well, I don't jest *know;* but this kind o' thing can't last allus,—luck'll come to a man sometime, an' I'm a mind to go an' try fur it thar. Git ye ready, Sis; we'll go fur it now—to-night; an' mind, now, don't be a tellin' nobody."

When Lieutenant Thurston passed the miner's cabin, soon after sunset, he thought he saw a laden donkey, whose rider was a woman, far up among the pine-shadows on the mountain road. It was indistinct in the gloaming, but the man who plodded behind reminded him of Joe. The matter passed from his mind, and he forgot it in thinking of something he did not see; for the only living thing at the cabin was the woman who sat upon the step, her chin in her hands, eyeing him, as he sauntered past, with all the vindictiveness of her kind toward anything that looks like respectable humanity—that is, "stuck up."

The days passed, and the weeks, and nobody

seemed able to answer the question, "Where is Joe?" The woman came to the commandant for bread, and declared herself cruelly deserted, and very badly wounded as to her feelings; and finally she departed, with a party of her countrymen who wandered like Midianites over the land, for some region where men were more faithful. As for Lieutenant Thurston, he kept his thoughts, whatever they were, to himself. He was suspected of a careless weakness for Joe's daughter — and small blame to him; and he was rallied upon that point by his companions. But he seemed to fail to see anything particularly pleasant in their careless remarks about the "lost child," and they desisted. It would not be strange if he should think of his wise advice to her that moonlight night, as somehow connected with her and her father's departure, and suspect that the character of his last interview with her was such as to render him rather odious to her thoughts than otherwise.

The summer months, with their glory of air and sunshine and balm, passed away, and when the earliest snowflakes of a mountain winter were sifted over the land Joe and his daughter were well-nigh forgotten. But the dames and gentlemen of the garrison would have been much surprised had they known that the gayest and brightest of them all, the life of their limited social gatherings, had a greater regard for the mere recollection of the old miner's beautiful child than he had for all of them, or for the names and faces in the far-away land where he had spent his boyhood and which he still called "home."

The lieutenant, his fellow-officers thought, was growing "odd." He borrowed the topographical charts from the adjutant's office and applied himself to the geography of the wild mountain ranges. He questioned the wandering hunters and prospectors, with the private hope that they might tell him something of the persons he was thinking of. But all were ignorant. Joe and his daughter had strangely dropped out of the world.

The young soldier began to think he had reached that period in life in which a man seems no longer to have any use for himself. He had grown tired of his daily life and his routine duties. His pleasures had become very tame and insipid, and the winter's inactivity, though only begun, seemed endless and irksome. His constant thought of the miner's daughter, which was the real cause of all this, he excused to himself under the plea of ordinary curiosity. But it was a curiosity which wondered if she had gone because of him, and if he ever occurred to her thoughts. The idea gained possession of him that he might find her, and that he would like to try. As he thought of it, it seemed that by some rare chance he might come upon her hidden among the hills of that almost unknown stream whose waters ran toward the Pacific thirty miles to the westward. All that men knew of the head-waters of the Gila then was told by returning explorers, of a mysterious stream whose current was disturbed only by the leaping of the trout, of uplands smiling in the greenness of almost perpetual summer, and valleys in which the traveller seemed to have entered upon a new world. The hills were full of precious things, and the unhunted game which started from almost every brake made it a kind of hunter's paradise. Lieutenant Thurston had heard much of this current geography. For a long time he had heard carelessly; but of late it had seemed to offer a fair excuse for getting rid of himself. When he had asked of the commandant a scouting party, and had been refused, he bethought himself of a hunting expedition, and asked for leave of absence and an escort. These he managed to obtain; and after three days of careful preparation, with eight men and laden mules, he wended his way, through the slush of melting snow, up the mountain; where old Joe and his daughter had gone before. The man upon whom depended his safety and final return was a Mexican guide, who confirmed all the stories of the Gila country, and who had led explorers there, he said, before Thurston was born.

Were this a journal of a traveller's adventures, the frosty solitudes of mountains where perhaps a traveller's foot had never been before might well furnish a page. Men write of the Adirondacks, and the strange wildness of regions where every summer the tourists come. But those experiences in which man becomes a companion of the silence that has been unbroken since time was young, are seldom told. The slant winter sunshine lingered along the aisles of pine, and tinged with a melancholy glory white peaks unseen and unnamed before. They drank of snow-born streams that passed in cold and tasteless purity away to unknown depth and distance. The holly hung its drapery of green and crimson upon the hoary ledges, and the greenbriar and bramble lay in matted impenetrability across the cavern's mouth. Great bowlders sat poised upon the edges of abysmal depths, seeming as though the mountain wind or the finger of a child might hurl them headlong. The hanging creepers and the gray moss clung to dizzy acres of perpendicular granite with tenacious fingers that defied time and the storm. Here and there the cold blue depths of a mountain tarn lay silent between gray peaks that had been mirrored there ten thousand years; and in its oozy edges were the sharp indentures made by the hoofs of the mountain sheep, the round imprint of the wild-cat's cushioned tread, the dog-track of the fox, and, hardening in the crust, the curious marks that always seem to have been made by some wandering barefoot child, where the bear's cub has come to lap before his winter slumber. And over all there brooded a magnificent silence that seemed a fitting respite from the volcanic thunders which, when the world was young, had strewn the valley with its fire-scarred rocks and thrust the bold peaks into the smoky air. The gray bird of solitude sat upon the crag and plumed his wing so near that the lone wanderers could see the yellow ring in his relentless eye, and winged his silent way to his unknown eyrie; and save him there seemed to be no inhabitant of earth or air. In glens so deep that only the sun at midday looked into their recesses, the hardy mountain flowers still bloomed, and the coarse grass was green and brilliant. The ledges dripped with the ooze of melting snow, and the slender icicles which grew each night fell tinkling into the rocky depths in the morning's sun. On the far summits, where the foot of man shall never rest, winter held unbroken sway. The gathered snow which propped itself against the pines on the mountain-side sometimes broke loose from its fastenings, and tumbled, a fleecy cataract, which flung its spray into their faces, and buried an acre in its rest. And then the muffled echoes died away, and the wanderers turned aside to wonder when the hour would come that should wrap them in cold suffocation and chill their senses into drowsy death.

Lineal distance is not to be measured in mountain wanderings. After many days of devious journeying, the lieutenant knew that the warm fires of the post were glowing scarce fifty miles away. He knew, too, that somewhere among the rocks, perhaps scarce a hundred feet away, were the dim trails, the blazed trees, the remembered landmarks by which men had come and gone before, and which shortened distance and made intricacies plain. But to be lost in the mountains is to be dazed, bewildered, insane. Men lose the faculty of observation, and wander in an endless and hopeless round. They sit down in final despair, when only a ledge shuts out the sight of home, and the voices of friends might almost reach their ears. The lieutenant was lost. He knew it, and grimly bit his lips. The guide was lost; and while he claimed familiarity with each shadowy glen, and old friendship with each cliff's imperturbable face, the leader knew that he also was wandering at random amid rocks and hills that had not known the presence of him or any man. With a contempt for unwarranted pretences that men do not cease to feel even in despair, he addressed the Mexican no word, as he himself quietly took the lead. The party rode on in silence. In the face of every man except the leader was the knowledge of a hopeless bewilderment amid scenes never known before save to the unclouded vision of the immortals. But when he spoke, he gave his orders with the bluff distinctness of the parade-ground. For himself, he did not think he cared. He had in his heart that high courage which, regardless of physical strength, is the result of early training in the family, the school, and the traditions of a courageous race. He was one of that throng of gladiators whose skill, rather than whose strength, the world is beginning to understand, and in whom is illustrated the contrast between him who saluted Nero in the arena, and him whose weapon is given him first by his mother, to be sharpened afterwards by himself at school, at play, and in the first lessons of a life whose prizes are open to every man. Yet this young soldier was not a remarkable man. He was only one of those who are carving out the destinies of a brilliant century through the difficulties of daily life. He knew that beyond those wild and rugged fastnesses there was a river, an open country, a plain, or some change that could afford view and hope; and as he rode silently at the head of his party, he fixed his eye upon some distant land-mark that might keep them from wandering in the endless circle of bewildered men, and help them to the end at last, whatever that end might be.

So long as the snow melted in the morning sun, they need not thirst; so long as the startled hare sprang up before them, they need not want for food; and the wilderness-beleagured commander led his followers on. At night, in some sheltered spot, the blaze of cedar boughs threw its ruddy glare into the brooding darkness. The fox drew near to wonder at the illumination, and the green light of the deer's bright eye flashed upon them from beyond the fire-lit circle. It was a wilderness where even the Indian seemed never to have come, and, in the tameness of astonishment, the beasts came near to them in seeming friendship.

Then the soldier would sometimes leave his companions in the silence of slumber or thought, and wander away among the rocks and shadows. He did not go to brood and think alone. Perhaps it seemed to him, as it has seemed to many men ere now, that He whose hand had reared these pinnacles drew near and filled with an unseen presence the sinless solitudes of the primeval and uncursed world. In helplessness, almost in despair, he may have looked upward through the mighty shadows to the sailing clouds and the calm stars. It is in the desert, amid vast solitudes and awful silences, that men may reach upward and almost touch the mighty hand. There are hours when no man is an atheist.

And one night, as he walked in the gloom, he looked back and saw the silent group painted in striking colors by the ruddy light of that campfire which has seemed so often to the wanderer the light of home. A faint glow went before him into the darkness, and he fancied he dimly saw the outline of a path. A little further, and that was again lost; but he thought he perceived the faint odor of new-delved earth. Here and there a huge bowlder lay in his way, and as he touched it with his hand he could feel the slimy dampness of the surface that had lately lain in the earth of the hillside. Then he sat down upon the dry, dead pine-fringes, beneath an overhanging rock. Here was almost a link with the world. The morning would be begun with a new hope. A blessed some-one had been here before him, and he longed for light to see those human signs again, and follow them to wherever they might lead. He had almost started up to return to the fire again, when a strange sound fell upon his ear, and he stopped to listen. It was as a whirlwind heard from far. "It is the wind in the pines," he said to himself, and still listened as it drew nearer and nearer. Then a crackling sound mingled with the roar, and presently a great white bulk in the darkness leaped with a dull sound into the valley before him, and spread itself out upon the ground. Then another fell with a mighty crash almost at his feet, and he crept still nearer to the protecting rock. And while the great roar gathered in sound, and the foaming white sea came down like a relentless doom, the pallid face of the one frail mortal who stood in its way was turned aside, and as the white pall settled at the mountain's base, its cold folds shut in a figure poor and weak as compared with the mighty force that overwhelmed it, but grander, indeed, than all, in capacity for a heroic struggle with death.

In the morning, the soldiers and guide looked upon a great heap of snow, whose outer edge reached nearly to their camp-fire. "He is dead," said they, as they counselled among themselves. At noon they started back toward home. . . Was it indeed backward? The eagles that watched their wanderings, and the gray wolves who gnawed their bones, will never tell.

But he was not dead. The hollow rock was upon one side and the white wall of snow upon the other, and between lay his bed of dry pine-leaves, prepared for him by the angel of the winds, and softened by unseen hands. As the hours passed by, a dim blue light came through to him, and showed him the crystal outline of his hopeless house. He called, and the dull sound he heard mocked his own voice. But he did not lack air; neither was he wanting in hope and energy. He could touch the mossy rock, and the earth; and they seemed of the world, and friendly. He was hungry, and the blue-white light smote upon his eyes and seemed to benumb his faculties. As he reflected, he would have given all his knowledge of geography — nay, all he knew beside — for the topography of the snowy world in which he was buried, so that he might tell upon which side the white barrier was thinnest.

Then, as the first gnawing and weakness of hunger came upon him, he began to delve. He knew that strength would fail in experiment, and that where he began he must continue. As his fingers grew numb and stiff in his work, he wished he might barter all his hopes of ease and affluence for a despised spade. Yet his prison was not cold. The snow was a thousand blankets, and the radiating heat of the earth became a steam.

After many hours, the opaline mass grew slowly dark again, and he crawled backwards through his narrow tunnel, to chafe and warm his hands, and rest. Rest came with sleep. "He giveth his beloved sleep," and the angels must have looked kindly upon the place where, beneath his spotless tapestry, one lonely pilgrim lay, like a play-wearied child, with his head upon his arm in tired slumber.

When he awoke, he knew from his watch that he had slept five hours. He was frightened to think how the time was passing and he not saved. Hunger waits not upon effort, and already the enemy was insidiously gnawing. But he did not immediately set to work again. On the contrary, he did something that, to the uninitiated, would seem the very opposite. He was not utterly without a solace and comforter, and this comforter is one that has accompanied men in much toil and weariness in this world. It comes to every camp-fire, and stills like a balm the cry of hunger and cold. It was a brown pipe. He leaned against the rock, and the incense of the Virginia weed ascended and was absorbed in the roof of virgin snow. After a while, calmness came to him, and he again crept into the narrow tunnel he had begun. Lying prone, he pressed the snow beneath him, creeping slowly forward. Wearily the hours passed. Sixty feet — seventy — ninety — a hundred. He looked backward through the long passage, and thought of the unknown distance yet to go, and his strong heart almost failed him. A hundred and ten — twenty. His head swam, and the blood from his numb fingers stained the snow. Ten feet more, and his hands were like sensitive sticks, and almost refused their office. Then he crept slowly back, and crawling to his couch, tried to chafe his stiffened fingers into something like life and feeling. Darkness had come again, and he lay there, not knowing if he slept, or if indeed he saw visions of another country, with orchards in white bloom, and paths beside rivers, and shining spires of fair cities above the mists of morning. Afterward his raw hands were swollen until at sight of them he almost smiled; yet he crept into the long tunnel again, and, with pain at every stroke, worked at his task for life. A huge bowlder intervened, and with infinite pains he delved around it. The slow hours passed, and he was still another hundred feet nearer the far-off world. He ate the snow from thirst, and the thirst grew as he ate, and his throat was sore and swollen. He was chilled, and drowsiness nearly overpowered him. He was afraid to sleep, for he dimly knew that sleep was death. He was weary with a languor he had never felt before, and the narrow backward track seemed too long to be traversed again. Weariness had overcome hunger, and all feelings had given place to utter exhaustion. And still with weary strokes he plied his task. He knew that light must soon come, or death. He could not waste strength in crawling back to his bed. He could not wind his watch with his numb fingers, and the long hours passed uncounted; and still, with that dogged energy with which strong men fight death, he delved on, with movements so slow and tired that with remaining consciousness he almost doubted if he were not asleep. Three hundred feet, — and when morning came again and shone dimly through the snow, he hardly noticed, and did not care, that, white and strong, it lit with the radiance of spring the confines of his living grave.

. . . .

The March sunshine lights up the narrow valley with a blithesome glitter, that seems brighter by contrast with the lingering snow upon the higher hills. The air is full of the balm and sweetness of the southern mountain ranges, and upon every hand are the evidences of that strange mingling of perennial spring and eternal cold which in more level countries seems a fable.

Strewn along the edges of a noisy stream are four or five log houses. Spots of brown earth dot the hillside; the uprooted bowlders have tumbled into the torrent, and on every hand are evidences of the spade and the pick. The little settlement, in the very heart of the southern Sierras, is very new, and as yet unheard of in the world of stocks and trade. Everything necessary to the rude life of the place is carried thither upon the backs of donkeys, and costs almost its weight in the precious dust — of which there is some considerable quantity hidden in these cabins. All around lie the peaks and valleys of an unknown wilderness, through which even the miner has hardly yet wandered. You might pass and repass many times within a few hundred yards of Biggs's gulch, and not suspect its existence. The veritable Biggs himself, accompanied by his daughter, passed around the spur and near the new snow-bank, about nine o'clock in the morning, on this tenth day of March. It was Sunday, and he carried nothing but a stick. Their errand was not this time the perpetual gold, but wild flowers for her and trout for him. But, after all, there was something in their Sunday's pleasure unsuspected by them. As they passed by, the old man stopped to look at the huge heap that had come so suddenly and so late, and whose outer crust was fast melting under the rays of the valley sun. As they stood there, his eyes, ever accustomed to notice the small things of nature, discovered a curious cavity in the snow, fast widening in the sun. He stooped to obtain a better view. "Suthin inside begun that hole, sis, an' the meltin' is a finishin' of it," he said, and inserted his fishing-stick. At the very entrance, it touched something soft. Then he broke away the crust, and there, before their astonished eyes, lay a blue-clad figure, the face downward and resting upon an outstretched arm.

It were useless to note the ejaculations of astonishment, some of which had a strong though unmeant touch of irreverence, as the mountaineer drew forth into the sunlight the limp figure, and the bright rays kissed the pallid and suffering face of the soldier who had fought with death and been almost conquered. It would have been entirely in order if the girl had screamed or swooned. She did neither, but her face took at once a flush and a pallor. "Wait a minnit," shouted the old man, somewhat flurried, and started off as fast as his elderly limbs would carry him. As he passed around the spur, the girl stood looking at the unconscious form, and her face showed a curious mingling of emotions. Then her eye caught sight of one bleeding, swollen hand, and as she knelt and lifted it she began to cry. Then she took the other; and it would seem that she thought to warm and heal them by contact with her fresh, wet cheek. As the moments passed, she drew nearer and nearer to him. She touched his cheek with hers, and smoothed back the damp hair. Then she suddenly left him, and ran to the bank round which her father had disappeared, and looked up toward the village. No one was coming. She glanced apprehensively around; not even a bird was near. Then, as if fearful of the loss of time, she darted back to where he lay, and, kneeling, lifted his shoulders in her arms, and pressed his head to her bosom as a mother would press her little child. Even as the tears fell down upon his face, a rosiness of pity and love overspread her own. "*Ay di mi,*" she said, "poor theeng, poor theeng." But in the midst of her caresses and lamentations, the soldier opened his eyes. He said long afterwards that he would have done so had he really been, as she thought him, dead. She just laid him down again, and sat apart in shame, daring neither to look at him nor leave him. Her father came with his companions, and as they carried him to the cabin the girl followed far behind — glad as a guardian angel for the saving of a soul, ashamed as Eve at the voice in the garden.

It is strange, indeed, how near the brink of the great gulf a man may go, and yet return. An hour more in the snow-bank, and the soldier had never seen the sunlight again. As it was, the sluggish blood was slow enough to resume its flow through chilled and stiffened veins. But as he lay beside the one window in Joe's cabin and looked out upon the scenes of a new life, it seemed as though he did not much care. The distant post, guard-mount and dress parade, the midnight tour on the guard-line, his loved profession, and the charm and glitter of arms, all seemed to be far-away and almost forgotten things. Day by day his strength came slowly back, and he was indifferent as to whether his friends knew of his fate or only guessed and wondered. He was enjoying the only absolute and unquestioned dominion a man ever exercises in this democratic land — the dominion of the convalescent. He seemed almost to have forgotten his lady mother; and the mild terrors of an infringement of the Draconian statutes regarding respectable connections no longer troubled him. Joe Biggs went his daily way to his digging, and the girl, who sat demurely at the little fire and occupied herself with the endless stitching of her sex, was his physician, if he had any. Sometimes, as he watched her, there was the old merry twinkle in his eye, and a sly smile dawned in his face. Perhaps he was thinking of how very cunningly he had found her again, or of the great ridiculousness of the current supposition that he came near dying in the snow-bank.

But he talked to her, and was rewarded by the interest with which she listened to the strange story he told her. And then he feigned to sulk, by no means adding to his general agreeableness thereby, and grew tyrannical, and declared that unless she came near, nay, even sat upon the bed-side, he would probably never recover. Once, as she sat there, he told her of his far-away home, and of his mother and sisters; and then he entered more largely into the subject, and described, even more clearly than her father had done, the characteristics of the two great races from which she had distantly, and very fortunately, come.

Upon bright days of the advancing spring, he walked about the little mountain hamlet that had as yet scarce so much as a fortuitous name, and was apparently much interested in the life of the mines. He went with the girl to his last camp, and they two looked with curious eyes at the camp-fire ashes that lay there leached and sodden, with a broken knife and a lost bayonet as mementos of the bewildered wanderers who had last been there. And they stood together at the shelving rock, and her face flushed, and her black eyes sparkled with pitying tears, as he told her of his days and nights in the snow. No wonder that he became to her the central object of all thoughts, and the great concern and care of her life. For she still chose to believe he was not strong, and made him savory dishes of mountain quails, and demurely cautioned him about his various imprudences. She believed she knew men, and their ways and doings. She had had the care of one, and a wayward one, for some years. As for Lieutenant Thurston, and his masculine submissiveness to all this tyranny, he was conscious of but one defined and positive feeling in regard to it: he had made up his mind that an indefinite continuance of it would suit him precisely.

One day he followed Joe to his hole in the hillside, and they sat together upon a log at the mouth of the shaft.

"My friend," said he, "I must go back to the post; will you lend me that mule?" It really was a diminutive donkey of which he spoke.

"Well, now,— sho," said Joe, "ye needn't hurry. Besides, ye can't find the way 'thout I go, an' I ain't got time."

"I'll find a guide, Mr. Biggs. Will you lend me the mule?"

"Y-e-s, of course," said Joe; "but," he added, with a twinkle in his eye, "how'll I git the animal ag'in?"

"I'll bring it to you."

"An' come ag'in yerself?"

"Certainly."

The elder man looked at the younger keenly and inquiringly. He was peculiar in the respect that all his kind are, and cared no whit for any man's dignity. So, between two who by this time understood each other thoroughly, the conversation was continued.

"What would you come back here for? *You* don't belong to this kind."

"I do not belong to any kind; and," desperately, "I would come back for your daughter."

"Don't ye do it 'nless ye come fair an' square,— I advise ye, now. I like ye, young man; I saved yer life, an' I'd do it ag'in. But if ye ever use what I done for you for anything as isn't square an' fair between my folks and yourn, it 'ud a been better for ye never to a come out'n the snow-pile."

"I tell you I will come again, and that I am an honest man, and a grateful one. What I mean is plainly what I say,"— and he rose to go away.

"Hold on, youngster!" cried Joe; "I knowed it, but I wanted to make sartin'. Bless ye, I ain't blind. Does she know it,— have you said anything to her?" he continued, in a lower voice.

"Well,— yes; I think I have said too much. I am afraid there is one thing that I have not sufficiently thought of. If I should do precisely as I wish, it would be very imprudent. I— I have not much money."

"Come with me; I want to show ye suthin' purty," and Biggs laid hold of the young man's sleeve, and started back toward the cabin. When there, he lighted the greasy implement contrived to do duty as a lamp, and crept under the rude bedstead. "Come on!" he cried from unknown depths; and the soldier went down after him and found himself in a kind of cellar, the earthen roof of which was supported by cedar beams, as mines are, — for the cabin had no floor but earth. "This is whar I lived afore I built the cabin on top," said the old man. "I've been poor all my life, an' now the luck has turned at last. This is whar I keep the stuff." Then he threw aside sundry old blankets, gunny-sacks, and dried skins, and disclosed three or four large glass jars, such as are used in packing relishes, and some small sacks made of canvas. He took up a quart bottle, and as he held it to the smoking light the dull yellow gleam of the metal showed it to be full. Then he lifted another, which held the same yellow hoard. They were all full. There, before his eyes, the soldier saw many thousands of dollars. The old man sat down upon a broken box, and eyed his treasures, and talked. He told how he had run away from whiskey and a cross woman, and, coming to this spot, had found "signs." He had made a dug-out, and killed game for food, and opened a drift into the hill-side. He said he had "sloshed around" the bottom of the hill a good while before he had concluded to really go at it. He had found pockets before, and "kinder knowed" there was one somewhere about here. He had a hard time, but finally "struck it rich," and at last came upon the pocket he had been looking for all his life. He was glad he had come; for, he argued, what good would it do a man "to hev a million, an' that 'ar woman too?" When his luck came, he was afraid, as men often are under such circumstances, and for a month did not even tell his daughter. Day after day he took out the veined and crumbling rock, sometimes almost pure gold. He crushed it in a rude mortar, and subjected it to the clumsy chemistry of the mountains, with instruments of his own contriving, and at night. Then he needed help, and took his daughter into the somewhat miserly secret. Finally he induced some wandering miners to settle in his neighborhood, for the sake of company and protection. They had all been successful to some extent, but none of them could do more than guess at the old man's success, with the peculiar miner's intuition in respect to such things. In the course of his conversation in the cellar, he made the startling announcement that he had twice been back to the post, and that it was only sixty miles away by his trail. When asked what he had gone there for, he answered, "quicksilver" and "suthin' to wear," and told how his daughter had remained "cached" in the mountains until his return. As he told this story, with evidences of its truthfulness all around him, the soldier wondered if this was not Aladdin, and if he were not dreaming. "Now, youngster," said the miner, in conclusion, "I've told ye this, so'st the arrangement needn't be one-sided. I tell it to ye, 'cause I think ye're honest. The pocket's petered, an' ain't wuth much now; but my lead's wuth more than I'm just now willin' to lay myself out on. I'm gettin' old, an' am goin' to quit."

They climbed the ladder and emerged again into the outer air. As they stood in the sunlight, it seemed more than ever a dream.

But to the old frontiersman must necessarily

come some relief after such earnest discourse. He turned away at the door, and as he departed, looked back and said, "Ye kin hev the jackass, an' be d———d to ye. I only said it to try ye."

The night passed to the lieutenant as a waking dream. He had lighted upon a wonder, and through the moonlit hours he tossed, questioning if morning would find all those jars of yellow metal real things. The wealth of this poor girl of the mountains exceeded his mother's dreams of monied respectability,— though he did that lady the strict justice to remember that she required of her ideals a little more than mere money. Aside from all this, was he willing to forego all there was for him in the far-off world, for this sweet child of the desert, and to accept her, and her alone, and forever, as just and full compensation for all there might be besides? A week ago he had deliberately concluded upon his course, and was surprised to find himself questioning now.

In the morning, a donkey stood at the door, accompanied by a companion. He was assured that the miner who was to go with him knew the way; and as he started, the girl stood in the doorway, shading her eyes with her little brown hand, with pleasure and regret striving for the mastery in her face. She knew he would return. He had told her that, and she believed him. In truth, she did not see why he should not. A young woman cannot be expected to understand the mysteries of a life she has never known or even dreamed of.

They met the old man in the path. He was

wiser, and had not much to say; but as they passed by, he shouted after them: "Bring me some quicksilver when you come." He had never been very romantic, even in his own affairs of the heart. It was not surprising that he should insist upon looking upon this as mere matter of fact. Old Joe was a man of very hard sense, after all.

For two days they plodded steadily on, the returning wanderer paying little heed to the road, and absorbed in his own thoughts, following in the trail of his leader. On the third day they caught sight of the floating banner on the slender flag-staff, idly flaunting its glories to the green world of silence and sunshine. The sight gave him a choking sensation. When he alighted at his quarters, they were inhabited by another; and the whole garrison, from the commandant down, and including that class with whom he had always been most popular, the ladies, looked at him as at one risen from the dead. He briefly told them his story, saying not a word of the personality of his rescuers. He learned then that his companions had not returned. But he had grown accustomed to startling things, and was not surprised. He had been dropped from the rolls, and his record closed as one dead. Even that failed to shock him now. He confessed to himself, with some surprise, that he wished above all things to get back to Old Joe's little cabin, and see that little uncultured womanly woman, who, he had almost come to believe, was the one angel of the universe.

The same night the commandant received a communication, addressed through him to the Secretary of War, tendering the unconditional resignation of First Lieutenant Thurston, Third Cavalry; and at the end was the startling declaration that, after so long an absence, he had returned to his post only to perform the duty necessary to a soldier's honor.

That night he locked his door and read his letters. There were several from his mother, and two or three from female friends who inquired when he intended to pay the long-deferred visit to his home. He read the delicate lines, and the faint perfume of old association touched his senses. But he laid them upon the fire, and moodily watched them turn to ashes. Perhaps they were never answered.

Four slow weeks went by, and the communication came that ended his military career forever. He carried it to his quarters, and locked himself in, and tried to realize his situation. He had been lost in the mountains; he had looked death, slow and cold, steadily in the face. In a few weeks he had tasted nearly all there is in life's cup, the bitter and the sweet. But through it all, there was no moment more full of regret than this.

Then, at the trader's store, there was the busy outfitting of a train of mules with all things necessary to a mountain life; and clad in homely gray, with slouched hat and spurred heel, citizen Thurston directed the enterprise. It began to be said among his brethren that after all Thurston was a shrewd fellow, and had undoubtedly found among the mountains something rich. But to the last he told no tales; and as the tinkling procession passed the house known as "Joe's cabin," the blue-clad throng looked their last upon a man who had once been one of them, but now passed out of their world forever.

There is a certain town on the far Pacific coast which has grown up of late years with the strange growth which is born of traffic in an opening mining country, and which agricultural communities never know. There is an elegant mansion there, and its proprietor is reputed very wealthy. Within are luxurious carpets, and shining wood, and marble, and plate glass. Fruits ripen in the yard, and rare flowers bloom on the terrace. He is a man, too, not alone of luxurious tastes, but of intelligence and public spirit. But he is mostly envied because of his wife. The curious people who have frequently scrutinized her elegant attire have also noticed that she speaks English with a little lisp, and apparently regards her husband in the light of a demigod. But they little know how the lady has changed under the tireless lessons of love, or by what slow processes the mountain nymph became at last the woman as cultured as she was always beautiful. And the man who sometimes looks thoughtfully at the old sword and crimson scarf that hang, somewhat out of place, over the mantlepiece, himself scarcely realizes how much he has accomplished, and how far-away and valueless is that respectability which comes by birth, as compared with that which, by faithfulness and honor, and sometimes through danger and suffering, a man may win for himself.

VII.

NEW MEXICAN COMMON LIFE.

THERE is a country far to the southwest in which everything is new, crude, and undeveloped, where the evidences of enterprise and the settlements of white men are few, but which is the seat of an ancient and Christian civilization, and whose capital is the oldest town in America but one.

Several centuries have elapsed since the Spanish tongue and Catholic faith came together to New Mexico. They antedate the settlement of Jamestown and the romance of Pocahontas. The then mighty Spanish power had founded a government here before the city of New Amsterdam had passed from the hands of its Dutch founders. The roads and mountain passes, traversed with such precaution now, were the routes of extensive trade long before the first wagon-road had been made across the Alleghanies. When the Delawares and Hurons were still engaged in their desperate attempt to hold their ancient possessions against the aggressions of the white men, the aborigines of this country had been converted to slavery and Christianity, always excepting those implacable and unconquerable tribes whose hands are against every man, and who were then, as they are now, the scourges of advancing civilization. There are churches here in which the disciples of the sword and the cross said mass more than two hundred years ago, and mines whose shafts have been closed almost three centuries.

Interesting as are the present aspects of this strangest of all the countries lying within the shadow of the American flag, the New Mexico of the past would be still more curious could we but read the story that is everywhere written in undecipherable ruin. The very names of the ancient towns, whose walls are now grass-grown ridges of earth, have been forgotten with their inhabitants. Almost the last vestige of the civilization of conquest is gone. All that the Mexican now knows he could easily have learned since the country came under the control of the United States, and in the comparatively short time during which American enterprise has had a foothold. Everywhere, even in places so wild and inaccessible that they will be among the last reclaimed, there are dim signs of a curious past which has gone without monuments and without a history.

The great feature of the country geographically is mountains — nothing but mountains; not the picturesque and tree-clad hills of the East, but bold and bare and brown, and piled peak upon peak, with the high plateaux lying hidden between for hundreds of silent and desolate miles. Here and there is a spring, and sometimes a ragged cluster of huts beside a few fertile acres. But on every hand the yellow and rugged peaks cut a frowning outline against a sky, the bluest and fairest in the world. These mountains are, however, the repositories of immense and varied supplies of mineral wealth, mostly undeveloped, and probably undiscovered. And they are not without inhabitants, for they are the domain, the inaccessible and chosen home, of the Apache. None but the Apache knows them, and none but he would be able to find sustenance there.

The centres of life and trade in the country are the small towns in the great valley of the Rio Grande, for miles along whose sandy and insect-haunted stream continuous villages extend. There are also many settlements under the shadow and protection of the military posts. Places most remote and dangerous are naturally the location of the military; and it is curious to note how soon a small settlement will grow up among the mountains or beside some tepid stream under the auspices of armed protection.

It is a land where nature in all her forms seems to delight in coarseness and ruggedness. Every shrub is thorny, and every undeveloped twig has a horny and needle-like point. The flowers are few and addicted to a universal yellow color, and trees there are none save those that grow sparsely on the banks of the streams, or stand dwarfed and crooked on the cliffs. But there is an interminable wilderness of *mezquit* — a thorny and ugly shrub whose beans furnish a staple article of savage food, whose roots are fuel, and from whose tough branches are made the bows which in the hands of the Apache so often send an unexpected and noiseless death to the traveller.

From topography, and discussion of resources

and prospects, all of which claim their share of interest for the future, and will be very carefully looked after and accurately described, we will turn to what is always a central point of interest in a strange land — the character and habits of its people.

In the question of the annexation of the immense territory, a part of which included New Mexico, to the United States, there were no more uninterested people than the New Mexicans themselves. They are not of that class who of their own accord long for freedom and sigh for the privilege of self-government. The difference between that rule that for so many years has been alternately a republic and an anarchy, and one whose great struggle for life was fought out almost unheard on these far shores, is one upon which the Mexican never speculates, and which it is doubtful if he ever perceived. To him, educated as he might be supposed to be by more than three centuries of residence in the new world, still cling all the peculiarities of the Latin race. Everything around him has changed. The power that sent his ancestors across the seas has long since sunk under that slow disease of which old monarchies linger and die, or perpetually slumber. The traditions of his country and his race are lost to him. His land has long since been invaded by Yankee dominion. He has seen the people who are here to-day and gone to-morrow — the weary and disheartened gold-hunter, and the adventurer of every name and class, — and they have smitten him with their vices and taught him none of their virtues. The alert and vivacious Saxon has established himself at the corner of every street in his chiefest villages; has brought him into contact with a new language, which, however, he has not learned to speak; has threatened him with new ideas; has changed his ancient real and doubloon to paper promises printed in green, and, withal, derides the religion of his fathers and is disposed to laugh at his saving ceremonies. But through all the Mexican clings unmoved to his religion, his language, and his social life. The plough with which he tediously prepares the soil is such as was used in the days of the patriarchs. His oxen are yoked with thongs binding the straight piece of wood to the horns, as was done in Virgil's time. He harvests his grain with a sickle of crooked iron, dull and toothless as that held by Ceres in a group of statuary. The wild hay upon the swale or mountain-side he is content to cut with a hoe, and carry to market upon the back of a diminutive donkey. The irregular, squalid and straggling village in which he lives is ancient beyond memory, and in its crooked streets generations of his ancestors have lived and walked, and left it unchanged. The bells which swing and jangle on an iron bar upon his church gable are perhaps pious gifts of some dead and forgotten cardinal of a hundred years ago. His Spanish ancestor was a man remarkable for his highly cultivated qualities of conservatism, jealousy, and love of dominion. His descendant is remarkable only for placidity. The supreme content with which the Mexican sits upon the sheep-skin in front of his door and watches the current of passing life, the satisfaction he takes in a life which has in it only the humblest lot and the hardest fare, is nowhere else to be found in nervous, restless, wandering America.

Rain is, or was, an unusual phenomenon of this arid country; and yet the Mexican's crops seldom fail him. The region is checkered with innumerable ditches, which twist themselves around hills and traverse sandy valleys, and are bank-full of turbid water. His squalid little villages gain their only charm from rivulets of water trickling everywhere, and his little farm glows with a peculiar greenness amid the browns and grays that lie around it in mountain and rock and plain. He solved the problem of irrigation a very long time ago, and did what the impatient Yankee would probably never have done. He is not an engineer any more than the beaver is one, and has been so far very successful without any admeasurement of gradients and curves, and without the use of transit or level; so that it has often been said, and more than half believed, that a Mexican can make water run up hill. Without the issue of municipal bonds or the forming of any joint-stock companies, he seems to have caused these snow-born mountain streams to follow him into the heart of primeval barrenness, and has made the desolation to bloom as the rose.

And yet his plow is his chief curiosity. Agriculturally it is no better than the Zulu adze, or the squaw's incompetent hazel eradicator. It is just a pole, with a second one fastened at a slight angle across the end of it. One end of this shortened stick serves for an upright handle, and the other end, sharpened, is the plow. A single pig, depredating in a meadow, on a wet afternoon, will turn up more ground, and do it more thoroughly than a New Mexican farmer can in two days. The contrast between this Egyptian tool and the glittering and elaborate instrument used by the Mexican's neighbor, the Kansas farmer, is as great as that existing between the clepsydra with which the gentle Nero beguiled his leisure hours, and the modern eight-day calendar clock. And yet the Mexican is in all probability the more successful agriculturist of the two. He knows; he deals with certainties. No farm journal will ever change his views as to soiling *versus* pasturage, fall plowing, the profit of wheat growing, Hereford and Shorthorn, or whether it pays to hoe potatoes. As to his plow, he is not so much to blame. All Spain uses the same model to this day. So do Cuba, Chili, and Old Mexico.

As might be inferred, the class which comes first and oftenest under the observation of the traveller is the common one of laborers and burro-drivers. But it is impossible that there should be no gradations in society among people of Spanish blood. Here and there through the country are pretentious houses, whose doors are closed to the common villager, and whose Dons and Señoras hold themselves aloof from common contamination. These are the thoroughbreds, who, amid these strange surroundings, trace back a lineage which is supposed to have had its origin among the knights and ladies of Arragon and Castile. In this wilderness exclusiveness, **what dreams of renewed Spanish splendor, what** regret for departed power, are indulged in, none may know. But sometimes the necessities of life bring about some intercourse with the commandant of a neighboring post, or some young army officer gains admittance under cover of his uniform, and then the stories that reach the waiting military world are to the effect that family greatness, as exemplified in these instances, is a myth and a flimsy dream, and exclusiveness a cloak beneath which is concealed a kind of respectable poverty. Tessellated marble, the carved balustrade and classic fountain, colonnade and balcony, have all been left out of the reputed demi-palace in which the grandees are spending their exile. It is the same earthen floor, the same unreliable roof, the same *chile-con-carne*, the same *frijoles*, the identical clammy cheese, that give to the villager his shelter, his fare, and his supreme content, through all his life.

To dance and to smoke seem to be the two great objects of Mexican life. In the village, the sound of the festive guitar is always heard, and the dance is well-nigh continuous. Not alone in the evening, but at midday, beneath some shade, or in an open court-yard, the passer-by stops, dances his fill, and passes on. Males and females, on whatever errand bent, join in the dance without hesitation, and quite as a matter of course. It is a habit that has become chronic,—the first amusement a child learns, and the last manœuvre his decrepit legs are made to perform.

Equally inveterate is the habit of constant and continuous smoking, and the corn-husk cigarette is the universal article. Men and women alike mingle smoke with every employment. Señoritas employ the intervals of the fandango in making and lighting *cigarras*, and the celerity with which the Mexican manufactures the small roll of corn-husk and tobacco, never once looking at it, and chattering and gesticulating all the time, is astonishing.

The New Mexican village is a complete nondescript. It has not its likeness among all the sordid villages under the palms, or the ice-huts of shores where shines the midnight sun. At the distance of a mile it has the appearance of an unburned brick-kiln. The sun-dried adobe is the universal building material, and there is almost no diversity in plan, pattern, or style. No attempt is made at regularity in the streets, which are simply narrow and zig-zag alleys, intended only for donkey travel and the convenience of the goats. The description of a Mexican town invented by some border humorist, describes them all: "Nine inches high, eighteen inches long, and a mile and a half wide." And this is really a description so far as appearances go. The luxury of a floor, of bedsteads and chairs, is almost entirely unknown. Wooden doors, stoves, and iron utensils are nearly so. Everything is of the earth, earthy. Beds and benches are banks of earth against the wall. Fire-places are slender arches, in which the fuel is placed on end. Cooking is performed in earthenware, and the favorite and standard dish of beans is quietly and thoroughly stewed for two or three days in an earthen jug.

In these villages, the sounds of industry heard

everywhere else in Christendom are unknown. There are no shops, and every man is his own carpenter, joiner, and shoemaker. Iron is the great necessity of civilization, yet here its use is scarcely known. The only wheeled vehicle the Mexican uses of his own choice is a cart in which there is not so much as a nail; and this unique triumph of the endeavor to make the ugliest, heaviest, and most inconvenient of earthly vehicles, creeps with shrieking axles over the mountain roads, eternally oilless.

The Mexican mode of life is almost entirely agricultural, and these villages are simply collections of people pertaining to lands that are tilled in common. There is a personage who is complacently designated as *El Indio*, constantly on the alert for spoil, and from whose incursions there is no escape save in union. Wealth here consists in a multitude of goats, together with a limited number of donkeys and oxen. In his use and treatment of these animals, the native is as peculiar as he is in other respects. Everything pays tribute to his larder and is included in his resources, except those things in general use with the majority of mankind. Cows are seldom milked and goats always are, and even sometimes the small pigs go short of the mother's milk, for which, however, they cry as lustily as do infant swine the world over. Pigs, lean and unhappy, are fastened to a stake by a lariat, while the donkeys are confined in pens. Dogs, innumerable and ill-favored, swarm everywhere, and domestic fowls roost among the household utensils and lay eggs in convenient corners. Red pepper, the famous *chile colorado*, the hottest sauce ever invented, is a standard dish, eaten by everybody. The manufacture of common soap seems not to be understood or attempted, and its place is supplied by a plant that requires no preparation for use, and that grows wild in the country. Wood for fuel is not cut, but dug, being the huge roots of the insignificant but universal *mezquit*. Butter is almost unknown, but cheese from goat's milk is a staple. There are dishes in the Mexican bill of fare of which the name conveys no idea, and which were never known among the gourmands and epicures. There is a beverage that is the very concoction of Beelzebub himself, made from that gigantic herb called by us the century plant. Acrid as turpentine, fiery as proof-spirits, its effect is more like insanity than drunkenness, and its use adds nothing to the general agreeableness of the race that, even when sober, is the very opposite of ingenuous.

What is a country in which the two articles leather and iron are not in general use? asks the political economist. Yet here the utility of both these articles in every-day life is practically unknown. Chains, tires, straps, hinges, braces, everything that requires lightness, strength, and toughness, is made of raw-hide; and, applied to the Mexican's uses, it is nearly indestructible. A dozen mules will chew a long summer night through upon a single lariat, and leave it unscathed; which, to one accustomed to examples of the perseverance of that sagacious animal in tasks of the kind, is sufficient testimony. The shoes of the Mexican, made of a thinner variety of the same material, always last until they share the fate of most articles of the kind in this country, and are stolen by the coyotes. Everything broken is mended with hide, or not mended at all, and without it the common operations of life could hardly be carried on.

The ancient primitiveness of New Mexican life is more particularly displayed by the dress of the common class than by any other one sign. Stockings and gloves are seldom seen, any more than they are among the peasantry of southern Europe. Generally, neither sex is encumbered with more than two distinct articles of clothing besides the head-dress, which last is with both sexes as elaborate as possible. The females wear a skirt and a single upper garment, in which, in maid and matron alike, at all times and places, is displayed a great variety of arms, shoulders, and bosoms. But no one ever caught a man without his *sombrero*, or a woman without the *rebosa*. The first-named is the most elaborate article of the hat kind, sometimes profusely adorned with gold embroidery. A Mexican's hat is a matter of profound importance, as indicating his respectability. It costs four times as much as his whole wardrobe besides, and even more than the donkey he rides. Shabby as he may be in other respects, his Sunday hat should insure him the respect due to a well-dressed man.

The *rebosa* is a garment as old as Spanish civilization, once of costly lace, but now a shawl, more or less gay, and sometimes elaborate, in which, indoors and out, the Mexican woman covers her modest head and hides her captivating face. Shoulders, arms and feet may be bare, but all that can be seen of her countenance is one eye and the end of her nose. Peculiarly graceful, as the females of her race generally are, long habit renders her especially adroit in the management of her headdress. Eating, smoking, drinking, talking, this constant shawl never falls, never becomes disarranged, never gets blown away. If ever in this country the traveller espies in the distance a figure upon whose head is neither hat nor shawl, he may begin to study the means of defence; for it is no friend, but an Apache.

Leaving out of account the goat, which seems to be a peculiarly Spanish animal, all the beasts of the field are of small importance as compared with the *burro*. These are very small, many of them not so large as the smallest pony, and many a cuff bestowed in lieu of forage from colthood up, has made him even more diminutive than nature intended. He is a melancholy brute, much given to forlornness of countenance and leanness of flank. Appearances indicate that, with all his reverence for sacred things, the Mexican has forgotten that the burro carries upon his shoulders the sign of the cross, and once played a prominent part in the most memorable ecclesiastical procession in the history of the church. He is tied in the street by having a blanket thrown over his eyes, and guided in his wanderings with his master by vigorous thwacks on either side of his patient head. He is loaded with everything that can be tied to him or hung upon him, and in such quantity that frequently all that can be seen of him are his four little feet, and those enormous ears that in all his kind have ever refused to be hidden, even by a lion's skin. He is the carrier of hay, of stones, of bales of goods, casks of water, firewood, and sometimes of a whole family of small children. His owner has a confidence in his powers of locomotion that would honor an elephant. Burdened with humanity or merchandise, faithful of disposition, frugal of habit, and tough of hide, the little slave toils through his hard life with an uncomplaining patience that makes him the martyr of the brute creation.

The small commercial transactions of the native remind one of the shrewd dealings of a schoolboy. Should the purchase of eggs become desirable, you must be content to buy them two, three, or half a dozen at a time. He will expend an immense amount of eloquence in attempting to convince the purchaser that they are worth fifty cents per dozen, while all the time he is really anxious to take half that sum. Should milk be wanted, he will swear by all the saints that the yellow and unctuous fluid is the milk of a cow, and not that of the goat from whose udders it is yet warm. If it be fowls, the hoarse old master of the harem will be extolled as young, tender, and precisely the bird for Señor's supper. Discovered in his small rascality, the varlet disarms resentment by a smile so bland and a shrug so expressive that you are convinced he means no harm in being an inveterate and incurable liar.

The female of every race and tribe differs from the male by a greater difference than is expressed by masculinity and femininity, and the New Mexican woman is in many respects more a woman and less a heathen than could be expected of her from her surroundings. Always neat in attire and cleanly in person and surroundings, comely and sometimes handsome in face and figure, always trying to look pretty, with a very weak side for flattery and admiration, coquettish in her ways and suave in her manners, tender and kind to those she loves, with a laugh or a tear always at hand, as have her sisters all the world over, she is in striking contrast with the sordidness of her daily life, the surly uselessness of her degenerated kindred, and the habits of the country in which she lives.

And while all this is true, there follows it a truth which is in itself a problem for the socialist and the student of human nature. Stated as a proposition, any form of society not cemented by a peculiar and almost indescribable spirit of chastity is sure to fall. Virtue must be regarded, venerated, inherited,— taught by the schoolmaster, the priest, and the mother. Such is not the case here. Prostitution and adultery go unregarded and shameless. Faithfulness to the marriage vow is not deemed essential, and the idea of absolute virtue seems not to be extant. The New Mexican women present the unusual spectacle of almost universally modest demeanor and gentle manners, fulfilling the ordinary duties of home and life in a manner far better than could be expected of them with their training and education, and yet without an idea of the meaning, as it is generally understood, of the word virtue. The fact is, so far as I ever heard, an undisputed one. It is undoubtedly a study worthy the attention of those who are given to social questions, and who have attained to advanced ideas upon free love, affinities, etc. The train of social debauchery passes by, and the grand result comes thundering after; for a large proportion of the population is more or less affected by that malady which is one of the direst strokes inflicted by the angel with the flaming sword who stands at the gate of the garden of forbidden pleasure.

No one need go to Rome to acquire a knowledge of what Catholicism is at home. The seat of the papal government, with the old man of infallibility throned in its midst, is not more thoroughly Catholic than is New Mexico. The passion for saints, relics, images, candles, and processions is universal throughout the country. Nearly all the villages are named "Saint" somebody, and Jesuitism may be said to be the established rule. The worst social vices are coupled with the deepest regard for everything that tastes of saintship and sacredness. Every hamlet has its church, or a building that was erected for that purpose. Each churchyard is a Golgotha which in some instances has been dug over many times for the purpose of burying the dead within sacred precincts. Exhumed skulls and large bones —a cheerful sight for those whose friends have been interred here — are piled in a corner, or within the railing that surrounds the grave of some occupant who has not yet been ousted from that limited freehold to which the poorest of us are supposed to be entitled at last.

Convenient appliances for the doing of penance are included in nearly every sacerdotal outfit. There are crosses large enough for practical utility, which penitents are requested to carry far out among the hills and back to atone for some unwonted sin. There are whips and ropes' ends for much-needed flagellation, and sometimes barefoot pilgrimages are prescribed to be made through a country where it would be difficult to find a rood that is not thorny. Lighter sins are purged away by lying all night upon a gravestone — a thing at the bare idea of which the soul of the Mexican quakes within him — or sometimes by bumping the head a great many times consecutively upon the church steps. Whether this last-named exercise is a mere form, or whether the saving thumps are given with faithfulness and vigor, manifestly depends upon the thickness of the skull and the thinness of the penitent's conscience.

The *fiestas*, or sacred days, come so often and are observed so generally that the ill-natured remark has been frequently made that they were invented to avoid the necessity of work, and lay the blame for all consequent poverty upon the saints. The motley procession that parades the streets on these occasions, firing guns, yelling, and singing, behind a tawdry image of the Virgin that is usually arrayed in pink muslin, with a black mantilla and cotton gloves, is one of the raggedest, noisiest, and most ludicrous performances ever called by the name of religion. Yet this unique form of the Christian faith is not wanting in its consolations. There are no free-thinkers and sceptics here. Under its influence the Mexican becomes, if not very courageous in danger, at least hopeful and resigned in death. Upon those occasions, unfortunately not infrequent in this country, when his companions flee in desperation from the Apache, still hoping to escape when there is no chance of life, he drops upon his knees and awaits his fate, calmly dying with a prayer upon his lips to that mother of Christ whose name is dearer than all others to the Catholic heart. Nevertheless, this statement is a reminder that we should be thankful that the sturdy Protestant is apt upon such occasions to die fighting if necessary — running if possible. A course of conduct the opposite of the Mexican's has saved a great many lives in these lonely cañons, and the desperate survivors of unrecorded skirmishes are not impressed by the religious aspect of the Mexican's case.

The love of isolation, the contentment with the condition to which they were born, the desire to remain forever environed by that changelessness that has sat brooding over his primitive world for centuries, which is the characteristic of the Spanish peasant in the old country, seems also to cling to the character of his descendants wherever they are scattered. Of all the homes of America this is the happiest; of all her citizens this is the most satisfied. The land that is new to us is very old to him, and all his straggling villages belong to another age and have remained to this. As he is ignorant, so is he careless of all things outside of his sierra-bounded horizon. He cannot be awakened. He refuses to submit to that pain which accompanies the parturition of an idea. He does not even understand that the skies are changing over his head, and that he or his children will be called upon to take step with the march of a great people, or be left by the wayside forgetting and forgot. Time will bring about none of its revenges for him; a changed life none of its compensations. There is something in race, and a great deal in what we call "blood." There are five kinds of us whose traits and faces are known to every school-child. But it is a mistake that there are not six. The Spaniard and his children are apart from all the rest, for six hundred years changeless at home and abroad. The land that has come under his dominion, wherever it may lie, has been from the day of his conquest under a spell also.

It is so with this. Even at this distance of time and space, with every vivid recollection blunted, it is easy to recall the old, familiar summer afternoon in Mexico. I remember how the señoras sat with folded hands about the doors, and looked with one unveiled and furtive eye upon the passers. Ancient and parchment-faced crones chattered and smoked at the corners of the little dusty plaza, and impish boys played at noisy games in the quiet street. The cocks and hens sauntered in and out of their owner's houses with an air of satisfied ownership, and venerable and bearded goats perambulated the crumbling garden walls. Unhappy pigs whined and pulled at their tethers, and kids furtively nibbled at the tail of a solemn old donkey who stood with closed eyes and hanging lip, asleep. There are rows of white tents, and moving figures, and curling blue smoke, and the distant laughter and careless song of soldiers. These are they who have come from far, whose lives are not the lives of peace, and who seem the invaders of a region that was ever before the land of dreams. I see the white tops of the Sierras gleam in the slant sunshine, and slowly the long shadows of afternoon creep over the scene, and finally there is nothing left in the gloom but the twinkle of the camp-fires, and the outline of the cold peaks against the fading purple of the sky. There is the red glow of open doorways at intervals far down the village street, but no sound save the tinkling of a guitar, the faint laughter of the dancers, and thin and far the bleating of the flocks. All is the perfect peace of contented poverty. All is to-day, and there is no to-morrow.

I wonder, as I recall such scenes, whether I shall live to see the day when these dry bones shall be stirred. The land is already touched by the farthest ripple of that wave which slowly creeps horizonward, burdened with life, energy, and change. There already is the camp of the advance guard who steadily widen the borders of that civilization which is destined to include within its boundaries a hundred millions of freemen.

VIII.

"PEG," THE STORY OF A DOG.

"GIT out'n hyar, Peg Watkins! Ef I come thar, I'll"—and there was a sound as of a broom lighting upon its brushy end, and the handle thereof striking the outer wall with a vigorous thwack.

"Now, in the name of wonder, who can this much-berated female be?" asked the doctor, as he heard the words and their accompanying emphasis. The doctor was the latest arrival. He was strange to the post and all its surroundings, having only six weeks before entered into a solemn contract with the high and mighty Medical Director U.S.A. in the city of Philadelphia, to do duty as acting Assistant Surgeon at any post to which he might be ordered, and to receive regularly therefor the sum of one hundred and twenty-five dollars per month, quarters, and a ration. The doctor was not in delicate health, and did not pretend to think that the air of the frontier would be beneficial in restoring a constitution shattered by hard work in his profession. This was what most of his kind had reported of themselves, together with other details of extensive practice and influential connections, and the regrets they felt at leaving it all at the demands of physical debility. The brusque sunburnt fellows he was hereafter to associate with had known many acting assistant surgeons in their time, and were not to be imposed upon. A new doctor means to the officers of a frontier military post a some one out of whom is at first to be fairly had a considerable amount of fun, and afterwards, if he should prove a good fellow, a new companion, considerable hospital brandy, and the service for which a doctor is supposed to exist. He is welcomed and treated accordingly, and with all these various ends in view.

When the doctor had alighted from the ambulance which had been sent to bring him three days before, his appearance was as startling in these solitudes as though he had just escaped from another world — which, indeed, he in some sense had. He was dressed in a gray suit, wore neat brown gloves, and, to crown all, a tall white hat of the "plug" variety, deeply and solemnly bound with black. The air of Chestnut street and the Continental Hotel seemed to emanate from him, as he stood there looking through the inevitable spectacles at the curious place that was for an indefinite time to be his official residence. A group of young fellows, all clad in blue, and each wearing the emblem of some comfortable military grade upon his shoulder, sauntered out to welcome him from the trader's store. "Here is Pills," said one. "Remark the tile," said a second. "Bad health — large practice," chimed a third, epitomizing the usual story. "Wish I was where he came from," sighed a fourth, "wherever it is." But they ceased to laugh as he came nearer, and greeted him with that solemn courtesy which is the usual thing when the object of it has been expected, and when previous remarks have not been of a character to be considered entirely respectful. As these really kind-hearted fellows shook hands with "Pills," one by one, the prospect for a great amount of fun out of a greenhorn did not seem to brighten. The new doctor was a kind of blonde Nazarite, whose face, it seemed, had never known a razor. He was so tall that the men around him looked up into his open eyes, and felt for a considerable time thereafter the impression of a hand that was anything but flaccid. "Bad health," remarked Thompson to his companions, shortly after, "bad health be d——d."

With the air of a man who did not think his surroundings very remarkable, the doctor sat oiling his gun when the broom was thrown at Peg Watkins, as aforesaid. The voice and the missile he knew were the personal property of the quadroon — or a shade darker — who did the culinary offices of the mess. But having been there but three days, he believed he might not yet have seen all the female denizens of the post. So, with the remark mentioned, he arose and went to the door, in expectation of seeing this creature, who had apparently been caught *in flagrante delicto*, make a hasty exit from the rear of the premises. What he actually saw was an immense yellow-and-white dog, with bristles standing like the spines of a roach along her back, and her head turned aside with that curious pretence of looking the other way that angry canines are apt to practise, while the pendent lip, drawn away from her square jaws displayed to some antagonist at the kitchen door a glittering array of ivory. This was the female. The doctor laughed as he thought of it;—"Peg" was only a dog.

But he was one of those men who are prone to have an extensive acquaintance among the hairy beasts who, in all ages and with all races, have chosen to be beaten, spurned, misunderstood, and murdered, as the humble friends and followers of man, rather than live in savage independence without him. As he watched her, with an amused expression upon his face, it doubtless seemed to him that the shaggy creature was one possessed of rather more than the ordinary amount of canine character. "Come here, Peg," he said, in rather a conversational tone, as he held out his hand. Peg was visibly disconcerted, and lowered her bristles and seemed astonished at hearing her name called in a tone of kindness. She crept humbly toward her new friend, and when she felt the touch of his hand fairly grovelled in the dust before him, and at last deprecatingly followed him into the house. For a long time she had been accustomed to be addressed with missiles and epithets, and driven away whenever her shaggy form appeared in a doorway, and had presumably stolen from the butcher and the waste-barrel whatever she had to eat. And through it all she had lain in the sally-port every night, watching and listening, the most vigilant sentinel of the command. She was an outcast, so entirely abandoned that it was only through inadvertence that she was permitted to live at all. As she crouched close beside the wall, with forlorn countenance and haggard, watchful eye, it seemed, had any cared to notice, that she felt, with such a feeling as her human masters often lack, her utter ignominy and disgrace. Now, in less than two hours after her first acquaintance with him, she lay in the twilight at the doctor's doorway, with self-conscious importance, and disputed the entrance of the commandant himself. So are dogs — and men — wont to forget themselves upon a sudden change of fortune.

There is a road, a monotonous and desolate yellow line across the desert, which leads westward from the Rio Grande across the southern border of New Mexico. There is many a long day's journey upon it in which there is no water, no shade, no house, no passing traveller — nothing. Over it have passed hundreds who never saw the end, and other hundreds who, if they did see it, never cared to return. Over plateaux where the tall cacti stand like ghosts, through cañons Indian-haunted and lined with graves and crosses, the melancholy path stretches for hundreds of lonesome miles. Yet it does not want wayfarers. Here, through the summer, thousands of long-horned Texas cattle drag their gaunt limbs along on the journey to California. Here is the man whose destiny it is to wander from place to place through life unsatisfied, surrounded by his dozen white-haired and boggle-eyed urchins who seem to have been born by the roadside, and ever accompanied by a woman whose most serious troubles are cured by a pipe, and whose amazing fecundity seems to be no bar to constant wandering. Sometimes, too, there are those who have a more definite purpose in their journeyings, and who escape from the ties of family and the law, and the manifold difficulties of civilization and old associations. But to all there is the same fatuous certainty of something better beyond, the same proneness to underestimate the length and peril of the road and the hard facts that lie at the end. But it is one of the roads of destiny, and by it do southern Arkansas, Texas, and other of the southwestern states empty themselves of their more unstable population.

Some months before the doctor's arrival at the post, several families of such had encamped at the spring, whose semi-circular disc of stone opened the tepid waters to the light a few hundred yards from the southern wall of the military enclosure. The circumstance was not an unusual one, and would have attracted no attention had not the party stayed so long and been possessed of unusual attractions. They wanted an escort of soldiers, and waited for the return of a scouting party, so that troops might be spared them — provided some other excuse for not furnishing a guard did not meantime occur to the mind of the commandant. The men were well-dressed and independent, and the women were some of them comely and all of them quite exclusive. There was one tall girl, who attracted universal attention as well on account of her beauty as her demure reserve, who turned a cold eye upon Thompson himself, who in his day had been (the word of a soldier must be taken in this matter) a famous woman-tamer. Tuck, the butcher's man — contractor's agent, he designated himself — had, with cosmopolitan impudence, visited the new-comer's camp the very first evening, and, contrary to all his expectations, had fallen desperately in love with this young woman, and would have been quite willing to forego all other attractions and sacrifice himself for her sake, but when he ventured upon his first remark to her, she not only failed to reply, but turned to the man who seemed to be her father or her guardian and addressed to him a question which left Tuck in no uncertainty as to the rejection of his overtures. "Miss Margaret" the rest of them called her; and though thereafter Tuck called her "stuck up," he nevertheless worshipped Miss Margaret from afar. She "didn't do nothin'," he said, and he noticed that when she was not reading a book whose binding suggested a different kind of literature from that to which he was accustomed, she sat apart, with her uncommonly white hands in her lap, and looked, as he was pleased to imagine, very unhappy indeed. Had this most unconscionable ass but known that she was only angry, and that even her anger never touched *his* most distant neighborhood, he would have been sorely puzzled to know how to account for it.

In the course of a few days it began to be suspected that the young lady held no relationship, unless a very distant one, with any of her party. The gallant and polite officers of the post were treated by her with some consideration, and they acutely made this important discovery: Thompson averred that she was a well-educated northern girl, who had gone to the south as a school-mistress, and had been jilted by some person to the said acute young officer entirely unknown. He acknowledged that she had not told him so, or in any way given him her confidence. But the Thompsons are all shrewd people. When asked if she intended making a residence in far-off California she said she did not know, and hinted that she did not care. The longer the party stayed the more imminent became the prospect of a sensation of some kind, on account of this fair-haired and blue-eyed young woman, who seemed strangely out of place amid her surroundings, and who had captivated all hands down to the butcher's man. There had never passed through these regions a traveller upon this most desolate of roads, one whose footsteps were so dainty, whose skirts and collars were so preternaturally white, and who coiled her hair round her head with so much feminine skill. But she was "queer." She was, in a sense, homeless among her companions. Disregarding the supposed danger from prowling Apaches, she took long walks alone; and Tuck subsequently stated that he once saw her far down towards the cañon, sitting upon a bowlder in the moonlight, apparently "thinkin'," and that beside her, alert and watchful, sat her sole companion on such occasions, an ugly yellow dog, who had always seemed to have an especial dislike to the contractor's agent.

One night, after tattoo, the man with whose family Miss Margaret seemed somehow connected came breathless to the commandant with the statement that she had "gone walkin'" early in the evening, and had not returned. Nor did she ever return. The most accomplished trailer of the post failed to account for the manner of her taking off. After a day and a night of fruitless search, all further efforts were abandoned as useless, and thereafter the theme was avoided, as a horrible reminiscence whose every detail was sufficiently expressed by the hated word, "Apaches." Thompson was most severely afflicted, and much exercised in the necessary concealment of a grief which this time was not one of that shrewd young officer's pretences.

But had she indeed been captured by the Apaches? Had her reckless walks ended at last in sudden capture, and a fate worse than death? Mariano, the scout, said not; and he knew. He declared that there had never been an Indian near the emigrants' camp, nor between there and the cañon, for three moons. Men would no doubt sometimes arrive at conclusions more nearly correct if they would study probabilities less and improbabilities more. If the commandant had been asked if there were any other means by which a young lady might be spirited away, he would have said unhesitatingly that there were not. He would have been, unconsciously all the time, thinking of the lost one as a woman. Men, here as elsewhere, go where they list, and there is little thought of how or of when they may choose to return.

Every Friday night, at an hour when the wilderness itself was asleep, there came rattling down the hill from the eastward a canvas-covered vehicle drawn by four vicious little mules. The officer of the day often heard the driver's coyote-bark, by means of which signal he and all his fellows are accustomed to arouse the sleepy officials of the desert post-offices as they approach. The sentinel, as he walked back and forth before the sally-port, watched it as the wheels ground over the gravel at the door, and heard the leathern sound of the falling mail bag. A sleepy word or two between the driver and the trader's clerk, the shutting of a door, the renewed grinding of wheels, and the overland stage had come and gone, so like a border phantom that it seemed doubtful, when the day came again, if such an institution existed. Sometimes there were passengers, but not often. Occasionally a desperate man, whose absolute necessities called him across a continent, loaded himself with weapons, and ran the gauntlet of discomfort and danger in the overland. People wondered sometimes why or how the line was run at all. The doubt was hardly a pertinent one. Some hundreds of thousands of dollars for a semi-weekly mail service, coupled with an agreement that the line must be prepared to carry passengers, will accomplish wonders.

The man who reported Miss Margaret's taking-off to the commandant confessed that she was not in any way related to him or to his family; that she became connected with them in eastern Texas by having been a teacher in his neighborhood. She had money, he said, was "offish an' book-larned," had started with him for California because she had some concealed purpose in going, and added that "she never tuk to him or his family much, an' war a leetle quar in her ways." He prudently forgot to state that on the night of her departure she had told the whole partly distinctly that, in her opinion, they would never see California, and in terse and elegant terms expressed her opinion of the slowness of Texans in general, and of these in particular. He also failed to state that she had taken with her a travelling bag, but had left behind her an immense trunk, which, with all its unknown finery, might be regarded as a legacy to his own not uncomely daughters. In fine, Miss Margaret's guardian lied; and the day following left the post with all his belongings, going westward.

More than a week after these events had occurred, and when the tender hearts of the gentlemen of the garrison had assumed that shade of subdued regretfulness for Miss Margaret's fate, that is said to be characteristic of the sex, early one morning while Tuck was plying his vocation at the slaughter-pen, he was surprised by the apparition of an immense yellow-and-white mastiff, gaunt, tired, and almost starved, who came crouching toward him, urged by hunger, and mutely begging for the merest taste of the raw meat in which the churl was at work. He was greatly astonished, for he had no great difficulty in recognizing Miss Margaret's surly guardian. He paused, with his bloody hands upon his hips, and as he looked, conceived a new hatred of the dog for her mistress' sake. "*You* kin come back, kin you? Drat your ugly eyes!" and he threw a stone at her. The creature yelped, and limped away toward the sally-port, too tired and hungry to even show her teeth to that other cur who refused a bone to a starving dog. When he saw her again, he said: "There goes that Peg." This was very brilliant irony on the part of Tuck, and he laughed a good deal to himself at the thought that the friendless dog should hereafter bear what he chose to consider the nickname of her lost mistress. Then, because the name of Miss Margaret's whilom protector was understood to have been Watkins, the servant, with unconscious drollery peculiar to her kind, had called her "Peg Watkins" the evening she became the doctor's friend.

As time passed, the doctor dissipated all the theories upon which the officers of the post had constructed their conclusions as to what, as a contract doctor, he ought to be. He accommodated himself to surroundings that might well be considered curious, in an hour's time. He seemed to have travelled much, knew his fellow-men very well, and was cool in all emergencies. He was not afraid of sun or rain, was a keen hunter, and an excellent companion, and could tell stories like Othello. He seemed to know the miner of California, the ranchman of Texas, and spoke familiarly of Paris and Rome. In a word, he was very far from being as "green" as his companions, having observed carefully the habits of many doctors, had expected. But there was something about the man that, after all, they could not quite understand. Thompson thought he was "curious" in that he seemed to have no earthly interest in those creatures who were ever to Thompson so near and yet so far. He never spoke of women at all. He seemed never to have had an affair. He never amused or entertained his auditors with stories of past flirtations. One night, not long after his arrival, the presence of the outcast mastiff at his feet suggested to some one of his companions the story of the lost lady—Thompson alluded to her poetically as "the loved and lost,"—and it was added that her name among her ill-assorted friends sounded like a schoolma'm's—"Miss Margaret." The doctor looked up quickly, relapsed into thoughtful silence, and without a single comment upon the sad story, began presently to talk of something else. In other respects also did they think him rather queer; for like many men of his kind, he liked very well to be left alone. Often, accompanied by Peg, he passed the sentinel at midnight, coming home from some purposeless wandering. He was, it seemed, not unaccustomed to life on the frontier. Only a year ago he had visited California, and within a few months had been in Texas. He did not allude to anything as the specific object of his wanderings, but he left the impression upon his listeners that he was either running away from, or chasing, some fleeting shadow round the world. Often, far beyond the midnight, when the officer of the day passed in his rounds, he could see the lonely man sitting in the lamplight, and Peg crouched watchfully in the open window.

The understanding between the brute and the man was so remarkable as to attract some attention.

Wherever the doctor's footsteps led him, the dog awkwardly waddled behind. Peg was now clean, well-fed, and carried her content to the extreme of being somewhat saucy. Her master was her world, and she cared for nothing and no one else. The inhabitants of the little community might pat her on the head if they would, and she reciprocated by hardly so much as the wagging of her tail. Hundreds of times her name was called from open doors and across the parade-ground. She scarcely so much as turned her head, and usually walked with great dignity in the opposite direction. All this may have been a kind of negative revenge for past indignities; for she had the general good at heart. Often in the watches of the night her bark came faintly back from the surrounding hills. There was a legend that she never slept. But she did — at midday, upon the doctor's bed.

The saying that time at last makes all things even, is only poetry, which is often far from true. But there was a notable instance in which the statement was fairly demonstrated. Tuck possessed two curs as ugly as himself, one of which was of Peg's own sex. Early one morning, as the butcher went to his avocation, accompanied by his two companions, they three met Peg walking with great stateliness beside the wall. With his dogs beside him, Tuck could not resist the temptation to utter a vicious "*sick 'm!*" With much more valor than judgment, the two dogs rushed to the onset. If Peg was frightened, she made no sign of it; and quietly taking the female by the neck, with one great shake she covered her white breast with her enemy's blood. A few minutes after, she appeared at her master's bedside, apparently unconscious of the stain. Afterwards, when told of the outrage by Tuck, the doctor called his grim friend to him, and, as he patted her, remarked: "Margaret, did you kill the meat-man's dog?" And the "meat-man" went away convinced that dogs and men may sometimes have a singular mutuality of interests.

The long summer passed, and autumn came with its nights of frosty sparkle and moonlit glory. The little walled post, with its bare parade-ground and its monotonous routine, dulled by daily use, seemed to grow irksome to the doctor. It was not strange that he liked better to wander through the long evenings among the near foot-hills, accompanied always by Peg. His associates had long since become accustomed to his vagaries, and paid small heed to his absence, as they whiled the dull night away with social games at cards — chiefly that captivating one that for some unexplained reason has been named "poker." True, they had concluded long ago that there was "something on the man's mind," and guessed, with a nearness to the truth they hardly suspected, that the position of "contract doctor" at a frontier post was, to a man of his attainments, little more than an excuse to rid himself of himself.

One night he lay on his back by the roadside, a gaunt cactus lifting its thin spire at his feet, and Peg beside him, looking at the stars. His thoughts were dreamy, but they were busy. This refuge in the wilderness was not satisfactory. Go where he would, he could not rid himself of a thought that had been with him so long that it was a part of him. He had lain there three hours, and in all that time had not evolved any new idea as to his further profitable disposal of that troublesome person, himself. He had already resigned his appointment, and questioned within himself where he should go. "If I could only find her," he ejaculated, "I would start for China."

The moonlight on his watch-dial showed it was one o'clock. The silence of the wilderness seemed to close around him impenetrably. Everything was asleep. The social game at the trader's store was undoubtedly played out, and he wondered, as he walked slowly homeward, whither the officer of the day, whose business it was to be up, had betaken himself. But he thought he heard afar off the sound of wheels amid the rocks of the cañon. When he arrived at the trader's store, the sound grew louder, and he paused, out of mere wakefulness and curiosity, until the phantom mail, which so seldom brought him any letters, should come. Soon the four little black heads were dancing along above the roadside chaparral, and the driver, his hand upon his mouth, had begun to utter his hideous coyote-calls. Jehu seemed merry; for the mail was from the west, the worst was passed, and home and rest were only twenty miles away. That is a long distance upon which to congratulate oneself at two o'clock in the morning, the moody physician thought; but happiness is a merely relative term.

A strap was broken, and while the driver mended it, and the sleepy clerk stood at the door, Peg inspected the wheels, the boot, and, cautiously, the heels of the mules. Presently she seemed strangely attracted by something inside. She arose upon her hinder legs, and with her paws upon the broken window-frame, struggled, yelping, to climb higher. This amazed the doctor, and he also came near. Then a feminine voice was heard inside, and a hand appeared in the moonlight, which the dog devotedly licked. Presently the door was flung open, and a somewhat muffled face appeared, and before the clumsy efforts of the dog could effect an entrance, her shaggy neck was clasped in some one's arms, and audible kisses rained upon her hairy face. "Oh, you dear old dog! where *did* you come from?" were words the doctor thought he heard. It occurred to him as being rather an eccentric proceeding also. He went to the window, and said "Peg,—old girl," and Peg thumped her large tail upon the floor, and turned from one to the other, and displayed the whole immense length of her tongue, and seemed agonized between two great happinesses.

Then occurred the following conversation, interrupted by little gasps and swallowings:

"Doctor—Daniels! Who—who—My goodness" (evidently recovering), "*is* it you?"

"Now, Maggie" (somewhat huskily and leaning very far into the vehicle), "where have you been?"

"Everywhere, sir" (entirely recovered); "to California last."

"Well, but where? — how?"

"This is what I have to say to you, Ed," — and the lady's voice grew strong in its tone of injury,— "that no matter how you or I came here, or where from, you must go with me here and now, or I shall just get out and stay here, as I'm sure I've a right to do. And then I've been so far, and am so tired, and — and — I think I must be dreaming, after all." And then this Amazon broke down, and began to cry.

The doctor never looked more earnest at the bedside of a very doubtful case than he did at this moment. He took off his hat solemnly, and wiped his forehead, looking down at the ground as though he had lost something there. With all that he had been looking for so long, there in the shabby vehicle, — with what he had been willing to go to China for there within arm's length, — he stood fighting his pride outside. Then a hand came forth and touched his shoulder, and a voice said "I'm very sorry, Ed;" and immediately Doctor Edward Daniels turned resolutely and climbed into the coach. It would seem that after so many years of estrangement and regret, after a thousand maledictions by each upon all the stars and fates that preside over matrimony, after a trial by each of every quack medicine for unhappiness that human nature is wont to suggest to itself, it only required four little words to do the business; and it was the woman, of course, who said them. He left everything behind, caring nothing for the morning astonishment of his late associates at the post, for the criticisms of his enemies, or the regrets of his friends. He was very glad to take up again the burden of a love that had been wilful, capricious and exacting, which had defied him twenty times in a day, which was nothing that he would have it to be. but which was nevertheless the love of a beautiful woman whose slave he was and wished to remain.

Jehu had been listening and chuckling to himself. "I reckon she's got him now," he said. "Hudup thar!" and he brought the long whip to bear with a keen snap under the off leader's traces.

The dumb friend lay at inconvenient length along the bottom of the coach, quite content to have her wrinkled neck used as an imperious lady's footstool. "I'm sure it's all very curious," said she, "and her name is *not* Peg at all. And Ed. —there were a great many nice things in that trunk. To think of the Watson girls wearing my dresses! — the hateful things."

"The Watson girls are very fortunate if some Apache squaw is not wearing them by this time," said the doctor; "and you — well, you are equally lucky that the same amiable savages did not get your back hair, especially when you consider the extraordinary beauty of it;" and the doctor felt obliged to satisfy himself as to whether the brown coils were yet his by placing a rather large hand upon the lady's head.

"I should not have cared if they had — at one time," said she.

Thompson strenuously asserted for a long time that he suspected Miss Margaret was a married lady. "Now, I never knew a girl to act just so," he said; "at least, not to *me*. They usually tumble to the racket sooner or later, and—"

But here the lieutenant was assailed with jeers and laughter to the extent that he rose in a huff, and walked out of the room—the back room at the trader's store.

IX.

A GOOD INDIAN.

IF the Lieutenant General of the United States Army ever made the epigrammatic remark that has been attributed to him, that "the only good Indian is a dead one," it is probable that he was not at the moment thinking of that lone and solitary variety of the Child of Nature in the West who has never given the military any trouble.

It is true that the Pueblo is only an Indian by the general classification; but it is hoped that the reader will not therefore prematurely imagine that he is again to be taken by a button and made to understand the author's views of the rights, wrongs, and general character of the dun-colored Ishmaelite who, with no history of his own making, has entered so largely and so falsely into American literature. The Pueblo is included among the tribes only by a mistake made in the beginning, and perpetuated through time. There is, indeed, no distinction of race more perceptible than that which exists between the patient and home-loving farmer of the Rio Grande, and the lawless freebooter who from time immemorial has been his inveterate enemy.

Those long, low, grass-grown mounds that lie in sequestered valleys and beside streams in all the nooks and corners of New Mexico and Arizona are all that now remain to mark the outlines of those cities whose names are long since forgotten, and whose last burgher died four or five misty centuries ago. Nor were these their only or most enduring dwellings. They hewed out of the living rock of the cañon's sheer walls, cities for the shelter of many thousand souls. They once peopled these regions, and hundreds of miles to the northward of them, with a race who lived under a common head, who practised many of the arts of civilization, who builded for permanence and beauty, who erected temples and monuments, who tilled the soil, who owned the ties of duty, family, and religion, and whose ancestors, still more remote and far than all these desolate remains, anticipated the oldest legends of discovery, and crossed the Straits of Behring before the Norsemen or Portuguese had dreamed of another world. The Pueblo is the small remainder of that people who preceded all that we call American antiquity, and who were more brave and more prosperous than any of the tribes and races that have occupied the land since they passed away as a people. You might not suspect it, as you see him in his humble village, and engaged in his patient toil. He is the pathetic last man.

In contradistinction from the Indian, as we know the man usually meant by that term, the Pueblo is purely a farmer, and has been so from time immemorial. All his tastes and inclinations are peaceful. In his intimate knowledge of his business, his laborious patience, his industrious contentment in what the sunshine brings and the soil yields, he is the model farmer of America, and reminds one of all he has ever heard of the patient husbandmen of Egypt and China. It is surprising to note how he is the teacher of those whose ancestors were his latest conquerors and oppressors. The whole curious routine of Mexican husbandry is borrowed from the Pueblo. His plough is made of two pieces of wood, the one mortised to the other at such an angle as makes at once the coulter and the beam. Sometimes, indeed, it is only the crotch of a tree, found suited to the purpose. Yoked to this are the gaunt, long-horned, patient oxen, tied together by a straight piece of wood bound to the horns. As one sees the brown-faced son of toil holding his rude plough by its one straight handle, walking beside the lengthening mark which can scarcely be called a furrow, through the low field yet wet and shining from recent inundations, urging his beasts with grotesque cries and a long rod, one can hardly help thinking that the rude wood-cuts that illustrate Oriental agriculture in the Biblical commentaries have come out of their respective pages and are there before him.

And it is the Pueblo who has modelled the universal architecture of the country. The low houses of sun-dried brick, with earthen roof and earthen beds and benches and floors, have an origin far back of the conquest, and though somewhat modified by it, are by no means the result of Spanish ideas of comfort and taste exclusively. The Pueblo, a farmer by nature, has from early times been surrounded by the Apache, his enemy always. Therefore the cluster of houses which formed the common village was each one a castle. He made no doors, and when he and his family retired for the night, they climbed a ladder to the roof and drew the stairway after them.

Their villages are still the nuclei of farming communities, and their inhabitants, in the majority of instances, yet enter their houses through the roof. The orchards of peach and apricot, and the laden grape-vines, as well as the low-lying little fields, are, with immense pains, surrounded by an almost inaccessible wall. The Pueblo shuts in his life from the world, and delights in personal isolation. His curious house and closely fenced garden are not so from motives of fear alone. In common with all the aborigines of the continent, he seems bent upon solitude amid the thousand changes which encroach upon him, and desirous of passing away silently to join his fathers, without a memento, a monument, or a word of history, save the meagre annals of his decline and death, told only by his conquerors. For hundreds of years it has been so, and the picture presented seems almost an impossible one to the restless American mind. For centuries beyond which the poor Pueblo has still his traditions, with decreasing numbers, with new surroundings, with the predatory Apache and the tyrannical and covetous Spaniard, and latterly the Yankee stranger ever peering over his garden wall, he has toiled on, clinging to ancient habits, intensely occupied with the sordid details of the humblest of all lives, and, through all, content. Nor will it be considered strange if, as they tell, the light required by his ancient faith is still kept burning upon his hearth, and in his heart he still cherishes a faith that in the light of some radiant morning the immortal One, King of all the faithful, will come again from the East, bringing deliverance with him.

But it is the recollection of a harvest-day among these patient and pathetic people that suggested all this. Far down the sandy valley, as one approaches, stand the long lines of brown wall, and far to the right glitter in the noon sunshine the slimy pools and yellow current of the mosquito-haunted river. The settlement, with the village for its centre, seems a large one. On every hand are the evidences of unwonted activity. The cumbrous carts, with their framework of osier, howl dismally on oilless axles as they pass you on the roadside, to return laden with yellow bundles. Here are four women, the eldest old indeed, and the youngest almost a child, who trudge along in the sand, each one's back loaded with fresh fruit. Did you ask for peaches? The eldest deliberately unloads herself by the roadside, opens her bag, selects a double handful of the largest and ripest, and presents them, with a motherly smile upon her wrinkled old face. She will take no money, and trudges on, leaving you to look after her and reflect that courtesy is by no means confined to the Christians who have white faces. Perhaps the small incident is characteristic; for with just such kindness did this poor woman's ancestors welcome the strangers from across the sea, so many centuries ago.

In the fields on either hand the reapers wade slowly along, patiently gathering each yellow stalk. Some distance away, a cloud of dust, and straw tossed high in air, and uncommon noises, proclaim the active operation of a primitive threshing-machine. Around a circular space some twenty feet in diameter tall poles are set in the ground, and between these, from one to the other, are drawn thongs of raw-hide. Within, the ground is covered with wheat, which is being trodden out by some twenty unbridled donkeys. The small urchins tumble and halloo in the straw outside of the enclosure, like children in a straw-pile anywhere in the world; and two women and a man in the centre of the ring so work upon the feelings of the donkeys that, what with gestures, and shouts, and sundry long poles, they go fast and faster, as diabolically mixed as Tam O'Shanter's witch-dance. To a man accustomed to close intimacy with the kind, there is ever something ridiculous and grotesque in the long ears and solemn countenance of the ass. Stir intense dignity and preternatural solemnity into unbecoming friskiness, and the scene becomes pitiably ludicrous. As you watch these who tread out the corn on the ancient threshing-floor that seems translated out of the Old Testament, you find yourself intent upon seeing how, with long ears laid back and flying heels, they revenge upon each other the indignities of their masters.

Somehow, as you approach the village, you gather the impression that all the women you meet are very large and all the men are very small. For aught I know it is a fallacy; but the average Pueblo woman is a creature whose dignity would not suffer by comparison with some of the queens of civilization. And you begin to discover that there are also girls, among whom the selling of fruit is a specialty. A row of heads are just visible above the wall, and before each there is a huge melon and a fruit basket. This is the temporary market, instituted without issue of bonds or previous arrangement, upon the arrival of every government train. I would there were some lone spot upon the habitable globe where the tricks of traffic were unknown. Here the fruit trade is rendered considerably more lively by the merry eyes, white teeth, and brown and sturdy shoulders of a company of merry market-women. Surely the long train of wrongs that have pressed to the verge of extinction a hospitable and gallant race have by these creatures been but seldom heard of, or are poorly remembered.

The village has the appearance of being composed of blank walls. Only the square tops of the houses, and none of the domestic operations, can be seen. But the loaded boughs of trees droop over the walls, and here and there are glimpses of trailing vines and pleasant vistas. But it is in the midst of a dreary land; and the stretch of yellow stubble between you and the bank, where the cottonwood leaves tremble lazily in the summer wind, the suggestion of rest, quiet, contentment and plenty behind the drab walls, and the holiday faces around you, contrast strongly with the bare brown mountains that rise on every hand. In any more favored country the simple pastoral scene, which remains long with you in the hundreds of monotonous miles yet to come, might scarcely be remembered at all. From villages such as this, fenced about with walls, upon one side of which grows the cactus, and upon the other verdure, fruit and content, the very name of this curious people is taken. "Pueblo" means only a town. The old name by which they call themselves, the name which expresses lineage and a country, I know not, and there are few who care what it may be.

Yet a little further, and there is another oriental threshing floor, upon which the scene is different from the last. The children and the persecuted and revengeful donkeys have vanished together, and the hands and minds of the two stoical persons there are occupied in an operation so striking and important in the operations of simple life that it was more frequently used than any other as a simile to teach the sons of the patriarchs the lessons which all men ought to know. It is the winnowing of the wheat. One of the persons is an old man, so withered of shank and so lean of face that he would seem to have been subjected to some process of drying for the sake of preservation. The other is a woman, and directly his opposite in all things. I cannot tell if it is always so, or if the picture was only made for me; but I lingered and studied it. She too was tall, and had a stolid and determined, but rather comely, face. Her head was bound in a folded shawl, but her hair escaped unconfined and lay about her shoulders. Her outer garment was not a gown, but the dress of her kind, so universally worn that it seemed a kind of uniform, being a blanket of black wool, bound about with a red sash. From the knee her limbs were bare, as were also her arms and shoulders. She stood with her left foot advanced, and her large arms held high above her head the saucer-shaped basket, over the edge of which poured the slow stream of mingled chaff and wheat. Considered merely as a bronze statue endowed with life, and without reference to any other faculties or qualities, this stalwart woman, who was entirely unconscious of herself, was the most perfect specimen of grace conceivable. When the padded queen of the ballet stands in the tableau, in an attitude meant to be the embodiment of gracefulness, but which is but a mincing and studied artificiality, then I know how far is any attempt of art from the grace that untaught nature attains, and think of the Pueblo squaw who winnowed wheat by the roadside in the afternoon sunshine.

There was still another personage there, who at first escaped notice. His presence was not essential to the work in hand, but it would be a mistake to underestimate his personal importance. In the slant shadow of the straw-pile lay a big baby boy, in the entire nakedness of nature. He flung his brown, round limbs high in air, in the lissome gymnastics of infancy, and while he gathered mysterious sustenance from the sucking of one of his fists, with the other he clutched awkwardly at the sunshine and other imaginary nothings that float in the air before the eyes of infancy.

It is a question whether the much-discussed subject of woman's rights really had its origin in the minds of cultivated and highly-educated people. Among all the aboriginal tribes of America, women have had their "rights" time whereof the memory of their brutes of husbands runs not to the contrary. And the truth is that those rights entail upon the sex, as well in civilization as in savagery, that concomitant of equal drudgery which the Logans and the Stantons and the Miss Dickinsons would be very unwilling to assume. To the privileges and labors of masculinity, the conditions of civilization seem to be an eternal bar. Once a robust Pueblo woman was selling piñons at the corner of the plaza at Albuquerque, and a sleek-looking infant lay in a blanket beside her. I asked her how old the youngster was. She complacently answered, "Day before yesterday," and pointed with her finger to that part of the heavens where the moon was at that inconvenient hour in the early morning, at which, as I am credibly informed, babies everywhere are in the habit of coming into the world. She was proud of the urchin, too, as all women are, and slipping her finger through his waistband, held him dangling and kicking like a large spider for our closer inspection. Such women as these are alone physically competent to maintain "rights."

So many strange stories are told and believed of the Pueblos — of their religion, social customs, and domestic life, — that it is almost impossible to sift truth from romance. But they are, at least, the only ones of the original races who have always been friendly to the white man. When General Kearney took possession of the Territory in 1850, in the name of the United States, the immediate release from the peonage and semi-slavery of so many years so affected the hearts of the simple people that for a long time they are said to have clung to the belief that the commandant was the long-looked-for "man from the East," come for their deliverance. Repeated enforcements of equal laws, protection from Apaches, and general and reciprocal good treatment, have conspired to place them in such relations with the great power destined before many years to absorb the whole central continent as none others of the aborigines enjoy.

It will not do to imagine that because the Pueblos are purely agricultural, they are incapable of defence. On the contrary, their whole history has been one of turmoil and strife. The Mexicans oppressed and the Comanches and Apaches murdered them; and these ancient and unremitting contests are the cause of that air of ancient ruin and dead history that so much of New Mexico now wears. It is not the crumbling church, and the foot-worn and dilapidated village street, that are the oldest things in Mexico. Far back of the conquest existed the semi-civilization seen in the Pueblo village of to-day. Almost unchanged, we see it still. The cities whose walls are grass-grown ridges now, perhaps had bustling thoroughfares and a teeming population while the mound-builders of the Mississippi valley were at their strange work.

But these are questions for the *savans*. It is

with the present, and with such things as are apparent in daily life, that this sketch has to do. I said that through all these centuries of conflict and change, it was strange to note that manners and dress had remained so nearly unchanged. But that remark needs this further explanation: that it is of course impossible that contact with others should have absolutely no effect, and here is an instance. It is not missionary effort — not even of the invincible phalanx of Jesuitism,— not Bibles, tracts, and preaching, that come nearest the heart of the pagan. The Indian of every tribe and latitude has obtained for himself a new character as the autocrat of the speckled shirt, and these conservative people are long since clothed upon with the new idea. Of all the girls, women, old men, and babies, in sight, there is not one, except the last, who does not wear calico as the material of some queerly-cut garment. The old man who stands watching the winnowing, with the somewhat imbecile attempt at helping, has on only three articles of apparel, and two of them are cotton. The statuesque woman wears beneath the black woollen uniform a snow-white garment of a not unfamiliar pattern, which, when worn alone, seems ever to have the indisputable merit of looseness without any corresponding virtue as a covering. The girls who stand a-row behind the wall are all clad in the material whose familiar print takes one back at a bound to the square stone buildings that are the wealth and pride of the diminutive commonwealth of Rhode Island. But scarcely as dresses are they worn, and it is only the material that is fashionable with these.

Here the idea of communism has been practically carried out for all these years. The village, with its walls and gardens and curious houses, has one common purpose in its occupancy — that of protection and society. There is no industry but agriculture. There are no stores, no shops, no sound of hammer and file. Every house was contrived for but two purposes: residence and defence. There are not even streets, and only narrow paths wind between onion-beds and currant bushes from house to house. Each family is self-productive of every needed article of domestic economy, even to the fire-baked pottery from which they eat and drink. The black woollen garment was dyed after nature's recipe, upon the back of the sheep, and the moccasins were made by the wearer. The clumsy cart, upon which the Mexican has been unable to improve, is shaped and pinned and tied together by the unaided skill of the man who expects to use it. The only article of any constant use or importance, not actually made upon the premises, is the cotton cloth heretofore referred to. It is a community in which there are no questions of finance, and that could live without money.

Strangely enough, in all these things there is no diversity of style. Like birds' nests, as they are made now, so have they been made from time immemorial. The porous earthen water-jug which hangs from the rafters in every house is of the same shape, with the same ornamentation, in every case. The old idea of the Biblical commentaries comes back again, when two women sit grinding at the mill, the loaf is baked upon the hearth, and the girls are seen returning from the spring, each with her tall water-jar upon her head. These people only need to live in dingy striped tents, surrounded by their goats and asses, and to be a little less heathenish in their faith, to reproduce within the bounds of an overgrown republic the days when Jacob worked for that grasping patriarch, his future father-in-law, and was cheated at last, and the father of the patriarchs sat at his tent door and watched the countless flocks that grazed the future inheritance of his descendants.

As these primitive agriculturists produce within themselves all they need, so they are learned in all that it is needful for them to know. Long before the little monkish knowledge they may have consented to acquire came to them from across the sea, they knew the times and seasons, and had a calendar in which the days were three hundred and sixty-five. They practised then, as now, their patient agriculture with a skill and success some part of which would be a boon to farmers who subscribe for agricultural journals and are engaged in the polemics of farming as a means of disseminating the surplus of information that they have acquired. They knew how to take the crude metals from their native beds, and mould them into forms for ornament and use. Their brethren of the south built colossal piles of hewn stone. The fountains they made in thirsty lands are playing yet, and the roads they built still lead to the gates of the Mexican capital.

They have, indeed, through all these centuries, gone backward and not forward. But the truth which is even now apparent, that for not one of all the original tribes of America is there any hope, will probably not be accepted as such until, within a few generations, the end shall have come. There is an isolation in the midst of surrounding life and activity, that accepts no compromise with death. Ever the patient victim of change, himself unchanging, and never the aggressor, with the material for a hundred histories, no one may know how heroic or pathetic, gone in the past, when the poor Pueblo shall finally leave his seed to be sown with a patent drill and his harvest to be reaped with a clattering machine, he will merit at least the remembrance that his hands were never red with Saxon blood and that his hearth was abandoned without reprisal.

But before he goes he will see the white man's magic in the engine rushing before its train down the valley of the Rio Grande, and the iron rail will usurp the place of the donkey-path before his door.* And soon the denizens of whitewashed towns will have scared the husbandman from his plough and the fruit-seller from the wall; and the noisy civilized crowd will forget, if they ever knew, that in these transformed regions there existed so peaceful and pleasant a thing as the home and farm of the Pueblo.

* Written ten years ago. The railway daily performs the feat described, and the time for studying the modern life of this last of his interesting race has forever passed.

X.

JACK'S DIVORCE.

HE was not black, though universally known as "Black Jack," and except that he had upon him the ineffaceable marks of sun and wind, might have been considered more than ordinarily fair. His hair was of a reddish brown, and his eyes had that steady and unflinching gaze which bespeaks for their owner honesty without blemish and vision without flaw.

It is not enough to say that Jack was merely a frontiersman, because in many instances that only expresses an accident and not a character. He had about him that something which, while it can only exist on the border, is yet a part of the man. Though not a negative person, he was one of those of whom a clearer idea may be given by stating what he was not than by explaining what he was. There is a whole world in which all the famous and remarkable doings of mankind are performed, of which Jack knew absolutely nothing; and in him I do but describe a class, of which he was a representative man.

Woman, in all the splendor of pearls of the ocean and gems of the mine, endowed with all the refinements of civilization, and the inheritor of all the tact and delicacy that result from ages of refinement — bland, bewitching, and fearfully and wonderfully made up, — he had never even seen. Femininity conveyed no such idea to him. The women he had known were only women in the broad sense in which female is not male. The wharfs and streets of crowded cities, the throng of the pavement and the exchange, the crowd and jam and bustle of trade, blooming fields and paved roads, were all crowded out of his conceptions of life and men, and he fortunately had no speculations and opinions to digest concerning them. He had never even heard the sound of the church bells, and, perhaps also happily for him, was steeped in Fijian ignorance of all the fateful differences in creeds which exist among those who diligently seek after the truth. He was benighted, but he was perpetually free from any attack of *odium theologicum*.

In his ignorance of all that is fashionable and most that is good among civilized mankind, he was even ignorant of the praises and luxuries men sometimes earn by dying, and the fair monuments and flattering epitaphs of Greenwood and Olivet would have filled him with astonishment. His was the rock-piled and lonely grave of the wilderness; and it had never occurred to him that a palace was necessary to the welfare of mouldering clay.

If the schoolmaster was ever abroad in western Arkansas, where Jack first saw the light, the benign influence never reached his mind. He could not read, and was ignorant of the primary rules of arithmetic and of everything else in the way of books. The immense literature of fiction and newspaperdom he had never even heard of; and yet he knew, traditionally as it were, some of Watts's hymns, and would repeat them with the same unction and pathos with which the childish and immortal lines are said by all who speak the English tongue.

But he was not a grown-up child. He lacked none of the great essentials that go to make up the remarkable biped whose ancestor was an ape and whose future is very doubtful. He spoke his mother tongue with a fluency equal to all the requirements of his life, and he spiced and strengthened it with that piquant slang which expresses so much in so few words that it is almost to be regretted that it is very vulgar to use it. His most peculiar characteristic, however, was not an educational one. It consisted in the seeming absence of anything like personal fear. Whole armies of men, surging masses that number many thousands, may, and often do, go through a long day of carnage without any instance of cowardice. But this is not the variety of courage meant. He limped, had lost a finger, and carried an ugly scar upon his cheek. But all these he had obtained at different times, and all in fighting with Indians. But not for glory. With no particular interest at stake, pecuniary or otherwise, he still wandered through the cañons and over the hills, alone, and solely bent upon killing the game he loved to hunt, unmoved by repeated encounters and escapes. Unless questioned, he never alluded to his adventures. He seemed to be ignorant of any manner of life among the conditions of which was included the common essential of personal safety.

There is a certain weapon which all have seen and with which far too many are familiar. The name of its inventor has gone down to posterity with something like renown. Skilfully handled, it is a weapon that few like to face. It is a small arsenal of rapid and sudden death, and a single man, skilled in the use of Colt's revolver, is almost equal to six men with old-fashioned arms that fire but a single shot. In the use of this pretty toy, Jack was a miracle even among his own companions. He was a walking Gatling, and the pair that were continually upon his person were worn smooth with constant handling.

This was one reason why Jack was not afraid of Indians. There was no moment when eye and ear were not alert. He frequently remarked: "They ain't got me yit; a man can't die nohow till his time comes." And in that bit of profound philosophy he believed with so profound and simple a faith that it seemed a pity it had not more sense in it.

But simple and honest as was the life of this gentle savage, he became the victim of one great trouble, and that of course had a woman at the bottom of it. It was the incident that made him seem more like the men around him, and demonstrated as well his kinship with the great mass of mankind.

Dolores was the handsomest woman Jack had ever known in his wild life; or, at least, she so appeared to him. She was Mexican — which is

Spanish. — had been once as fair as a brown-colored nymph, and was still as coquettish as it runs in her race to be, and as false as the profane word Shakspeare uses as a comparative in this same connection. She was only a laundress in the military post hard by; but her eyes were black and her teeth were white, and she caught Jack on the tender side which all such men present to female blandishments.

Bold as he always had been, he must therefore surrender to this fragile señorita. She had had many lovers. She could hardly count them upon all her fingers. Some she had discarded, to-wit: all she had ever had, at odd times, of her own race. And some had discarded her, namely: certain American Lotharios, who could be faithful long to none. But she was not broken-hearted, nor indeed very sorrowful, and had steadily replaced vacancies by new recruits. And last came honest Jack, whose heart she accepted without hesitation, and whose money she spent without remorse. Doubtless for her sake Jack might have left off risking his life amongst the Apaches. There was no telling but that he might in time have been induced to live in a town and sleep upon a bed.

It must be understood in this case, as in all others of the kind, that a man's liking for a woman is not controlled by any trait in her character. Dolores was still maturely handsome; she knew men very well; and she practised the art of coquetry with the skill of all her sex, added to the historic proficiency of her race. It may be that there had descended to her, through a long line of forgotten ancestry, some of the cunning graces and charms, and some of the velvet-covered trickery, which long ago distinguished the dames of Arragon and Old Castile. She had at least the softness, the subtle smooth suavity, which gives to the women of the Latin race a peculiar attractiveness to the bluff American.

So she married the hunter, after the manner of the country; and well it was to one whose vows sat with such habitual lightness, that the ceremony was of no more binding character. It was *bona fide* to Jack, however, and they two lived together in a very small house near the outer wall of the post. Perhaps Dolores never intended to cling with very great faithfulness to him alone. She probably argued that it was for the present convenient; and, judging him by her standard, calculated upon his roving life and the faithlessness of men in general for final freedom when some new inducement should offer. But, as stated, it was a part of Jack's personality to be faithful. He had no other idea than that he was bound hand and foot, and had never read history and thus become acquainted with the illustrious examples there afforded of matrimonial unfaithfulness. And as was natural to one of his ignorance and simplicity, he expected a reciprocity of feeling.

In a few weeks, Dolores began to use her fine eyes upon various of the uncouth masculines she met, after the old fashion, and Jack began to grow moody, and to look hard and determined out of his blue eyes, and by and by there was a look upon his face that the veriest death-seeker in all that desperate country would hardly have cared to defy, and when at home he certainly kept his house and his family to himself.

But now there came and stayed at the trader's store a man who wore barbaric gold and a linen shirt; one whose fingers were long, and exceeding nimble in dealing cards, and whose countenance had about it a look of mingled bravado and cunning. He came as a traveller, and stayed for weeks; and ere long he and Jack's wife were exchanging glances of recognition. Fraud and foxiness were so plainly written upon his person that it was easy to believe that to defraud Jack, or, if not Jack, then some one else, was what he stayed and waited for.

But meantime the hunter had ideas and purposes of his own; and, with a silence that was ominous, he kept those purposes to himself. He seemed always waiting and watching for something; and the man who has many a time waited and watched among the rocks and hills, and many a time come off victor through vigilance, does not usually wait and watch for nothing. What he waited for finally came, and with it his idea of reparation and justice.

As was not uncommon, he took his gun and canteen, and went away to the mountains. But he seemed to go regularly, and generally returned on the third day. Strangely enough, he brought back no game, but looked clay-begrimed and tired. So far as known, he still found everything to be, to use his own expression, "reg'lar." Nevertheless, it was a fact among the knowing ones, that the dull hours were beguiled by the gambler at Jack's cabin, during these frequent absences of the owner. A month or more passed in this manner, and Jack's look grew colder and harder every day. No common man could have passed unquestioned. But there was an evidence of purpose in his demeanor and a method in his coming and going, and those who knew him quietly awaited results. Meantime, possessing all the qualifications that are valued and admired in such a country, and having been faithful to all and wronged no one, he had many friends; while his enemy, if such the gambler might as yet be called, had none.

Several times hints were given to the latter, by those who acted in the interests of general peace, that a day of reckoning might come to him. But he considered himself in luck in having so simple an enemy, and stayed on. He did not know his man; that was the general comment. More than once, when Jack was absent on his apparently fruitless expeditions to the mountains, a tall figure that looked like his had been seen by some sentinel walking his beat to approach the cabin, and to glide noiselessly away in the darkness.

One starry October night, when Jack had been gone only since the morning, he suddenly walked in among the story-tellers and poker-players at the sutler's store. All turned toward him, with inquiry and surprise in their faces. He looked very grim, and closed the door carefully behind him. "Men," he said, abruptly, "come along with me now, an' I'll answer the questions ye 've been *lookin'* at me for more 'n a month. An' purvidin' I don't do nothin' desp'rit, will ye agree not to interfere?"

A half-looked and half-spoken answer was given, and four men went out with Jack, among whom certain uniforms did not disdain to appear. At the door he untied a donkey, such as are common in the country, and drove the animal before him toward the cabin. The hunter was foremost, and without ceremony pushed open the door and entered. At the same moment, with the dexterity of long practice, he whipped out of its place the inevitable revolver, with three strides was across the room, and in a moment after the monte-dealer was looking down the bore of it with an expression of countenance which indicated that he regarded it as being several inches in diameter.

"Now," said Jack, in the peculiar tone which indicates earnestness without any doubt, "*My* time has come. You an' this woman must git up an' go right along with me. Mister, you orter know me. If ye want to shoot, ye kin hev a chance; but I'm apt to hit, an' I'll try, so help me God."

This fearful adjuration was uttered, not as the common profanity of an angry man, but in a tone and manner that gave it a fearful meaning. "Git up," said he, as the gambler, with paling face, seemed to say something conciliatory. He arose instantly. "Now," for the first time addressing the woman, "git your traps together. Quick," he said sharply, as she seemed to hesitate, "ye shell hev yer lover's company from this night to all etarnity."

Though a scene in which the comic was not altogether wanting, there was still something terrible in it. The woman, her olive roses blanched with terror, moved about, gathering her apparel into a bundle. The gambler glanced furtively at the door, and at his own weapon lying upon the table. But Jack's eye was upon him, and the implacable weapon was in his hand. Finally he placed his hand in his bosom and drew forth a plethoric bag, opened it, and poured some of the shining pieces into his hand. Frightened as she undoubtedly was, a glitter came into the woman's eyes as she saw them. There was no situation in life in which the chink of the dollars would not be music to her. But Jack's face only changed to take on a look of intense contempt, as his enemy pitifully offered him first the handful and then the bag. He was again mistaken in his man.

When the woman at last stood with her bundle in her hand, Jack pointed to the door, and bade her and the gambler move out together. He caused the woman to mount the diminutive donkey, and the gambler walked behind.

Straight up the slanting mountain-side they started, the implacable husband taking the gambler's weapon from the table as he left the room. Away in the starlit gloom the strange procession passed, and as the donkey picked his careful way among the stones, plodding safely and patiently after the manner of his kind, the last sounds the bystanders heard were the wailing and sobbing of the woman, the stumbling footsteps of the gambler, and, behind all, Jack's long and steady stride. And all these died away in the distance, and in the silence of the night the witnesses of the scene stood at the door of the deserted cabin, and looked at each other, and afterwards went back to the store, each one privately gratified, and none caring to say so.

After three or four days Jack returned empty-handed. He was questioned now, for human curiosity cannot be restrained forever. A grim humor was in his face as he said: "I've purvided for 'em. They've meat enough for three weeks;" adding, "any of you as wus particularly fond of him air informed that he wus well wen I kim away, o'ny a *leetle* lonesome. But he don't know enough to find his way back here, an' I reckon he'll hev to fight now."

And Jack thereupon cleaned his pistols, got together such things as hunters carry, said he believed he'd "go back to Californy," and at sunrise started out upon that pathless journey toward the northwest, that to him was only a question of time and life, and has not been heard of to this day.

Some months after this, the Mexican guide of a scouting party led the soldiers, hungry, bewildered, and parched with thirst, to where he said there was, years before, a spring among the rocks. They found it, and near it a deserted "dug-out." From this to the spring a well-worn path was made. When he saw it, the eyes of the professional trainer opened wide, but when he approached the hut he threw up his hands with a gesture of extreme astonishment, exclaiming, "*Madre de Dios!*—it was a woman!'"

Upon the floor still lay the sodden fragments of a woman's shawl, and not far away the coyote-gnawed remains of a man's boot. What had become of the late residents of the lonesome place, no one could tell. But here at last was Jack's mystery; the house that he built for them, and in which Dolores and her last lover met a fate that will never be known.

There have been men very like Othello, who never heard of Shakspeare. But the Dolores and the Desdemonas do not greatly resemble each other, —at least not in New Mexico.

XI.

COYOTES.

HE has been called an outcast by a notorious poet. He is universally conceded to be a sneak, a thief, and an arrant coward. He is a lier-by by day, and a wanderer o' nights; a dissipated wretch in whose whole history there is not a redeeming trait. He has an extensive connection, but no family. He is disowned by the dogs, and not recognized at all by respectable foxes. The gaunt gray wolf who sends his hoarse voice across the ravine in a howl the most dismal and harrowing that ever disturbed midnight and silence, will have no fellowship with the little thief who seems to have stolen his gray coat, and would fain be counted among his poor relations.

And yet the coyote is the representative animal of the border. It is his triangular visage, his sharp muzzle, especially fitted for the easy investigation of the smallest aperture into other people's affairs, his oblique, expressionless eyes, that should have a place in the adornment of escutcheons and the embellishment of title-pages. The buffalo, who is his successful rival in such matters, occupies the place because his shaggy stupid head is big; but the buffalo is not the representative of anything more than stupid ponderosity. He has roamed in countless thousands over his plains for hundreds of years, and during all that time he has never even bellowed. There is no degree of pleasure, anger, excitement or passion that can induce him to make a sound other than a guttural groaning that ill becomes his size. That great equipment of lungs and throat and nostrils is good for nothing in acoustics, and while he might make the valleys to echo, and might almost shake the hills, he spends his life in galloping, fighting, butting at sandbanks, and eating. Especially does he affect the latter. His life is one long process of deglutition and rumination. He never stole anything. He never made the moonlit hours hideous for love of his own voice. Colossal in size and fearful of aspect, he is yet so dull as to be incapable of self-defence. None but a great booby would deliberately get himself exterminated by running alongside of a slow-going railway train, to be shot by kid-glove sportsmen, and even by women, three or four score times, in the back, with silver-mounted pocket pistols. His stupidity is illustrated every day by the countless bleaching skulls and faded tufts of brown hair which mark his death-place at the hands of people to whom the riding of a mustang would be an impossible thing and the killing of a jackass rabbit a wonderful feat of skill and valor.

Not so his neighbor and actual master, the coyote. He will lengthen out the days of his years until his voice sounds hollow and thin and aged in the watches of the night. Nothing but infinite pains and insidious strychnine will end his vagabond life. As his gray back moves slowly along at a leisurely trot above the tall reeds and coarse grass, and he turns his sly face over his shoulder to regard you, he knows at once if you have with you a gun. The coyote is a reflective brute, and has an inquiring mind. Only convince him of the fact that you are unarmed, and he proceeds to interview you in a way that, for politeness and unobtrusiveness, is recommended as a model to some certainly more intelligent but slightly less obtrusive animals.

As he sets himself complacently down upon his tail at the summit of the nearest knoll, and lolls his red tongue, and seems to wink in your direction, he is so much like his cousin, the dog, that you can hardly refrain from whistling to him. Make any hostile demonstration, and he moves a few paces further on, and sits down again. Lie down in the grass and remain quiet for a little time, and by slyly watching him out of the corner of your eye you will discover that he has been joined by a half-dozen of his brethren and friends. Slowly they come creeping nearer and nearer, and are cautiously investing you upon all sides. Our curious friend has an object in all this, aside from mere frivolous curiosity. He knows that all flesh is grass, and now wishes to find out—first, if you are dead; and second, supposing you are not, if there is anything else in your neighborhood that is eatable. You rise up in sudden indignation, and scare the committee away. In such case you have offended the coyote family deeply, and they retire to a safe distance, and bark ceaselessly until they have hooted you out of the neighborhood. That night he and his friends will come and steal the straps from your saddle, the boots from under your head, the meat from the frying-pan (and politely clean the pan), and the pony's bridle. Nothing that was originally of animal organization, or that has the faintest flavor of grease, though it be but the merest reminiscence, comes amiss to him. Through a thousand variations in his family history, and through all the vicissitudes of a hap-hazard life, the disposition to be continually gnawing something remains unchanged. There is no more formidable array of ivory than his, and his greatest delight is ever to have something rancid between his teeth.

There is a distant collateral branch of this extensive family, which has been for ages noted for the artistic and incomparable roguery of all its members. The first beast with which a child becomes acquainted is the fox. He has, since that far dawn of intelligence in which illustration became, as it is still, the chief means of teaching, illustrated more pretty fables than all other beasts. He has beautified more stories and picture-books, and employed more artistic skill. In reality he possesses but one advantage over the coyote, and that consists in his proverbial swiftness of foot. His brush is no bigger or bushier, and his coat no grayer or thicker. Probably neither of these rivals in the science of thievery can lay any great claim to personal beauty, and, considering his want of speed, the coyote is the better beast of the two, in the particular industry in the pursuit of which they are both distinguished.

Upon the great plains of the Southwest, and in the mountains of New Mexico, one is sometimes puzzled to know where a beast so wanting in ferocity and so slow of foot can possibly obtain his daily provender. The truth is that he has to live by his wits. No one ever saw a starved coyote. He does not confine himself to any particular diet, and wherever he may wander or rest he is evidently always intent upon his next meal. He would greatly distinguish himself in that ancient industry, the robbing of hen-roosts and the abduction of domestic fowls, only there are none in his dominion to steal. But he is not discouraged, and does not abandon his profession on that account. He has the Chinaman's epicurean fancy for birds' nests, and follows the mountain quail to her bundle of twigs, and daintily laps the inner sweets of a dozen eggs, and retires like a man from a free lunch, slyly wiping his chops with his tongue. In the dead hours of the night he creeps upon the covey resting in the coarse grass, their tails together and their heads beneath their wings, and even the wary old whistler who leads his interesting family daily over the intricate miles of their habitat himself dozing, and throwing his sprawling forepaws suddenly over as many as he can, leaves the rest to whirr screaming away in the darkness, and learn from him a lesson in family vigilance for the future.

The jackass rabbit, doomed to fame partly on account of his grotesque auricular development, but also because of his beady eyes, his supposed foolishness, and his extraordinary swiftness in continual races with the only thing that can keep anywhere near him — his own shadow, — frequently falls a victim to the cunning of this marauder, at whom, under ordinary circumstances, he might be supposed to sit upon his hinder legs and smile derisively. Jack is sometimes tempted by a damp and shady nook to lie upon his back like a squirrel, and, with his ears conveniently doubled under him and his gaunt legs in the air, to sleep too soundly. Then the coyote creeps cautiously upon him, licking his lips, and as silent as though his voice had never waked the lugubrious echoes. He may be an hour in the task, but finally makes a spring not the less effective because it is very awkward, and the poor rabbit takes subjectively his last lesson in gnawing.

The virtue of perseverance shines brightly in the coyote. All these things require an inexhaustible fund of patience. Of course, he fails in many of his nefarious designs, but none the less does he try, try again. There is a notable instance in which this quality alone brings him victory, and that is in his contest with the buffalo. In this, since the supply of meat must necessarily be large, he makes common cause with all his hungry relatives. The old bull, after many years of leadership, and after becoming the father of a horde of ungrateful descendants, is finally driven forth by the strong necks and ingratitude of his younger associates, and ruminates with two or three of his own class, retired patriarchs, while the herd wanders afar off and forgetful. Then the coyotes take him in charge. Wherever he goes they follow. He dare not lie down, and weariness helps to overcome him. Finally they begin to harass him openly, and with increasing boldness A gray assassin is upon every hand. The buffalo is too imperturbable a brute to succumb to mere barking, and his enemies finally begin to bite. The contest may last several days, and be fought over a territory many miles in extent. But the old monster is worried, crippled, and finally brought down, and a snarling feast is begun, which is continued until the last bone is picked bare. The beef is none of the best, but our friend is content with substantial blessings.

But all the coyote's other modes of obtaining a livelihood are mere by-play to the great business of his life, which is stealing. For a long time it has been supposed that a cat approaching the cream-jar, and a weasel intent upon coveted eggs, were the ideals of sly cunning and predatory silence. But it is time our coyote should have his due; and there is no doubt that, in the exercise of a preternatural talent for silent appropriation, he excels all the sharp-smelling and light-footed night-wanderers. He has a curious *penchant* for harness, rawhide, boots, thongs, saddles, and old leather generally. He gnaws the twisted raw-hide lariat from the pony's neck, and bodily drags away the saddle and chews it beyond recognition by the owner. He enters the open barrack window, and steals the accoutrements from the soldier's bed-side and the shoes from under the bed. He will walk backward a mile, and draw after him a raw-hide that is dry and juiceless as a board. It would seem that he did not all these eccentric things for the sake of food alone. In the majority of instances, the articles are beyond mastication even by a coyote's tireless jaws. He steals, as men do, because he is a born thief. He is greatly gifted in every accessory of his chosen profession. In the olfactory sense he is a phenomenon. The savory odor of the camp-fire frying-pan reaches him at an inconceivable distance. With drooping tail and abject head, he comes stealthily near like a wilderness phantom, and his appearance in the darkness is the very picture of treachery. He is patient, and will not be driven far, but sits down a hundred yards away, he and all his kin, and invests the encampment, and longingly licks his lips, and waits. Ere long, the little bright fire, that is like a glowworm in the wide darkness, and the tired, lounging figures around it, are surrounded by a cordon of patient, harmless, hungry thieves, who lick their jaws and faintly whine in expectation.

These are the times, and only these, when the coyote is silent. Upon all other occasions his voice is his pride and glory, and he sits upon his tail, and throws back his head in the ecstasy of discord, and gives it to the wind and the night in a rapid succession of discordant yelps which seem ceaseless for hours together. Indeed, the coyote's bark is the prominent feature of night in the wilderness. To one unaccustomed to it, sleep is impossible. In spite of the knowledge of the brute's cowardice and general harmlessness, it is impossible to banish restlessness and some feeling of fear. After the fire dies out, as the sleepless and discordant hours pass, you long for morning and peace.

Coyotes and Indians are supposed to be on good terms always. They are somewhat alike in general characteristics, and have a supposed mutuality of interests. They both object to the invasion of the white man, and both are contemporary occupants of a country that cannot long remain the home of either. But the coyote's dislike to the invader seems to be only an unreasonable prejudice, for he has been furnished more feasts upon the carcasses of causelessly-slaughtered buffaloes in a single year than the Indian would have given him in ten.

But our gray-coated friend makes a near approach to respectability in one item: he is a creature of family, for whom he duly provides. Any morning in early spring, upon some dry knoll, may be seen three or four little dun-colored stupid-looking cubs, lazily enjoying the warmth. At the slightest alarm they tumble, with more alacrity than gracefulness, into the mouth of the den, from which they never wander far, and many hours patient digging will not unearth them. Not far away may be seen the mother, uneasily watching the course of the intruder's footsteps. But provision for the support of a family is not carried so far as it is with the foxes. There are but few delicate morsels carried to the den, and the adolescent thief must mainly subsist upon his mother's scanty udders until he has attained his teeth and his voice, when he is launched upon the wilderness world fully equipped by nature and instinct for the practice of all the variations of music and theft, and to follow in the disreputable ways of all his ancestors.

He is a brute who is entitled to respect for his very persistent and professional course of knavery. He understands his business, and follows it. He makes a success of it. Contemptible in body and countless in numbers, he forages fatness from things so despised of all others that he becomes almost a producer upon the just plan of coöperative industry. He is utterly careless of the contempt that all other beasts seem to feel for him, waiting for his revenge for the time of their feebleness and decay. Like all cowards, he can fight desperately when he must, and there is many an ugly scar of his making. Winter and summer, in heat and cold, he wags his way along the prairie paths with the same drooping, quick-turning, watchful head, the same lolling red tongue, the same bushy ornament trailing behind, ever mindful of a coyote's affairs, ever looking for supper, the figure-head, the feature, the representative of the wide and desolate country of which he comes more nearly being master than any other.

XII.

A GUARD-HOUSE GENTLEMAN.

LIEUTENANT CHARLES SMYTHE — Smith, all the same, but Smythe looks better in the register — was commandant of the post, and unquestioned autocrat of a territory comprising sixteen square miles of trap-rock, *mesquit,* and sand. But supreme authority was never vested in one more unappreciative of its privileges and responsibilities — possibly because he was so seldom called upon to exercise his prerogative that he almost forgot his distinguished position. Certainly his thoughts were very far from all troubles of this kind that July morning, as he sat in the inner room at the trader's store, sole occupant of the apartment. There was a round pine table, covered with a red artillery blanket, and the earthen floor had been swept away until each leg stood upon a little pedestal of earth. Many a game of "poker" had been played there, and the small box of "beans" still sat upon the cloth; but the useful piece of furniture had its sole office at this moment in being a rest for the lieutenant's feet. He was trying to read a copy of the "Herald," very new in being only three weeks old; but his eyes wandered away from the dull columns, through the small window, and out upon the foot-hills shimmering in the sunlight and the blue Sierras with their streaks of snow.

The air was heavy with silence. There were no bees to hum, and no twittering of small birds added cheerfulness to the time. Only occasionally, near the spring, the spiritless yellow-breasted and fidgety little lark, who seems to be careless of all climates between Maine and Texas, sat and swayed upon a tall weed. The usual ravens sailed in lazy circles, or sat in rows upon the ledges, and sociably croaked to each other. And these were the only living things. But the commandant was not taking any lively interest in these irresponsible denizens of his dominion. It is doubtful if he saw them at all, for his mind was boozing in one of those inane reveries that are the precursors of sleep. The "Herald" slipped from his fingers, and a faint wish that it was night half developed itself in his indolent head. Then, remembering his dignity, perhaps, he roused himself enough to yawn, and to remark to the group of deliberative ravens that he wished something would happen. Whereupon something did happen, which, in that dull region, was enough to keep him awake for the rest of the day. It was a circumstance wholly unimportant in itself that attracted his attention, for it was only the sound of a voice from the outer room. Voices are common enough, and there has even arisen an opinion that there may be upon occasion too much of them. Nearly every individual has one of his own, and some of them are harsh and some are soft, but each is characteristic of its possessor. As there are eyes that are never deceived in the recognition of a face, so there are ears that remember voices that were heard casually months or years before. Generally such voices have some marked peculiarity of their own; and such was the case here. The tones were low, perfectly polite, and the accent was that of a German educated in the English tongue. At first the commandant listened through the open door, with only that degree of interest which attaches to a stranger in a locality where strangers are infrequent. Then it began to remind him very dimly of something or some one more than a thousand miles away. Finally, as he sat there with one hand upon the back of his chair and the other upon the table before him, and in an attitude that indicated a hesitating suspicion, the whole scene came to him like a remembered dream. Moments accomplish these things in reality, and they are by no means worked out in the dull words it is necessary to use here. The inspector's office at Fort Leavenworth; the group of officers who sat there, and among them, yet far off, the man whose voice he seemed now to hear as he heard it then, as he stood in the constrained position of "attention," his bright black eye and regular features marking him more distinctly from his humble position, his concise answers and clear definitions imparting information to his superiors, and leaving the impression upon the casual visitor that one August Stein, private in the 5th U. S. Infantry, though but a detailed clerk, was perhaps the ablest man in the office of the inspector general of the Department of the Missouri. But it was not from these things alone that the listener remembered the man whose voice he thought he heard. It was partly from the peculiar look darted after him like lightning as he left the room, which, seen again under any circumstances, would mark the man. It is the look which distinguishes that class of men, of which there are fortunately few, who for a sufficient stake will face any danger and commit any crime, who disdain all law as not meant for them, who may even fascinate when they will, and who are the Machiavellis of social life.

And this was undoubtedly the voice of Stein. The five years of his enlistment could not have expired. His regiment was stationed four hundred miles away. Discharged for disability, he would hardly come to these ends of the earth for a home, and — the gentlemanly soldier was a deserter. This was why the commandant listened and hesitated, why he doubted if it were not better and more merciful to let the soldier go, and keep the secret. For, as his mind threaded out the story, he remembered all his former impressions of the man, and among them that he was one to whom the ranks would be insufferable — a humiliation nearly always ended at last by the only way possible. As he thought of all this in his listening attitude, he nodded his head in final certainty, and said as to himself, "I thought so — I am not mistaken."

There was a feeling of regret, not entirely acknowledged to himself, that this man's evil genius had brought him so near the only one by whom he could possibly be recognized. Here was a voice betraying its owner at an inconceivable distance from where it had last been heard, and that owner entirely ignorant that his unconscious gift was about to bring upon him his life's greatest misfortune and disgrace. Here, after travel and toil, at this last stopping-place in the wilderness, with freedom and safety in view, were to begin those troubles that would probably end in the Tortugas. As the commandant pondered these things, the voice ceased, and he rose and entered the room as the stranger turned to go out. A glance lighting into a gleam of recognition in the peculiar eyes, and down toward the cañon, through the sage, Stein was gone like a flash, with all the vigor and determination that belong to such men. Immediately in front of the door stood a train of laden asses, whose burdens were baskets, bags, and household utensils. Standing near were three or four Mexicans, and mounted upon one was a woman whose shawl had fallen from her face, and who watched the flight with clasped hands and startled manner. These things the commandant took in at a glance. They were common. In this country, no man travelled alone, unless it were in some desperate emergency in which safety was of secondary importance; and here, he thought, were a travelling party in whose company the deserter had reached the post. His flight, causeless under any ordinary circumstances, had a strange effect upon the girl. Her brown cheeks blanched, and as she watched the fast retreating figure her eyes had in them a kind of desperate look.

Stein's flight was in full view of the half-dozen

soldiers who stood beside the sally-port. They understood the situation, and at the merest sign from the commandant three or four of them were in pursuit. The girl slipped from her donkey, and, with frantic gestures and a torrent of Spanish, attempted to hinder their progress. Almost heedless of her presence, they passed on, and she sat upon the ground with covered face, and rocked herself to and fro. Her companions looked stupidly on, and, apparently regardless of either her or the fugitive, awaited results.

In half an hour the deserter had lost in one of the most desperate ventures of life, and had taken his place in the guard-house among men as desperate and hardened as common crimes and misfortunes ever placed in chains together. But before he entered there, the woman, who seemed in some degree to have regained her composure, found means to come near and speak to him, in Spanish, words which the commandant did not hear and no one near him seemed to understand. As he listened, there seemed to come into his melancholy face, and to gleam from his black eyes, a new hope and purpose. With a glance eloquent of defiance and hate, which took in at once the commandant and all his minions, the girl turned and was gone. The handsome, sinister, defiant face he remembered long afterwards in connection with this strange scene; and though she watched his footsteps from afar, and haunted the purlieus of his command, he was ignorant of her presence, and never but once, and then under very different circumstances, saw her again. Long afterwards, he knew that she had stayed behind; that she had taken up her residence with the Mexican guide, and that there, with all the cunning of her race and more than its faithfulness, she had watched and waited.

The guard-house of a frontier post is one of the necessary means by which the few control the many. It is not a light and airy place. There are no soft luxuries and comforts there, and idleness is unknown within its grimy walls. Had he been a king's son, there was no better place for him; and here the unfortunate deserter took up his abode. The commandant passed him as he worked among the prisoners. In this lonely nook of the desert, the guard-house gang, as they sullenly wandered with clanking chains wherever there was work to do, was always a reminder that even a land that was lacking in every feature common to the world was not without its crimes, and not wanting in its means of punishment. As he came near, the prisoner threw aside his broom, and asked permission to speak.

There was never a soldier who had nothing whereof to complain in his best estate, and most certainly even a deserter can urge good and personally satisfactory reasons for the act. This was what the commandant expected, and he deemed it wise to forestall his prisoner:

"Are you not a deserter?" said he.

"I am, but—"

"Are you not aware that desertion, according to the law under which you voluntarily placed yourself, is not a remedy for wrong and admits of no excuse?"

"Certainly, sir, and I do not wish to make any excuse. I only wish to show *you*, if possible, that there was justification, *for the sake of your good opinion.*"

Now, words like these the commandant had never heard spoken by one man to another under like circumstances. Here was one in the chain-gang, guilty by his own confession of a crime that ought to keep him there, talking of "good opinion." The commandant had not been accustomed to think that an officer had any opinion whatever of a private, in or out of the guard-house; and he went away pondering the curious case he had gotten upon his hands— a man with the jewelry of crime upon him, still claiming respect, and tacitly advancing his claim to be regarded as a gentleman by one who also claimed that distinction.

Ere long, the two or three ladies of the small garrison began to inquire concerning a very good-looking prisoner who had been seen piling wood and carrying slops in their back areas. Contrary to orders in such cases, savory morsels were passed out to him through windows, and dainty meals were enclosed in napkins and sent to him. All this the commandant saw—and did not see. Nay, more; he became convinced that the man who had excited so much pity was daily fed from his own table, much to the envy and dissatisfaction of the other prisoners, and he, the commandant, was so careless that he neither saw nor heard.

By and by it was discovered that the prisoner was possessed of great clerical ability, and he was placed in an upper room so constructed that a window opened from it through the wall to the outside of the post. He was required to make topographical drawings and to copy the letters of the post adjutant; and in order that he might be near his work, he was allowed to sleep in his room. All night a sentinel paced to and fro beneath the window, and immediately under him was the guard-room.

As time passed, little by little his story came out, all of which, when it reached their ears, the tender-hearted ladies of the garrison did religiously believe. Much as his condition had been improved, it was a pity (said they) that this much-wronged and much-enduring man (who was so interesting and so handsome) should still be compelled to wear a ball and chain. Feminine bets were freely offered, ten to one and no takers, that the prisoner would not, and indeed could not, escape. But by this time the commandant had received circulars from headquarters, in which they had been at the pains to print a description of the deserter, with especial instructions for his apprehension. The ladies could feed and pity the unfortunate, but, for a wonder, they did not succeed in ridding him of the odious jewelry. This was particularly set down against the hard-hearted Smythe, who had much to silently endure at their hands, and who had seen with what vigor a pretty miss of twenty could govern a post, and had known whole districts that were, in his private and unexpressed opinion, governed by the commanding officer's wife. But, had they only known it, the ladies of the garrison need not have troubled their heads upon this point. There was another woman equally interested in the case, in comparison with whose efforts theirs were as nothing

Much against his will, the commandant had come to know that the prisoner regarded him as his friend. He was no thick-headed military machine, who takes all things for granted. He did not say it or act it, but it was apparent nevertheless, that he entirely understood the feeling of leniency, sympathy, or whatever it was that had a place in the commandant's mind, close beside his sense of duty and right. So interesting a piece of humanity had the deserter become, with his skill, his good looks, and his influential friends, that the commandant did sincerely wish he had never seen him. But there was at least one act of kindness that he thought he could show the prisoner with perfect consistency: he could counsel him in regard to his approaching trial. One day he offered as much, and the deserter showed him an elaborate defence to be used on that occasion. He had imagined with astonishing acuteness every stage of the prosecution. Without access to any of the books upon military law, he had remembered and used some former study of them with an erudition and faculty of arrangement which caused the amiable commandant to retire with dignified precipitancy from the position of volunteer legal adviser.

By this time Stein had gained a complete ascendancy over the whole guard-house crew. He was their friend, and they his; and, indeed, the denizens of the garrison generally had a very tender side for him. By some means he became possessed of money. The Mexicans living near, men and women, acting as guides and laundresses, passed in and out unquestioned and almost unobserved. They had always done so, and were regarded as harmless and useless people. Sergeants and corporals of the guard thought it so small a matter that one of these women should frequently speak with the prisoner, that the circumstance was never even mentioned. It was hard indeed, they probably argued, that the prettiest and proudest of them all should not be allowed to stand sometimes in the cool night below his window, and chatter to him in a voice so low that even the sentinel could hardly hear, even if he could understand. Neither, surely, was there any harm in there being always somebody flitting around in the moonlight and watching the prisoner's window. She was only foolish, they thought — or probably very much in love, which is the same thing.

Smythe did not positively know, but nevertheless guessed, that his prisoner meant to escape, and might possibly succeed. He had done his whole duty; his orders were strict. One day he was by chance in the little room where Stein worked and slept. Upon the little cracked mantel-piece, in plain view, lay a large carpenter's chisel. The commandant took it up, turned suddenly upon Stein, and asked him how it came there. "I stole it from the shop a month ago, sir," said the undaunted prisoner.

The two men looked at each other, straight in the eye. "Stein," said the officer, "you are my prisoner, and having caught you I do not intend that you shall escape. I laid no trap for you, and personally wish you not the slightest harm. Nevertheless, I wish you to distinctly understand that I mean to keep you. This is an old game, and of course I understand it perfectly. Would you like to go and sleep upon a board again, and take your fare with the fellows below?" and his eye rested a moment upon the prisoner's shackle-rivet.

The prisoner, standing at "attention," turned slightly pale, and his peculiar eye had a look in it that the officer returned with one of equal resolution. "I understand, sir," he said, "it was my fate that brought me here, not you. I could have gone some time since, and did not. I give you my word of honor that I shall not try to escape while you command the post."

It was the first time that Lieutenant Smythe had ever been given a "word of honor" by a private soldier, much less by a confessed deserter. He looked again at his man, laid the chisel—already battered upon the edge—down where he had found it, and walked out of the place.

A month passed, and the expected new officer came to command the post. The prisoner immediately became restless. It was evident to Smythe, now no longer responsible, that the gentleman of the guard-house contemplated a *denouement* that would somewhat astonish the new commandant. Yet he wondered how, in the face of difficulties that would have caused most men to calmly submit to evil fate, he intended to remedy his ills. It happened in this wise:

There came a night of wind and storm rare in that region. The clouds scudded across the sky in quick succession, and the favorable elements of noise and darkness were plentifully contributed. About midnight, Smythe was awakened by the new commandant, and informed with a rueful face that the celebrated prisoner had escaped. It was strange, he said; he had given that man a double share of vigilance ever since he had been at the post.

The orders required the guard-corporal to inspect the prisoner's room every two hours during the night, and in making one of these untimely visits the object of so much unappreciated solicitude was found to have placed himself beyond the reach of annoyance. The ponderous ball and chain lay upon the floor. The pallet where he had lain was fancied to be yet warm. Under the table lay a leaden rivet that fitted the hole in the ankle-ring of the discarded shackles. It was simple enough — he had dropped from the window.

Upon the mantlepiece lay a battered and heavy carpenter's chisel, and with this the prisoner had hammered the head of his shackle-rivet until it had been broken off and removed. He had then inserted the leaden one, made from a musket-ball, and worn it in that manner until opportunity came. He was gone irrevocably. In these barren hills, on such a night, nothing less than the chance that had captured him once could take him again, and before the dawn he would have safely crossed the Mexican boundary. But would he have made the desperate venture on foot, and without a guide? And what of the sentinel who walked beneath the window? The wall was white, and the night was not wholly dark; why had he not been seen or heard? Strangely enough, in cases like this the first thing, the essential difficulty, is always the last thing thought of. When the sentinel was sent for he was found lying beneath the window, limp, silent, dazed, his discarded musket lying beneath his hand. "*Aguardiente*," said the reflective Smythe to himself, as he turned away, and walked off to his quarters and his bed more than ever regretting the unlucky morning he had uttered his wish to the ravens, of all birds; for, quoth he, there are no bars that can confine, no circumstances that can daunt, the combined forces of brains, unscrupulousness, and love. But Smythe did not say much; the following morning he even sat up in his bed and smiled to himself as he thought of the explanatory letter the other fellow would have to write about the escape of the prisoner whose personal description was posted in the adjutant's office, whose safety the department commander had stated he was solicitous of, and who, he was privately glad to know, was gone about his affairs.

It was almost a year afterward, and Lieutenant Smythe seemed to have forgotten the little episode of the guard-house gentleman. He had, in fact, been ordered elsewhere, and was occupied with new duties and surroundings. One of these duties necessitated a journey of four hundred miles, from a post upon the lower Rio Grande, to Santa Fé, to attend the sessions of a general court-martial. It mattered little in the execution of such an order that it was a region of uninhabited distances as rugged as they were long. There are cañons, passes, wild defiles, and endless miles of alkali and sage. There are Apaches as well, and Mexicans who are reputed no better than the copper-colored Ishmaelites who murder and are never seen. No town or tavern ever greets the eye of the tired wayfarer. Camp-fire ashes, in little heaps beside the trail, tell him what he too must do when night comes. No man makes the journey alone, and he and his companions may while the time away as best they may, so they be but watchful. And for the first day there is watchfulness—a vigilance that scrutinizes every movement of the gaunt cacti upon the hillsides and hears every movement made by quail or rabbit in the sage. The second day there is also care, but less of it. The way is long, and the thoughts wander, it may be to New England, but to the homes and fields of long ago wherever they may lie. The third, and all other days, are but periods of weariness and of wishing one were at his journey's end. There are no Indians; there is nothing but earth, and air, and sky, and silence, and that deep monotony that shall never be broken by civilization and the uses of man.

The lieutenant rode alone. Far behind him he could hear the clank of sabres and the jingling of bridles, and was carelessly satisfied with the nearness of his escort. He was busily thinking, and was tired and worn with the eternal vigilance of such a journey; tired of his fare of hard-bread and ham, coffee and dried beef; tired of himself. Sometimes, perhaps, he almost slept. Anon a brawling stream from the mountain snows crossed his trail, and his gray horse stopped to drink. Again the steep rock rose above him a thousand sheer feet, and below him yawned a chasm black with depth. There were glades, too, where the miniature oak, with its bright green leaves and its thickly-clustering acorns, gathered in tangled groves over acres of uncropped grass. Yet it was all the same: it was New Mexico, with her skies forever blue, her sparkling air, and her stony and inhospitable bosom.

The trail widened; there were two paths now instead of one. The lieutenant did not know how long it had been so; and when he came to think of it, had no recollection of how long it had been since he had heard the clank of sabres behind him, or paid any attention to the nearness of his escort. He waited and listened, and all was as silent as chaos. He rode back, and his escort was not behind; forward, and they did not appear. They were gone in the silence, and the officer was alone — and lost.

But these paths were made by men, and must lead somewhere. Smythe was wide awake now, and spurred his horse on, he knew not whither. The guide was with the soldiers. "They are not lost," he mused; "I am." And he rode on, faster and faster, as time passed and no sign of humanity, known or unknown, appeared. The low sun of the afternoon reminded him of the coming of an inhospitable and supperless night, for the sumpter-mule was with the escort also, while he was with the gnomes and uncouth fairies who inhabit these stunted and primeval shades. He had ridden far, how far he did not know. The glens were already cavernous and black in the shadows, while the slopes and hill-tops shone with a yellow glory as of stained glass. He knew that he had climbed higher and higher. Sometimes, as he looked back, he caught a glimpse, through some long cañon, of the vast plateau below, stretching away for a hundred miles. Around him appeared a new earth. There was water everywhere, and the herbage was the grass of another zone, green and bright with rain and sun. Oak and pine stood clustered together in silent parks, with mountains still above, and leagues of rock below.

Smythe stopped and looked about him. Would they ever find him? Could he ever retrace his steps? Did men or did deer make these now innumerable paths? It was with a feeling approaching despair that he sat down upon a bowlder and watched the horse greedily crop the grass. Had he not been lost he would have been entranced by the scene around him. But presently he imagined he heard something — a metallic sound, faint and far and dim; a dream of the tinkling of a bell, or a waterfall. Intently listening, he was sure he heard it again. He rode forward along the glade, and presently found a steep incline and a winding road. Far down lay a nook in which were clustered some little adobe houses. There was a rocky stream brawling among its bowlders, and here and there moving figures that were not Apaches. Standing closely in a huge enclosure there were hundreds of sheep, and from among them came at intervals the muffled tinkling of their drowsy bells. Smythe sat upon his horse and looked down upon the scene. The last red rays of the sun shone aslant through the valley, and tinged with rose-color the gray rocks and earthen roofs. The blue smoke lay like a wide and fleecy mantle above. The astonished officer fancied he could detect the odor of primitive cookery and hear the sound of voices. A huge brindled sheep-dog paused in his journey from house to house, stood for a moment looking up the hill at the gray horse and his rider, barked, and went his ways again. He rode down the steep incline; and as the long mountain valley opened before him, he thought of Eden and the solitary loves of those two to whom it was, like this, all the world.

It was not strange that Lieutenant Smythe's appearance spread consternation through the little hamlet. A woman saw him first, and darted away. A man's swarthy visage appeared around a corner, and again disappeared. The dogs stood afar off and growled. Presently, however, came one with a quick step and unabashed demeanor, and laid his hand upon the horse's rein.

"It would seem, Lieutenant Smythe," he said, "that you and I were fated to meet in strange places. Are *you* lost, or a — *deserter?*"

"I am lost," said Smythe, and he scrutinized the face of Stein, as wondering if it was necessary at last to fight it out upon equal terms.

"At any rate, the meeting is an unexpected pleasure," said the other, and Smythe was requested to come into the little house, while some one led away his horse. He found a fire and a seat, but also discovered that he was left entirely alone. A half hour passed, and a swarthy person brought beans, cheese, and meat, and placing them upon the little deal-table went away without a word. Drowsy and hungry, the officer ate, and afterwards nodded in his chair by the fire. No one came, and deep silence rested upon all the spot, without and within. It was a hospitality that was left him to partake of or to leave; and presently he lay down on the huge pile of sheepskins that was evidently meant for a bed.

It was all oblivion to Smythe, until, awakening, he knew that some one was placing a rude breakfast upon the table. Without, he heard the bleating of sheep and the tinkling of bells. The servant retired, and he found the earthen water-jar with its attendant basin, bathed, and again ate. While the sky behind the eastern mountains was as yet but a red glow, the door was opened, and his horse stood there, with a Mexican, who beckoned him to mount and follow. As he climbed the hill and looked back, the sweet vale lay bathed in sparkling dew, the flocks had disappeared, and the place seemed uninhabited. The Mexican with his donkey plodded on before, and Smythe, wondering, was fain to follow.

Some rough miles were passed, and suddenly Stein was encountered, sitting quietly upon his horse at a place where the trail turned northward. "I know," he said, "where your party are. Follow this man, and you will find them." He paused a moment, and added, "There is a strange story between us, of which it is useless to talk. We shall in all likelihood not meet again. I was never a criminal, and am here in peace after many mistakes and misfortunes,— or follies and crimes, as you may be pleased to think them. Be so kind as to excuse my scant courtesy; it is necessary that I should have this much hereafter to myself. If I chose to keep *you* a prisoner, do you think they would ever find you? No matter; I gave you my promise once, and kept it. Will you return the compliment now?"

"I understand. You and your happy valley shall never be molested by my fault. I give you my word of honor."

"*Adios;*" and as the officer looked back, he saw, disappearing among the low oaks, and for the last time, the character who, in all his reminiscences, bears the title of "The Guard-house Gentleman."

XIII.

WOMAN UNDER DIFFICULTIES.

THERE is a being who is the embodiment of beauty, gracefulness, kindness, and unaccountable caprice. Wise men spend their lives in a futile endeavor to understand her, and die with every conception of her incomplete. She is at once our ideal and our possession. She is with us, but not of us. Living our lives, breathing our air, the co-subject of all our vicissitudes and sorrows, with a thousand others of her own, she has yet a life apart, filled with her own thoughts, her own conclusions, and her own peculiar opinions. She fills daily our sole conception, our full measure of belief, as to what a woman ought to be and is. Beside her, there is no other creature worthy of the love which is her inheritance, or the dignity that comes of universal motherhood. She is human, a woman, and she never yet came to a conclusion that was logical, or formed an opinion she could give a reason for, or possessed the remotest conception of abstract justice. She reigns, the irresponsible queen of the civilized world, with her feet upon our necks; and we are willing she should, the grayest cynic of us all. She gives us all there is in this life to give, and all she has, and yet keeps a world of her own to herself —a world we cannot enter. The gem and glory of creation, the recipient of the profoundest idolatry of which the mind is capable, the nearest and dearest of all, she yet lives indescribably apart, and radiates an essence that is to us like the faintest glimmer of the farthest star. With the passage of centuries she has added to her own loveliness, until she has no comparative in the Rose of Sharon, no peer in the white Lily of the Valley. Were it but known that in the hereafter she would not be changed, and would welcome us there with the smiles and tears that beguile us here, the hopes of mankind would take new directions, and the milennium, when it came, would be but an unimportant event.

And yet no creature is so entirely susceptible to surrounding influences, to the strong teachings of nature, wildness and loneliness, to rough associations and uncouth companions, yet still preserving the distinctive characteristics that belong to sex rather than to race. The women we know and daily see, whom it is a part of our religion to respect and a part of our lives to love, are only typical women — specimens of the grade of beauty and refinement attainable under the highest form of civilization. There are thousands of others, worthy and womanly in their way, who are not as these. Nay, our ideals are scarcely even in the majority.

There are many rough and honest men, whose faces are brown and bearded and whose hands are hard with toil, who have never even seen the graceful creatures whose white shoulders gleam through tulle, whose footsteps patter upon errands of extravagance over every paved street, and whose faces bloom in rows at the theatre. There are unfortunates in whose early recollections are not included the ineffably genteel whisper of the matronly silk, as it passed up the church aisle on Sunday morning in the decorous company of fair broadcloth and a gold-headed cane. To this man, the being who blushes at the mere mention of an indelicacy, whose hair is indeed a "glory," whose palms are pink, whose garments are a wonderful triumph of mind over cloth, whose movements are tempered with gracefulness, and whose very language is the result of culture until worn platitudes are sweet upon her tongue, is one so far off that he would scarcely picture her in his dim imaginings of angels.

But he has his companion, like him, and eminently suited to him. In his home, and to accompany him in his wanderings along the frontier, he needs no other. Neighbor she has none. Of the crowded street, and the jam and jostle of pavements, she knows nothing. Her amusements are lonely, her occupations homely and masculine. All she has, and most that she hopes for, may be included in the dull routine of one room, one hearth, one changeless scene. Life to her is the rising and the setting sun, the changing seasons, the cloud, the wind, the frost, and the falling rain. She knows the tricks of horses, the straying of the herd, and all the economy of the corral. Business to her is the small traffic of the trading-post. Strangers are those who occupy the white-tilted wagons which she sees come and go on the far horizon. Friends are all those who have white faces and Christian names, and enemies those whose faces she seldom sees and who are the wily and inveterate foes of all her race. Of such as she, the denizens of cities know but little; and she deserves a history because of her very isolation.

Wherever the frontiersman has occupied a place in Western annals, his wife has stood in the background. The women of the plains, of Colorado, of Arkansas, and of Texas, are of the same genus with the women of the Wabash and the Missouri, only with differing surroundings. None of them are of the class of the "piney-woods" maiden, whose life, appearance, and general character became known to us through the veracious narratives of Sherman's "bummers." But the men who write of Buffalo-land, who wind off narratives of Western life for trans-continental newspapers and magazines, or who verbally detail to a knot of listeners their Othello-like adventures, have little to say of the daughters of the wilderness. The sun-burned and slip-shod woman who hunts cows in the creek "bottoms" upon a bare-backed mustang, who folds her hands behind her at the cabin door, and in a shrill voice gossips with the passing stranger, and whose careless cookery furnishes forth a bill of fare as changeless as time, does not figure largely in the overdone stories of the romance of the frontier and the adventure of the border.

Why should she? Her precise pattern in these respects still lingers amid encroaching fields in the ague-haunted fens of the Wabash and amid the brown sand of the Missouri bottoms. But there are other and more remarkable characteristics pertaining to the woman of the far West. She is there, not from carelessness and ignorance of any better place, but from necessity. Her surroundings are not those of choice, but of what is nearly allied to misfortune. Indolence and innate untidiness are not the causes of her poor larder and her comfortless home. There is no broad line drawn between her and thrifty and prosperous neighbors. For hundreds of miles there are no more comfortable and prosperous homes than her own; and, with a patience that might have a touch of sublimity were it not so nearly unconscious, she waits for better things. And when these better things come, if they ever should, when population and prosperity encroach too near, then, following the instinct of migration, for God's purposes, as strong in humanity as in the beasts, she and her husband will move again. The grotesque procession of lean and melancholy cows, multitudinous and currish dogs, rough men and barefoot girls, and, lastly, the dilapidated wagon, with its rickety household goods, wends never eastward.

The sod house of western Kansas, the cabin of Texas, and the adobe of Colorado, are not all so fortunate as to have a female mistress. The fact is proclaimed afar off by an essential difference in appearance. There was never yet a lonesome borderer who planted a vine or draped a window or swept the narrow path in front of his door. Men seldom do such things, while the virtues of good housewifery are, in a greater or less degree, the natural qualifications of every woman. In many a wilderness nook, the blooming plant that is cherished beside the door, the drapery of the one small window, the clean-swept hearth, the row of shining tins, and the small evidences of needle-and-thread industry, proclaim that however poor the place may be, if it hold a woman her hand will still find something to do in the way of adornment.

There is nothing strange in the fact that the Indian squaw is always a slave. Yet the savage goes but little further in that direction than his enemy the frontiersman. In all times, races, and circumstances in which crudity and toil preponderate over ease and refinement, woman bears the burden of the misfortune. But the rule of compensation exists everywhere. The sun and the wind are kinder than are late hours and furnace-heated chambers. The slavery of the field is infinitely more conducive to strength and happiness than the slavery of the corset and the high-heeled shoe. Maternity is not a terror and a peril to the woman of the border. Life, with all its hardship and isolation, gives her at least all it has to give. The days may be days of toil, but the noon brings its hunger and health, and the night its deep sleep of rest and peace. That wearying round of ceremony, that daily attendance upon the mirror and weekly investigation of the fashion-plates, that thought of Mrs. Smith's bonnet and Mrs. Brown's children, and the bank-account and the milliner's prices,—all the unseen and untalked of, yet wearisome and monotonous burdens of fashionable life, are here unknown. And the compensation is great. Untrammelled by stays and ceremonies, the border woman has what few of her sex but her entirely possess — health. Not a fictitious and deceptive rosiness of cheek and gracefulness of carriage, not whiteness of hands and willowy slenderness of waist, but rude, awkward, brawny health. The women who, all over the eastern United States, are the chief adornment of beautiful homes, and the wives and daughters of what are called, by way of general designation, Christian gentlemen, who cause mankind daily to forget Eden and Eve and never to think of the fall, and who are the mothers of daughters as brilliant as June roses and who fade like them, and of sons who are men at twenty and old and *blasé* at forty, are not expected to credit all this, or to have the slightest desire for an exchange of circumstances, which to them would be impossible. The facts are only mentioned to show that the pity for those who live thus is often misplaced, and that there is no circumstantial misfortune that has not also its reward.

I know of no woman inhabiting the border wilderness who has not some of the refinement that belongs rather to sex than to race, except the Indian squaw. A woman whose face bears evidence of a relationship with any of the dominant races of the world, has something about her, wherever you find her, that is more or less womanly and attractive. The borderer's wife does not swear, or chew tobacco, or offer the least suggestion of indelicacy in action or word. She is "green," constrained, and often awkward; but her face is not more coarse, or more incapable of that surging rosiness that is the tattling index to a woman's thought, than any other. If I may be allowed to coin a phrase, I would say that the standard of delicacy by which her sensibilities were governed was a different and broader one than that in common use. She associates with men, and rather coarse ones. She is intimately acquainted with them, and interested in all their affairs. She is accustomed to wildness and danger, and learns to be strong of hand and nerve, and cool in sudden emergencies. It may be set down to her credit that, while she will run if she can, she will also fight if she must. Yet there are no circumstances that can ever entirely divest a woman of her essential femininity. I have been amused to note that a woman who was complete mistress of a recalcitrant mustang, and every day brought him under subjection by a by-no-means-dainty application of the end of his lariat, and who ruled with a high hand all the hard-headed and sulky denizens of the corral, would utter the little cry of her sex and ingloriously retreat at the sight of one of the harmless little lizards who infest the prairie paths of the Southwest.

In society, women dress for women; in certain other walks in life, they dress for men; and left alone, they dress for themselves. The story of the first garment, made out of the world's fresh green leaves, tells only a part of the story. Here on the border, the old business of the sex — to look pretty — receives as much attention as it does anywhere. There is not much choice of material, — calico is the article. Valenciennes and Mechlin, and all the cunning variations in name and material which make up the lexicon of the modern dry-goods clerk, even the cant about "chaste" colors and "pretty" styles, are utterly unknown to the belle of the border. As she tilts back in a hide-bottomed chair like a man, it is easy to perceive that feet that are not always coarse are encased in brogans constructed with a special view to the roughness of wayside stones, the penetrating quality of early dew, and the gravity and persuasiveness of kicks administered by them. The neck, sunburned, but not always wanting in due proportion and natural whiteness, is ignorant of collar or confinement. Waist and limb are untrammelled by any of the devices which are supposed to be so necessary to style; and the hair, combed straight and smooth, is twisted into a tight little knot behind, which, as compared with the composite mysteries that within the memory of people still fashionable were carried about beneath the bonnets of our wives, remind one of a small wooden knob. In the frontier toilet there is sometimes a lack of the two essentials of starch and snowy whiteness. Cleanliness there is, to be sure; but it is a cleanliness of material and fact, and fails in any suggestion of daintiness. It is upon the useful and inexpensive calico mentioned that the efforts of feminine taste are mostly expended. There are ruffles, and bias stripes, and flounces, and a hundred pretty and fantastic devices that it is beyond masculine technology to describe. Yet, there are no prescribed fashions for these vagaries in dress. Each woman expends her ingenuity according to her ideas of beauty. The style of a calico gown may seem a small item in describing the characteristics of a class, but the adornment is so universal that it becomes a noticable feature. It is infinitely to her credit, too, being the evidence that barbarism is not the result of hopeless seclusion, and that taste and care will hold a place in the hearts and efforts of such women in their struggle with wildness, until that time shall come in which civilization shall complete her task.

If anything thus far should lead to the impression that comeliness, not to say beauty, is impossible to the women of the border, that impression needs correction. Under the severest tests, the frontier often has a comeliness of its own. It is not the paltry prettiness of gait and manner to which so many of our queens are deeply indebted; not the charm of soft words and cultured address. These, indeed, make us sometimes imagine beauty where there is none, and procure gentle thoughts and husbands where there is little else to recommend. Frontier charms, where they exist at all, make models of stalwart and untrained grace. Health itself is beauty, and that unfashionable kind is common enough. It were well if absolute ugliness everywhere were the result only of age, hardship, and decay, and it is pleasant to think that at least here youth seldom wants its round curves and its crimson glow. There are border-women whose hair falls in troublesome abundance and will not be confined; whose cheeks, if they could know immunity from the hot caresses of the sun and the boisterous kisses of the wind, would show the clearest white and the bonniest bloom. There are limbs that shuffle slip-shod along the trails in search of lost animals, of whose round strength the owner has little thought, and arms that split firewood and bring water from the spring, whose whiteness and mould would fit them rather for the adornment of golden clasps and folds of ancient lace. To see these women is to know that the old-time talk about "unconscious beauty" is a fallacy. The consciousness of beauty, and due appreciation and use of it, is its great aid in the absolute enslavement of mankind. Was there ever the phenomenon of a pretty woman who did not know it? As for men, there are thousands of them who, being fantastically homely, believe themselves to be reproductions of the Apollo Belvidere.

For so long have women been accused of an inborn love of gossip, that mankind, in their haste to accept ill-natured doctrines, are ever ready to concede the truth of the statement that she cannot live without it. I am satisfied that, in some poor way, she can manage to get along without a next door neighbor. It is stranger still that when, by an extraordinary chance, the cabins of two neighbors are in sight of each other, the fact seldom adds anything to the happiness of the two female occupants. Do they often see each other? Do they waste kisses when they meet? Are they inseparable friends? There is not a surplus of any of these things. Two women, here as elsewhere, with no third party to divert attention, are not apt to love each other with fervor. What is better, they do not pretend to. But neighborship bears a broad meaning in these regions. The chronicle of Jones's wife's affairs is reasonably well kept by Thompson's wife, who lives ten or twenty miles away. And this without any of the facilities for what is usually termed gossip. The wayfarer who has lost a pony, or who wanders in search of straying cattle, is the disseminator of most valuable items of neighborhood news. As he sits on his horse in front of the door, with his knee on the pommel and his chin in his palm, he relates how he has "heerd" so and so. And in return the dame delightedly tells of her own affairs, — the "old man's" luck, the measles, the "new folks," etc., etc., and always ends with "Tell Mis' Jones to come over." These things, and more, the result of his own acute observations, the simple cow-hunter tells to "Mis' Jones." But that lady does not usually "come over." That is a mere form, gone through with for politeness' sake. Sometimes she may come, but not for the visit's sake. Here, as elsewhere, there are mysterious gatherings in the middle of the night, and the cry of infancy is heard in the morning. If it were not for their babies, these curious "neighbors" would probably never have any other acquaintance than that which comes about by proxy.

The life of the woman of the frontier, while in its nature transient, seems at the same time to be that to which she was born. She and her male companion never think of that fact, and are themselves unconscious of the wandering instinct that brought them hither, and that is the characteristic of the class to which they belong. If they were placed in an Eden, they would never wait to be thrust out by an angel with a flaming sword, and would be anxious to go of themselves, satisfied of the existence of a better country. But the spot they leave never again returns to native wildness; while there they have accomplished a certain purpose as the forerunners and vedettes of civilization. Their home was the wilderness, and they came next after the savage as occupants. Slowly they creep up the valley of the Arkansas, already growing too tame for them with its two hundred thousand lately-gathered people. The twinkle of their camp-fires sparkles upon the verge of the desert, wherever in the solitude men may abide or human hope can find a foothold. Past the utmost of the western forts, over a road that stretches like a path through hundreds of miles of barren silence, they straggle toward Arizona and far-off realms of which, as yet, they neither know nor wish to know anything. Everywhere, in scattered nooks and in sheltered corners, are located the rude homes where they have stranded, and where they await a return of the migratory determination. Each home is the centre of those surroundings and appliances which are the absolute necessities of existence. But they make no better homes. Without knowing it, they did not come to stay; and as they repeat the old story of a better country beyond, they do not know that, with a different meaning and in another sense, they tell not only their own, but the story of wandering, restless, longing humanity everywhere.

Thus does woman take her part in a most unexpected place in the struggle of life. It is not an unimportant one. She brings into the world a constant levy of recruits, to be trained in infancy to wandering, if naught else. It is not an extravagant statement to say that without her the final accomplishment of the end for which isolation, wildness, and poverty are endured, could not be attained. In that which we, with a degree of egoism, call life, she occupies but a poor place. Her character, her ideas of things, and the incidents of her daily life, are so far from the absorbing interests which occupy the citizens of the great world of churches, schools, banks, gas-light, and society, that they are scarcely the subjects even of curiosity. But she is still a woman, and an example of the capacities of her sex in the exercise of that virtue which, more than any other, is characteristic of woman—the virtue of silent endurance. If her hard life on the far border lacks idyllic interest, and needs, to cover its hard outlines, the purple garment of romance and poetry, it is a compensating reflection that with its unconscious purpose it still goes on, and that, with the carelessness of all her kind, she reciprocates the indifference of the world.

XIV.

THE PRIEST OF EL PASO.

THE town of El Paso del Norte is a bright gem upon a green ribbon of fertility between frowning mountains. The green velvet ribbon is the valley of the Rio Grande, and El Paso is the jewel that lies upon it. Such, at least, is its description as set down in the chronicles of the fathers.

This important point in the Mexican empire was no longer young when Cincinnati was a hamlet in the wilderness and St. Louis was a French trading-post; Indiana a beech-grown wilderness, and Illinois a wide and inhospitable jungle of tall grass. Then the Conestoga wagons carried the trade of the young city of William Penn to the valley of the Ohio, and the waiting heart of a continent lay unheard of and uncared for, biding its time amid dense forests, and mighty rivers that crawled for thousands of leagues through an endless world of silence. The three generations that had already lived and died in El Paso had not cared for these things, or even heard of them. The priest, in his gown and hat, went his ways in the streets, and the laden donkeys stood in the market-place. The immediate descendants of a people who had brought with them across the sea at least their primitiveness and content, passed their days then, as now, forgetting and forgot by all the world. Then, as now, the days were days of sunshine and the nights were nights of stars. The rich grape-clusters ripened in the yellow rays, and the wine-vats gave forth their odors through court-yard doors, as the blood-red juice mellowed and grew rich within, and crept through chinks and grain-holes, and lay in odorous pools upon the floor. And the church was there as now; the same in its barbaric attempt at magnificence, only the huge cedar beams of the roof were not then covered with a gray mould, and the central arch had not sunk and cracked until its keystone hung perilously in its niche. The brown sandstone slabs in the yard tell us all that, as we read, in the ancient and half-effaced characters, of the Dons and Señoras who, in the Year of Grace 1700, and thereafter, went to their rest in the peace of God.

But least of all things did these good people suspect what their grandchildren should live to see. The Jesuit himself, best judge of the course of empire and sage prophet of political changes as he is, did not imagine that one day the boundaries of an infant republic would widen until, within sight of his church and within hearing of his chanting, and only upon the opposite shore of the river his brethren had discovered, should arise a Yankee town, named after a great mechanic who was also a lawgiver and sage, and not less a heretic and an unbeliever; and that yet a little further, and still within sight, should float in his own sunshine that silken, sheeny, starry thing, the emblem of free men and a free faith. Still less did he imagine that most fateful of all the invasions of his faith and of Mexico — the iron track that narrows and glistens afar to the northward, the rushing engine that scorns his narrow ford, and the unearthly howl that echoes through the cañons that were sacred to primeval silence.

It was seventy years ago. But the old man with whom the two strangers talked did not tell them of the changes between seventy years ago and now. Those seven fateful decades were not on his thoughts, and not in the story he told. But his long white beard and thin and scattered locks and shrunken limbs suggested it; and as he seated himself in the leathern-bottomed chair, its cedar framework polished and black with age and use, they were the words he used as a beginning: "Seventy years ago, Caballeros, — seventy years."

It was a curious chamber in which they sat. The walls were high and mouldy, and the cobwebbed ceiling was far up in shadow. The one tall window had lost all its glass except a few of the lower panes, and the cotton cloth that supplied its place fluttered as the autumn night-wind wandered through. By this dilapidated window they had first seen the interior; for, wandering through the rambling streets at midnight, one is curiously attracted by a light which has no companion in all the silent town, and which burns dimly in the narrow window of a crumbling church. Standing upon the grass-grown walk beside the wall, they had seen within a tall figure, upon whose shoulders lay the thin white hair, and who, prone upon the earthen floor, stretched his attenuated arms toward the Mother of Sorrows in supplication that was rigid, silent, pitiful. He was alone. The lamp smoked in its bracket upon the wall, and the small flame in the little fire-place served but to throw grotesque shadows through the narrow space. The star-lit darkness enfolded the old town in a shadowy cloak. The door-lights were put out, the last guitar was silent, and the far peaks seemed to guard in the darkness a scene strange enough to unaccustomed eyes at noonday, and sombre, silent, and mysterious at midnight beneath the stars.

They were strangers; it was their business to learn. Who could he be that prayed so long and silently? Presently he rose up and passed out into the body of the church, and a moment afterward the bell upon the gable rang a few sonorous strokes. At the sound in the stillness some sleeper may have turned in his bed and uttered his shortest prayer, and turned again to sleep. To go around and walk up the aisle of graves, and stand in the open door, was something which, prompted by the curiosity of youth, was soon done. The old man stood there, the bell-rope still in his hand, cautiously listening. They could not tell if there was surprise in his eyes as they entered, but it was a courteous tone in which he bade them wait where they stood. They heard his slow footsteps as he went back through the darkness. Presently he came again, the lamp held above his head, peering through the gloom

"Would you pray, señors?" said he, in the piping treble of age. They told him they came not to pray, but to talk. He hesitated a moment between doubt and courtesy, and then, bidding them follow, led the way over the hard earthen floor, past the altar-rail, at which he bent his decrepit knees, by images whose faces had a ghostly look in the dim lamplight, and into the room which seemed his chamber, and where they had seen him as he prayed.

He turned to them with a gesture that had in it a mixture of courtesy and irony, waved his hand around the room as if to say, "Here it is,—look," and seated himself in the one old chair and gazed into the dying fire. The place had a faint mouldy smell, and that suggestion of falling gradually into extreme age that is difficult to describe. The earthen floor was worn until it was as hard and smooth as stone. Upon one side were presses whose doors had parted from hinge and hasp, and whose panels dropped away piecemeal, and within them were to be dimly seen glimpses of yellow linen, and scarlet vestments, and faded and tarnished lace. There was surely nothing there that was worth a question; and as the old sacristan — for such seemed to be his office — still sat with his back toward them, looking at the glowing coals, they asked him none.

But in the midst of mouldiness and decay one small object attracted attention, from its seeming freshness. Against the wall, and immediately beneath a crucifix, was a frame of dark wood, some four feet long and about twelve inches wide. It shone with frequent polishing, and within it hung a curtain of green cloth. It might have passed unnoticed save for a suggestion of concealment and that these two minds were more intent upon discovery than a strict regard for politeness. They were there to see, and should they not know what lurked behind that small green curtain? It mattered little, perhaps, but as one of them touched its corner with his finger the aged man rose up with a polite deprecating gesture, at which they stood ashamed. He took the lamp from its place and trimmed it afresh. Contrary to all expectation there was interest and pleasure in his eyes as he approached the panel with the lamp in his hand, and tenderly raised the curtain. "Look," said he; "the hand that made it was a cunning one. He who painted those lines was a great artist—one of the greatest of his times; but none will ever know it. In the old land across the sea are great paintings, and the names of the makers of them are immortal. Yet he whose hand made this was as great as they. He and they might have worked together and you might know who I mean—which is not possible. You do not know; you will never know. There were few who did, and they are dead. There is nothing left but this—only this poor thing. Ah, he was a poet, an artist, rich, and a grandee. He was as handsome as a god and as learned as a sage. And this is left, señors; there is nothing else."

Whatever opinion either of them had formed of the old man, they were undoubtedly mistaken in it. His eyes had lighted with a new fire as he spoke. He was not the peasant and churl they thought him, and no one need have been mistaken who now saw the animated look in his keen old eyes, his clearly-cut and once handsome features, and the lithe figure that even in age seemed rather of the camp and the sword than of the bell and gown.

When one in the guise of a peasant descants upon art, the piece named ought certainly to attract a moment's attention. The carefully-covered specimen within the frame was a piece of vellum, dried and horny with age, on which was traced in colors which had lost none of their brilliancy a single Latin sentence. The head-letters had about them all the intricate and graceful beauty of the old art of illumination, and in elaborateness of design, brilliancy of coloring, and gracefulness of detail, the work was that of no unaccustomed or unskilful hand.

But as the strangers scanned the picture — for picture it might really be called, — the words themselves seemed remarkable. There was a meaning and purpose in them, and in the place they occupied. The legend ran thus:

"*ET NE ME INDUCES IN*
TENTATIONEM,
SED LIBERA ME A MALO."

"Lead *me* not into temptation, but deliver me from evil." It was only a sentence from that immortal form of prayer which has been sent upward by millions of hearts for these eighteen hundred years, the essence and meaning of all supplication. "Lead me not into temptation"; why was it written here, where the world seemed shut out, even without a cell and a priest's vows?

"If these words have a history, father, and the man you speak of made them, will you not tell us the story?" asked one of them.

There are two conditions in which age delights: one is silence, the other, extreme garrulity. The aged man, be he soldier, statesman, or priest, lives mainly in the past. When he is silent he thinks, not of what he shall do and accomplish and be, as he did when he was young, but of what he was and what he remembers. When he talks he tells of those things, often tediously in detail; and either the condition of silence or of discourse is his chief delight. And a smile crept into this wakeful old man's features again, as he heard the request. "Why not, my sons?" he said; and as he changed his address from "Caballeros" to "sons," he expressed the feeling of gratification that warmed his old heart. The strangers could guess by the commonest rules of that lesson of life as yet so ill-learned by them, that the sacristan's heart clung to this spot and its story with a concentrated affection. A memory of something greater or grander or better, something congenial to him through all the dreams and thoughts of a lonely life, kept him near the spot.

"Why not, my sons, since there is ever something more in the commonest life than appears upon the surface? My race is one that loves glory and art and beauty, but we love also God and Holy Church. You are from the north, and the blood in your veins runs cold. Your reformers—the heretics who have led so many astray, and have traduced and denied the Church which alone can save — were strong men here," and he touched his forehead, "but they were cold here," placing his hand upon his heart. "You can understand your Luther, but you cannot understand the gallant Knight of Pampeluna, brilliant in armor and flushed with glory, who founded the Society of Jesus. The sword and the cross — your cold race can never understand that." He had arisen as he spoke, and stretched forth his thin right arm as though he measured an antagonist's rapier.

"But the story, father," said one of the listeners; "you have forgotten the story."

The sacristan sank again into his chair, and the sadness came again into his face. "The legend upon the wall reminds me of that," he said. "It was placed there seventy years ago. It is a long time — a very long time. The world has changed since then;" he added, "else you would not be here. But I will speak, and afterwards you shall judge.

"Don Juan Salano was of a house that claimed a drop of the bluest blood of Spain. Its members stood ever near to greatness of lineage and greatness in deed. But Don Juan was the princeliest of them all, men said, because God made him so. Shall I describe him to you, my sons? Then I will say again that you cannot understand him: he was not of your kind. He had an oval face, eyes that shone in anger or kindness, and the form and bearing that a soldier and a noble should have. How beautiful his eyes were, and how tender and strong his voice! He was the manliest man in Spain.

Men admired and respected him, and women loved him, many a one. He was learned in all the learning of his time — though it was nothing then, — and last, he was a soldier. He could not have been otherwise. It is in his race, as I told you, to love the cross and the sword. I will not tell you of how he fought in the wars of his country. I do not love to talk of the old days of glory and strength. They sadden me. But I tell you that had my country remained as she once was, had her sons begotten their like again, our country had ere this been the mistress of the world, and our holy church the church universal. Ah, she had fallen before you were born; she was falling when Don Juan Salano died; but I know what she was. God's will be done.

"But Don Juan loved not only glory; he loved also the church; and when he was as young as either of you, my sons, he became a priest. Do you smile? Ah, *carramba!* your cold race knows nothing of either glory or religion. I need not tell you how he became a priest; only that it was duty, love, conscience. Do you know what I mean by the last? No, you cannot even understand that. Well, it was that Don Juan had sinned all the sins of noble youth, and in time he would make atonement, and purge them away and forget them.

"He asked of the council a mission, and they sent him here, — even here. It pleased him, for he knew not that Spain's daughters may be beautiful even in their descendants, and frail everywhere. They are all dead now who remember aught of the priest who came to the parish of El Paso del Norte from across the sea. But I, who am old, have heard them tell of his noble face and his graceful bearing, which even a priest's garments might not conceal, and of those of his people who wished he were still a soldier.

"You think he made a mistake. It is like your people thus to weigh and calculate. He did not. Many of our religion have borne the pyx and chalice who could strongly wield the sword. Many times has the rosary hung in the rapier's place.

"I told you in the beginning he was a great artist. After he came to this spot he was doubtless lonely, and his life much changed from what it had ever been. So he beguiled the time with colors. In this very room he did it, and his easel sat there by the window, and where I sit was his seat. At one time he painted the Mass in the cathedral at Barcelona. Then he made a head of the dead Christ, and many others. They hung here and in the church, and there were many of them, for he labored rapidly and diligently. It was his life, his occupation. He did nothing but paint and pray. How beautiful they were, and how his soul was absorbed in them!

"The last he ever made was a Madonna; not a sad and tearful mother of Christ, but one whose features had in them a radiance, not of faith and glory, but of human beauty. Ah, and the face was one that those who sleep yonder have told me they knew, and all El Paso knew. It was the gem of all he did, and a curtain hid it in its place, and those only saw it who chanced to catch a glimpse.

"By and by his soul became absorbed in art, and he almost forgot he was a priest. He knew he was forgetting, they say; but while he did hard penance, he still painted. He loved it; he was an artist, my sons; he could not help it.

"Once upon a time there came a dignitary of our empire to El Paso; one who travelled in state, great in power and influence. There accompanied him others only less than he. He came to this church, and scarce waiting to pray, passed on and entered this room. Perhaps he had heard of the priest and his work. He stopped and gazed. He called his companions also, and bade them look. He was astonished and surprised. 'Where is he who made these?' he said; 'bring him to me, for I have something to tell him to his own great good.' And they that were there said, 'It is only the padre Salano who did it.' 'What?' said he, 'the priest? I care not; he has that in him that should not rust here.' Then the priest came, and the Señor saw his presence and face. 'Father,' said he, 'if thou wilt come with me thou shalt have that which shall better please thee, for surely thou art mistaken in thy calling. Wilt sell these? Name thy sum.'

"Then Salano hung his head, and turned pale, and when at last he would not sell, the Señor departed, thinking strangely of the man, and wondering that priests were oft such geniuses and such fools; 'but,' said he, 'thou shalt hear from me again ere long.'

"On that same night the priest locked his door — that same door, my sons, — and was for a long time alone. What he did God knows — His will be done. But it is certainly told how a great smoke arose from the chimney-top, and in the morning he lay there so prone in prayer, so wrapped in deep devotion, that none dared disturb him. This that I tell you is indeed true, that pictures, canvas, colors and easel were never seen again. The fire consumed them or the flood drowned them, and the priest came forth sad and very silent, and went his ways and did his offices with a new humility. In a day following the few who ever entered here saw the panel in the wall. It was the last; he touched brush or canvas no more.

"But, my sons, a man may pray full oft, 'Lead me not into temptation,' — he may write it in colors never so beautiful beneath his crucifix, and may cast away in bitter self-sacrifice all that may hinder him aught, — and there may still be left one whose beauty he can neither make nor mar, and thoughts of whom he may not burn or put away. I have told you that this priest was lordly, learned, and beautiful. I said he was also a painter and a soldier. I may end by saying that he was also a man. He might burn his priceless Madonna; but the beautiful face that had crept into it he could not so easily put away. It was there — upon the street and in the open door. Do you know women, my sons? If you do you are older than you look, and have learned most of what there is to know. This priest had defeated but the first and least temptation. He was accustomed to admiring eyes, for there are men from whom admiration is scarce concealed. The demi-gods are few, but there were those who believed this man to be one. There is no tale-bearer who delivers his message so easily as a woman's eyes and a woman's rosy cheek. The Doña Anita did not admire the glorious priest, she did not love him, — she adored him. She was not a lunatic in any greater sense than many have been since Adam. But the mass had come to be a ceremonial, not for her soul, but for her heart; not for God, but for the priest who officiated. Think you I am telling a strange thing? Doubtless; for your race are cold, as I have told you. Yet she did not bring her love and lay it at his feet. Women are born with a better knowledge of men than that. But there was no land to which she would not have followed him afar off, no fortune she would not have shared with him. Yet without hope, since he was a priest.

"But I said he was a man, and he knew all this. Nay, it was not that which troubled him; it was the other fact that he carried in his heart the image of the Doña Anita. The Madonna's face was also her face, and perchance she had heard as much. He met her in the street, and a thrill passed through him if her gown but touched his garments. He saw her face as she knelt at the altar-rail, and — God pardon him! — he could have thrown away the Host and fled from all his vows and duties. You know that this priest was a heroic man, and was a priest for conscience sake, and for that cause had abandoned that only other thing that is dearer than love

—fame. Those who knew have told me that from vesper-bells to matins he lay all the night upon this floor and prayed to be delivered. He was wan and worn with penance and fasting, and yet, perchance, between his eyes and the Blessed Mother, as he prayed, came that other human face clothed with a nearer love.

"You think, as you listen, that there can be but little more of a story like this. But I am old. It pleases me to tell all, and you will listen. It came about, by and by, that the priest and the Doña Anita understood each other, whether they would understand or no. While she disguised less and less as she drew nearer and nearer to him across the great impossibility, so grew more and more upon him the irksomeness of his holy office. But they dared not speak, scarce even look, the one to the other. There have been many battles fought in men's souls, harder and more costly than the battles of kings. This man was no coward, and had conquered once. But he was beleagured now indeed, for he loved his enemy.

"It is told that one night in this room the priest thought he was alone. He walked back and forth, not quiet and calm, but anxious and almost despairing. As he passed by, his shadow fell again and again upon the window, and there was one near who saw it each time. There are times when men, and priests, lose faith in penance and prayer. This may have been to him one of those times. Presently she who watched the window knew that he stopped opposite it and stood still. Then there was the sound of a hurried movement, the faint clink of metal, and finally the outer door was opened, and there stood at the threshold a figure in plumed helmet, the baldric upon his breast and the bright scabbard upon his thigh. The lamplight shone upon him as he looked about him, not guessing that any saw him. Ah, my sons, it was not altogether boyish. In thinking and longing, doubting and loving, can we wonder that it came upon him to once more know in secret the feel of the sword — the sensation of a far-gone life? The best of us do much that we would not wish the world to smile at, and a soldier may not be blamed if he hides among a poor priest's effects the plume that has waved in the smoke of battle, and the sword he has drawn in the defence of his country.

"If we were women, we might know how she fell, who watched him then. It would seem that she forgot the reality and saw only the vision. She came toward him, and as she drew near to where he stood, he saw her. He did not flee. I have said he was but a man. She came very near, — nay, seated herself at his feet. 'Tis an old story. As she took his passive hand, perhaps he could look down into the beautiful eyes. Women are not slaves, neither are their lovers; but sometimes they dispute who shall be the humblest. The town was asleep as it is to-night. The priest forgot himself in the soldier and the man, and stooped and kissed, not her hand — the first woman's hand that had touched his for years, — but her very lips.

"Men are men everywhere, and the priest remained a priest until the Sabbath morning. High mass came again. I go not so far as to tell what may be in men's hearts. Even if his offices at the altar of Holy Church were heartless, many men's have been so ere now. We cannot tell. But the Doña Anita came and knelt at the altar-rail. The priest gave her that which is the body of Christ. No wonder, as he saw her face, the flood that is without volume or sound, and which none see, overwhelmed him. He dropped the chalice from his hands, tore the robe from his shoulders, and, coming out from his place, passed through the startled people, out at the open door, and hastened away from his office, from the bosom of Holy Church, from honor, conscience and hope forever. The legend was written in vain, and stands in its place only to remind us all, my sons, that love will conquer where fame, glory and wealth may be beaten in the contest."

The old man arose and took the lamp again from the bracket, and bowed toward the strangers. When, past the altar and images, and through the shadows, they again reached the open door, the weird hour of early dawn was upon the world. He stood in the doorway, and the light wind played with his thin locks, and the lamplight glanced across his sharply-outlined features, as he bade them farewell. The man was as remarkable as his story; and one of his guests turned before he departed, for another word.

"Father," said he, "we are grateful to you for your courtesy, and express our thanks; but will you not tell us who you are?"

"Others could tell you that, my son, even better than I can. But you are strangers. My name is mine only by inheritance, and not by baptism. Men call me Garcia, for so the Church has named me; but my father was a soldier and a nobleman, and I disclaim him not. I am the son of Señor Don Juan Salano, for whose soul's repose I nightly pray, and my mother sleeps in the last place but one, on the right hand as you go out. God go with you. *Adios.*" And the old sacristan turned and went back among the memories and shadows, to recall, perchance, the beautiful face of that Doña Anita who was his mother, long since mouldering in that "last place but one as you go out," and upon the fallen priest who was his father.

XV.

A FIGHT BETWEEN BUFFALOES.

HE was a scarred and shaggy veteran, and his general appearance indicated that he had been making a good fight of it for a week or more. Yet he seemed to be unwilling to accept the fact, beginning to be very obtrusive, that the day of his dominion was over. Like many a human imitator, he was uncertain upon the delicate point of his personal status, and lingered sulkily upon the outskirts of society. I dare say that in the maintenance of his dignity he had thus come back to the herd, and scowled at his descendants, and pawed, and groaned, and made himself generally disagreeable, innumerable times. For the long hair upon his neck was tangled and pulled until tufts of it were loose and unkempt. The outer fibres of his short black horns hung in filaments and splinters. His wicked little eyes had a reddish look, and his venerable beard was limp and froth-wet beneath his chin. Nor were these the only indications of his unhappy condition. Sundry long, oblique hairless lines appeared upon his flanks, and he put his left fore foot down tenderly, very likely remembering at the same time a square jounce he had lately got in the shoulder from some strong-necked youngster who had taken it upon himself to castigate his father.

He stood meditating upon the outskirts of the herd now, and pretended to be eating grass, and it was as nice herbage as a bull whose teeth were likely none of the best could desire — the first tender growth of the early spring. But he did not seem to enjoy it, and ate as one eats whose mind is preoccupied. At intervals of a minute or so he would look around over his shoulder quickly, and groan, and stand as if thinking, and then pretend to eat again. To this distressful pantomime, not one of ten thousand other shaggy grazers paid the least attention. They were busy. I could hear them cropping the grass as I lay there, with a continual rasping sound. It was only too evident that, of all those cows to whom he had been attentive for so long, who had so often been combed into curliness on the happy mornings of the long ago by his tongue, and whom he had led and herded, and fought for, — of all the little, stupid, hump-backed calves, so far as he knew, his own offspring, — there was not one who did not wish him disposed of according to buffalo destiny, or who cared how soon his monumental skull should be left standing on its base upon the bleak hill-top, with scarce so much as a thigh-bone or a faded tuft of brown hair by way of obituary.

But this old one was still a buffalo and a bull, and he kept creeping nearer and nearer to the herd. It may have been only yesterday that he had come back defiant and in a rage, shaking his head, and breathing out threatenings and slaughter, declaring unmistakably that there had not been a fair fight, and that if the company desired to see a handsome and scientific combat, some youngster had better come out and indulge himself with a ride upon his venerable ancestor's horns. I cannot say positively that all this unseemly bragging was done by the old one, but it is likely that it was, and much more, and that under the sting of repeated defeats he had made himself so odious to his rivals that he was now glad to nurse defeat and a sore shoulder upon the outskirts of the herd, but still near, and waiting for his present unpopularity to blow over.

I might have killed him by this time, and ended his troubled career; for he was lawful game and a fair shot, and that was what I had come for. But I grew interested in his precarious fortunes, a serene spectator behind a bank and a convenient bunch of sage. He reminded me of something I had dimly seen in my observations of my own species,—he was so valorous, and yet so prudent. But presently a calf came slowly, and in an investigatory way, toward him. A very immature and foolish animal he looked, with his little black nose wet and wrinkled, his little brown flanks distended with fulness, and the white milk-froth depending in long threads from his lips. Boggle-eyed inexperience doubtless moved him as he came slowly near his father, and the two had just touched noses amicably, when his mother also took it into her head to come. Then came another cow, and another, and presently quite a little company of females had gathered there, and the battered old warrior began to look about him very complacently. This was what brought about a very unfortunate difficulty, and made an unpleasant forenoon of it for the old one. I wonder he did not think of the result. He might have known that he was supposed to have had his good time, and had arrived at an age when the young bloods of the herd would not longer look complacently upon his hoary gallantries.

A fellow almost as big as the old one must have seen this social gathering from some distance, and threw out certain intimations of his approach. Little plumes of dust, very skilfully cast, rose gracefully in the air above the crowd, and there were certain ominous snortings and lugubrious groans. The old one stopped chewing, with a green mouthful between his teeth, and listened. The cows looked about them complacently, with an air that seemed to say that, while the disturbance was an unseemly one, it was none of theirs, and crowded off to one side. Very soon the antagonists were facing each other. The old boy straightened out his wisp of a tail to a line with his back, gathered his four black hoofs together, arched his spine, and placing his nose close to the sod, stood shaking his huge front as though he wished finally to satisfy himself as to its freedom from all entanglements that might hinder him from tossing this ambitious youngster over his head, and breaking him in twain.

I have often wondered at the quality of that unreasoning valor characteristic of the higher animals, compared to which the highest human courage is but ordinary prudence. These two did not stop to think. One was old and lame, and knew he was; and the other would have engaged any antagonist whatever whom he had never seen before. Any two droop-horned farmer's bulls will get together and fight it out to the death of one or both, and merely for the love of it. It is not for fame, or glory, or even for jealousy or the gratification of revenge. Midnight, and any lonesome hill-side, are good enough. There is no parleying, no boasting. Have at you, Sir Hereford! — *Whack!* and when those two curly frontlets come together, it is worth one's while to be there to see.

Taurus, in all his kinds and varieties, is the lordliest of beasts. Where are such gladiatorial thews as lie along that neck? where such gnarled and supple might as resides in those creased and corrugated thighs? When such a one has grown tired of his little field and his limited acquaintance, how easily he walks out and away from them, and goes yahooing and wow-wow-ing up and down the lanes of the neighborhood! He did not escape; he does not care who sees or hears him, and throughout his wanderings he marches with inimitable and deliberate stateliness. And yet the career that should spread consternation through a parish is usually brought to a close by one barefooted small boy, who drives the colossal monster back to his field and his harem, and can do it with only a bit of a stick to scare him with, and with a torn hat full of blackberries under his arm.

The other buffalo came slowly, and twisting his tail from side to side in circles that were very deliberate and grand for so small an organ. I shall never understand why, in the economy of nature, this inadequate appendage was ever hung behind so huge an animal as a buffalo bull, though upon occasions like the present he undoubtedly makes the most of it. He took pains to cause it to be distinctly understood that every hair he wore was angry. His eyes rolled in continually-increasing redness. His black, sharp horns were encrusted with earth gathered while he had been tearing the sod to pieces in the ecstasy of valor. His nostrils were distended, and he halted in his slow advance to toss the broken turf high over his shoulders with his preliminary pawing. He was a tactician of no mean abilities after his kind. He made pretences of flank movements, and turned his shaggy shoulders, first one and then the other, toward his antagonist, as asking him if he dared to come and smite him in the ribs. But the other was equally learned in the arts of the field, and stood shaking his huge head, as who should say, "Come hither and be annihilated."

But this by-play of battle could not last long. They by no means intended to take it out in vaporing. I, who saw it, found the desire to see it all momentarily grow upon me. It was not by any means that I had always, upon the occasion of a fight, felt an uncontrollable desire to stay. But this fight was not mine, and I was not even in sight. But, recalling sunny afternoons in crowded amphitheatres, where many a *picador* was overthrown, and many a curved horn was thrust remorselessly into the bowels of blindfolded horses, and five tawny bulls died like Cæsar to please a roaring crowd, I was never more interested than now. I wondered why I was thus alone — why there was no one to watch with me this Titanic battle. And there was. Peering over the edge, like myself, sat a little gray thief of a coyote, and beyond him another and another. I could hear him faintly whine, and could see him wipe his attenuated chops with his red tongue, and leer and long.

The challenger advanced to within a few feet of his antagonist, getting angrier and angrier as he came. Suddenly there was a dull crash, which had in it something Homeric. A rattling onset of that kind leaves one in no doubt as to why the horns of buffaloes have a dilapidated and splintered appearance at the apices. Then there was a long and steady push, in which every tendon of the huge bodies seemed strained to the utmost tension. After repeated vigorous thrusting, accompanied by tremendous snortings, there was a strategic easing off, and then a sudden collision which pressed the two heads to the earth in an even balance of strength. Neither beast dared relax a muscle or retreat an inch, for fear of that fatal charge upon the flank, or that perilous twist of the neck which means defeat.

And now the cows returned, and looked complacently on, and the very calves began to shake their stupid-looking heads in the first vague instinct of combativeness inspired by the battle of the bulls. The young lordlings of the herd distended their nostrils, elevated their tails, and yet forbore any active interference. It was a duel *a l'outrance*. A moment's relaxation of the tremendous strain only resulted in the shaggy heads coming together again with a dull thump, and a renewal of the stubborn pushing that might have moved a freight-train. It became a matter of lungs and endurance; and the froth began to drop in long, tenacious strings from their lips, and their eyes to glare dimly through what seemed clots of blood. I could hear their labored breathing even where I lay, and see the strained tendons stand out across the thighs and along the thick necks.

But this dead-set of strength could not last. Every moment of time was telling upon the failing strength and shorter wind of the valorous old crusader, who still fought for the loves of his youth. His lame foot slipped, and a knowledge of this slight disaster seemed to reach his antagonist more quickly than a flash of light. No skilful fighter ever urged his advantage more suddenly. There was a huge lunge, a sound as of horns slipping upon each other, a spring forward, and the horn of the younger bull had made a raking upward stroke through the flank of his antagonist. The fight now became more one-sided, and more bloody. Again and again the old one tried to make his old ward of head to head, and as often his more active antagonist caught him behind the shoulder. With the red agony of defeat in his eye, and the blood flowing from the long wounds in his flanks, he still refused to be conquered. With failing strength, and limbs which refused any longer to serve him, he finally stood at bay, with open mouth and hanging tongue, pitifully panting, unable to fight and disdaining to retreat. He was pushed, and yielded sullenly. He made no attempt to shield his flank, and patiently endured all that came. The original plan of non-interference was now abandoned, and the young lords of the herd began to gather round him, and snort, and shake their heads, and give him an occasional maledictory dig in the ribs, by way of expressing their contempt for him. The cows came and sniffed at him, and indulged themselves in spiteful feminine butts, and walked away. Their manner seemed meant to imply that they had always regarded him as a disagreeable old muff, and that they were glad of an opportunity to express their heartfelt sentiments in regard to him.

Through all this the old bull stood sullen, — whipped, but still obstinate. Gradually the herd left him to himself, and the vast crowd of spectators and intermeddlers wandered slowly away. It was no more to them than some other man's misfortune is to the reader or to myself. He did not even look around. He was forced at last to accept his sentence of banishment, and go and live as long as he could alone, or in the odious company of other bulls like unto himself, and fight his last fight with the coyotes, and die.

But that calf came out to see him again. I say *that* calf, because it seemed to me to be the same who had brought on this last unpleasantness, — though, for that matter, they are all alike. The calf came, and arched his back, and elevated his nine-inch tail, and pawed, and gave his venerable parent to understand, in the plainest terms, that he held himself in readiness to give him a terrible drubbing, if he had not already been sufficiently gratified. It was exasperating to see the young milk-sop imitate the actions of his seniors, while the poor old bull did not so much as look at him. But his calfship was inclined to push matters, and finally made a pass which placed his foolish head with a considerable thump against the old one's nose. He stood a moment with the air of having hurt himself a little, and ambled off to his mother.

The old one did not move, and seemed hardly to notice this babyish persecution. But I suspect it broke his heart. He wandered slowly down toward the sedge, limping and sorrowful; and I lay there, forgetful of the long army gun beside me, only regretting that there had been no one to bet with upon the result of the battle, or to stand boldly up and confirm this story afterwards. The sun rose high in the heavens, the wind veered, there was a sudden panic, and the vast multitude disappeared beyond the hills, leaving me to plod back to camp guiltless of blood,—the three coyotes looking after with familiar indifference,—and to muse meanwhile upon the problem of universal injustice and disaster, only to be accounted for by recounting to ourselves that ancient and somewhat diaphanous narrative of Eden, an apple, a woman, and the devil.

XVI.

CHICQUITA.

IF you stand upon a certain bluff, on the south side of the Arkansas river, a few miles above the mouth of the Purgatoire, in the earliest dawn of morning, you will be a witness of a scene not easily forgotten in future wanderings. Eastward stretches dimly away the winding, sedgy valley of the dreariest river of the west, treeless, sandy, desolate. All around you are the endless undulations of the wilderness. Beneath you are the yet silent camps of those who are here to-day and gone to-morrow. Westward is something you anticipate rather than see; vague and misty forms lying blue upon the horizon. But while the world is yet dark below and around you, and there is scarcely the faintest tinge of gray in the east, if you chance to look northward you will see something crimson high up against the sky. At first it is a roseate glow, shapeless and undefined. Then it becomes a cloud-castle, battlemented and inaccessible, draped in mist, and hung about with a waving curtain of changing purple. But as it grows whiter and clearer, the vague outlines of a mighty shape appear below it, stretching downward toward the dim plain. What you see is the lofty pinnacle that has gleamed first in the flying darkness, sun-kissed and glorified in the rosy mornings of all the cycles, the last to catch the fading light of all the days. It is Pike's Peak, ninety miles away.

Perchance before you turn to leave the spot, you may absently glance at your immediate surroundings. If you do, you will have before you at once the two great types of changelessness and frailty; for at your feet, scarce noticed in its lonely humility, is a single low mound, turfless and yellow, unmarked by even so much as a cross or an inscription, but nevertheless telling that old story which never needs an interpreter, that here rests another of the wanderers, and that there is no land so lonely that it has not its graves.

There may be a story more or less interesting connected with every one of the unmarked graves of the border. The rough lives that end here have all a history. But no one remembers it. Here, as in busy streets, the lives which, once ended, are deemed worthy of remembrance, are few and very far between. But this lone and wind-kissed mound upon the hill-top, albeit unmarked and seldom seen, has about it some slight interest not common to the rest; for it is the grave of a woman, and one of the strongest and most faithful of her sex. This is her story.

Years ago, a victim of the nomadic instinct named Lemuel Sims — a man who had first forsaken his home in the Missouri bottoms for a gold-hunting expedition to California, and after many changes, had again started eastward, — found himself stranded upon the inhospitable banks of the Arkansas, within the magic circle of protection around old Fort Lyon. Sims had grown middle-aged in wandering, and had consumed almost the last remains of that dogged persistence and energy in migration which is the characteristic of his class, by the time he had reached a spot than which it would have been hard to find one more entirely wanting in attractiveness. But he was not alone, for he had a wife who had been his companion in all his journeyings, and three daughters, who had irregularly come in upon his vicissitudes. In sending those guests who are often unwelcome, but are never turned away, it has been remarked that our fates are not always kind; and it is certain that the elder Sim's Penates had been especially inconsiderate. What he had needed was boys; boys to whom should come kindly the lot of the rancher, of the Indian fighter, the hunter, and the poker-player,—who should diligently follow in the footsteps of their wild predecessors, and live hard and die suddenly.

When Sims came to this, his last residence, the order of march was as follows: First, Sims, a hundred yards in advance, and across his shoulder the long rifle that now has a place in museums, but which has made a larger subordinate figure in American history than all the Winchesters and Sharps. Secondly, two mules and an old wagon, Mrs. Sims at the helm. Thirdly, three cows, some calves, and five dogs; and behind all, two freckled, brawny, barefoot girls. The third and youngest, the darling of the family,—too young, indeed, for service,—occupied a cosy nest among the household goods, and peeped out from beneath the dilapidated wagon-cover, plump, saucy, and childishly content. She had acquired the name of "Chuck," abbreviated from Chicquita, "little one;" and amid all the changes that befell her thereafter the name clung to her, regardless of its inappropriateness to such a woman.

The Sims "outfit" was only one of a cavalcade of such, strong enough for all purposes of society and defence. Months had passed since the family began this last move. The long summer days were gone, and the nipping nights and scanty pasturage were the cause of the premature ending of the journey. Having stopped only for a night, they had concluded to stay until spring, or some other time when a return of the migratory disease should seize them. But the rough house of cottonwood logs which Sims made, with the help of his family, was a sheltered nook which soon became home-like. There was game in abundance, and what was not immediately consumed the old man exchanged for groceries at the post. What was still more fortunate, Sims's house was near the route of travel, and he found he could indulge his love of gossip as well as furnish an occasional meal to travelers. When spring came, the stock had multiplied and grown fat. Impelled by the force of circumstances, unwonted industry was the order at Sims's. A small garden was inclosed, and it came about that by June the frontiersman and his family found themselves prospering beyond anything in their past history. The shanty took upon itself the dignity of a house— or, as it was more fittingly called in that country, a ranch. "Sims's" became known far and wide, and the proprietor began to think himself gaining upon the world both in money and respectability — two things which, in the present unfortunate condition of society, are not equally distributed. But this new era of prosperity was not due to Sims's management. It grew mainly out of the fact that he had three daughters. The unfortunate constitution of the family was the cause of its unwonted thrift. Any passably well-appearing white woman in such a place is an enticement not to be resisted by the average plainsman, and "Sims's gals" were celebrities over an extent of country half as large as the State of New York.

But as time passed, and the small herds increased, the females became objects of a still profounder interest. They were spoken of as heiresses. Nevertheless, at the pinch, no amount of money could have married either of the two eldest daughters. They were tall, gaunt, and angular. They were as ignorant as Eve, and had so long performed the duties which generally pertain to masculinity that either was a fair match for a cinnamon bear. Not so with the youngest. The most courtly and polished dames in the land seldom display so much in the way of personal beauty as this one rose among the thistles. Fair-skinned and blue-eyed, strong and graceful, petted from infancy and nurtured in comparative ease, healthful in sentiment as in body, she was the especial attraction, and came seldom in contact with the rough characters who frequented her father's house, and who were generally treated by her with the high disdain of a superior creature. And she had the mind of the family. Her opinions were the law of the house, and she occupied her autocratic position without embarrassment, and ruled without check. Old Sims was her confidential man-servant, and her mother was only her privileged associate and adviser. As for her big sisters, they continually rebelled, and always obeyed, though her caustic strictures upon their hoydenish behavior toward the male visitors at the ranch were unheeded. There is a mysterious law of primogeniture by which children embody the characteristics of distant ancestors, and completely ignoring the nearer family traits and circumstances, reproduce the vices and virtues that are long forgotten and the lineaments that have been dust for a century. There must have been some rare blood in the Sims ancestry, for this last scion of a race which had been subjected to all the influences of the frontier—hardship and toil in the Alleghanies, ague and laziness in the Missouri bottoms, and poverty always,—was totally unlike her family and her surroundings. The great feet, gaunt limbs, big brown hands, coarse complexions, and carroty hair, of her sisters and mother, were things they had apart from Chicquita. Nobody knew how she had really learned to read, or by what mysterious process she had become possessed of certain well-thumbed books and estray newspapers. No one ever inquired how her garments came to fit her round figure with a neatness that was a miracle to the uninitiated, or why the coils lay so neatly upon her shapely head. Finally the pervading force that directed all things in and around the ranch came to be almost unquestioned. A beauty with a will has always been a power in her immediate world;— a beauty with brains and a will is sometimes the most complete and powerful of despots.

The Sims family had now been five years in this locality — an unprecedented stay in one spot. Mainly through the ability of the youngest child, now a mature woman, aided by the circumstance of a fortunate location, they had acquired cattle, money and respectability. The money and the respectability were easily cared for, because Chicquita carried them both upon her person. But the herd which was gathered nightly into the corral was the lure of final destruction. The charmed circle which was drawn around the post was an uncertain and indefinite one, that might be near or far, according to the occasion; and the incursions of Apaches are governed by no conventionality. After long delay, and frequent smaller thefts, came the final raid that took all.

Old Sims and Chicquita started to go to the post. The presence of the latter was necessary to keep the former from getting drunk and falling into the hands of military minions, to be incarcerated in the post guard-house,— as, to say truth, had occurred to that convivial person before. In the perfect peacefulness and serenity of the early morning, it seemed impossible that death and ruin could lurk so near. As the old man dug his heels into the flanks of his mule, and Chicquita looked complacently back from her seat upon a pony only less wilful than his rider, the two little dreamed that it was the last time they were ever to see Sims's ranch.

As they threaded their way along the intricacies of the trail, Chicquita of course in the lead, the old man labored diligently to bring out the capacities of his mule, wherever the path was sufficiently wide to permit his riding beside his daughter. In truth, he had something to say to her concerning those matters in which girls are always interested and about which they are always unwilling to talk. A confidential conversation with his daughter was one of Sims's ungratified ambitions — a thing which in late years he had often attempted, and as often failed in accomplishing. She cared for him, was kind and loving enough, but seemed to have no ideas in common with him; and do what he would this morning, he could not keep pace with her. When two persons are thus together, there is often an unconscious idea of the thoughts of one in the mind of the other; and the girl, for this or for some other reason, kept constantly and persistently in the lead. But the subject was one that bore heavily upon the old man's mind, and, despairing of nearer approach, he presently called out from behind:

"Chuck!"

"Well, what is it?" came from the depths of the sun-bonnet in front.

"I want to know now, honest, which of them fellers which air one or 'tother on 'em allus around our house, you're goin' finally to take. It looks as though Sarey, bein' the oldest, shud hev some kind of a chance, — an' she did afore you growed up; but now it 'pears as though she'd hev to wait. Now, as atween them fellers. I'd like to know, an'" — plaintively — "'pears to me like I've a right to know, which uv 'em you're goin' to take. I couldn't be long a choosin' ef 'twas me. W'y, Tom Harris is big an' hansum, an' rides forty mile every week to git a sight on ye. I can tell from that feller's looks thet he'd swim the Arkansaw an' fight anything fur ye."

The face in the sun-bonnet grew red as a peony at the mention of the name; but the old man did not see that, and continued:

"But I'm mainly oneasy on account of there bein' two on 'em. When Tom an' the slick-lookin' feller from Maxwell's is there at the same time, they passes looks wich means everything that two sich fellers can do fur to win. I don't like 'tother feller, an' neither do the old woman. He'd do amost anything, in my opinion; an' ef you don't make choice atween 'em soon, them fellers 'll fight, an' that's *sartin*."

The face which had been rosy grew slightly pale as he talked. The old man had told his daughter nothing she did not already know, but she was startled to think that the hostility of the two men had been noticed by others. The question with her was not which one she would "take," as her father had expressed it, but how to rid herself of the disappointed one. Therefore, woman-like, she had encouraged neither of them. To her acute mind the affair had been a trouble for weeks, and the words of her father gave her new cause for disquiet.

Old Sims, having thus broken the ice, would have continued; but his daughter stopped him with an exclamation, and pointed to the sand at their feet. Sims approached and peered cautiously at the spot indicated by his companion. There they were, not an hour old, the ugly, inturned moccasin tracks of four, eight, a dozen Indians. In a woman, timidity and wit are often companions to each other, and Chicquita reined in her horse with a determined air. "I don't like that," said she; "I'm going back. It can do no harm if the herd is driven home, and I am going to see it done;" and she turned her horse.

"W'y, now," said Sims, "wat's the use? Sich things aint oncommon; come on."

"You can go on alone, if you think best," she answered.

Before he could reply, she was gone; and, irritated by what he considered a useless panic, he doggedly continued his journey toward the post. The sight of an Indian trail eight miles from home seemed a poor cause for fright, even in a woman, Sims thought, as he kept on his way. He fancied it was not that which had caused her to retreat; it was to avoid any further conversation upon the topic he had broached. "Cur'us critters is women," he profoundly remarked to himself, as he jogged on.

Sims spent that night, unconscious of all its horrors, happy-drunk in the post guard-house.

An apprehension that she could hardly understand filled the mind of the girl as she urged her pony toward home. Her father's words added to her excitement, and she thought of what Tom Harris, strong, daring, and handsome, would be at such a time. His tall figure, cheery face and handsome dress, as he sometimes sat upon his horse at her father's door, blithe and fresh after his ride of forty miles for her sake, came vividly before her. Even in the midst of her anxiety and nervousness, she felt that she and Tom, united in purpose and effort, could do anything in this world. Such were the strong woman's thoughts of the man she loved because he was even stronger than she.

Two miles from home, the rider's heart sank within her at the sight of a column of smoke on the verge of the familiar horizon. Frightened indeed now, she urged her pony to his utmost, and at the crest of the hill that overlooked her home, or the nook in which it had once stood, the truth burst upon her that while her father had talked to her of her lovers, and while she was yet speculating upon the footprints in the sand, the torch had been applied, and now herds, house, mother, and sisters were all gone.

It is not a romance, or a tale of hair breadth 'scapes, or a narration of the adventures of a second-class hero in a dime novel. It occurred then as it does now, every year upon the frontier. It was the burning of a home, and the murder and captivity of its occupants. One who desires to tell a marvellous story for the delight of the groundlings must find a more uncommon incident than this. It was to Chicquita a moment of conflicting grief and terror, with an overwhelming sense of utter loneliness and helplessness. The beautiful and subtle sense of woman may guide, but it can neither guard nor revenge. There seemed no help, and the girl wished in her heart she had gone with the rest. But she was not so entirely alone, for as she came nearer she saw the tall figure of Tom Harris, newly alighted from an all-night ride, standing beside his panting horse, so entirely occupied with a despairing contemplation of the smouldering ruins that he had not as yet noticed her approach. But when he quickly turned and recognized her, his grim face took color like a flash. In truth, Tom's paleness was not the paleness of fear. Words were inadequate to express the bitterness with which he had cursed the Apaches, as he stood looking at the burning house, and thinking with a pang that *she* was among the victims. But when he turned and saw her, all was thenceforth fair and serene to Tom Harris. With a frontiersman's quick perception of circumstances and situations of this kind, he understood, and asked no questions.

"The 'Paches are clear gone with everything, Miss," he said. "They must a' done it in ten minits. Come, light down now, wont ye? The pony's about done for, an' —W'y now Miss, 't aint no use a grievin'. Ye can't bring 'em back, an' ye can't catch the Injuns,— not to day. I'll be even with 'em if I live, but I've known a many such things in my time, an'—"

Tom stopped, for he had a sense of how tame and meaningless his rude efforts at comfort were to the silent and horror-stricken woman before him, whose whole mind seemed engrossed in a struggle with the calamity that had befallen her. The well-meaning fellow went away and waited some distance apart. And while he stood there the white despairing face grew still whiter, and she slipped helplessly from the pony, and lay a lifeless heap upon the ground. This was the time of the frontiersman's despair. In all his life's vicissitudes, there had been none like this. He knew nothing of what he ought to do in the case of a fainting fit, and was afraid to try. But he stripped the thick blankets from his horse and the pony, and hurriedly spread them in the shade by the bank side. Then he made a pillow of his saddle — a thing he had often done for himself; and with a redness that rose to his temples, and a thrill that went to his fingers' ends, he lifted the girl, and, strong as he was, fairly staggering under the burden, laid her upon the couch he had made. He took his own soft scrape, with its crimson stripes, and spread it for a covering, and filled his canteen and placed it near her, possibly with a question if she would ever drink from such a thing as that. Then he sat down afar off, and listlessly picked holes in the ground with his long knife, and whistled softly, and sighed within himself. Tom loved the woman who lay there, and because he loved her he was afraid she would die, and besides, was afraid of her, herself. Most men experience the same feeling once in their lives.

But there had been another and an unseen spectator of all this. We cannot tell by what peculiar conjunction of the planets things in this world fall out as they do, but while Tom was executing his plans of comfort for the girl, "the slick-lookin' feller from Maxwell's" was watching afar off. He came no nearer, because he did not at first understand the situation. The burning building suggested Indians, and he wished no nearer acquaintance with them, should they still be there. But while he looked, he saw and recognized those two, and a pang of jealousy entered his heart. Then he stayed at a distance because he desired to keep for future misrepresentation the circumstances of which he had been an unseen witness; and finally he rode away, baffled and puzzled, and pondering in his heart some scheme that could harm his formidable rival.

The afternoon passed slowly away, and still the anxious and unhappy Tom Harris kept watch. Occasionally he crept on tiptoe and looked at his charge. She seemed asleep. Finally he hobbled the two horses to prevent escape, gathered some of the vegetables that were left in the ruined garden, and stifled a strong man's hunger with young radishes, green tomatoes and oilless lettuce. He could afford to wait, for he was engaged in what he wondered to think was, in spite of all his anxiety and perplexity, the most delightful vigil of his life. He did not know that hours ago the occupant of the couch had opened her eyes, had touched the crimson-barred scrape, had seen the stalwart sentinel afar off, and had lain quiet, exhausted with anxiety, and perhaps oppressed by the somnolence of grief.

Through the long watches of the night the sleepless frontiersman paced back and forth, listening to the chatter of the coyote and the gray wolf's long drawn howl. He scared away the prowlers of the night, and listened and waited. Anon he crept close to the couch of the sleeper, and listened to her breathing, doubtful if she were not dead, then crept away again with the happy consciousness that Love and he had all the wilderness to themselves.

In the early morning he heard the clank of sabres and the hum of voices, and a troop of cavalry appeared from the post,—among them old Sims, red-eyed and trembling, but sobered by apprehension and grief. The man from Maxwell's had conveyed the news,—acting doubtless more from a sense of the delightfulness of the task of carrying ill tidings than from any sense of duty or desire to be of service. They left men and means for conveying the girl back to the post, and old Sims returned with her. It is but a mere unimportant episode, that she cast the glamour of her womanliness over the commandant's wife, and sat at her table an invited guest. That was the first lady Chicquita had ever seen; and to her, as the days passed, the story of the tall lover and his night watch, and all the girl's hopes and thoughts about him, became as an open page. And as for Tom Harris, the soldiers had given him something to eat, and he mounted his horse and accompanied them on the trail. His step was as light and his heart as merry as though he had slept in his bed; for as he looked back the last time the face he saw was sad and white, but the eyes were those of a woman who looks after one she loves and hopes to see again.

Frail of body now, but strong of purpose, the unconquerable spirit of Sims's daughter employed itself in directing the building of another house upon the spot that had been so long her home. In a month she and Sims were again established, in the little prairie nook, in a cabin not unlike the last, but surrounded by a palisade which bade defiance to Indian assault. The two were by no means poor; and while the old man drowned the past in half-drunken inanity, the dependants of the house did the work the two daughters had once done. Chicquita, stately and sad, but softened, seemed always to wait and watch for some one who never came, and of whom she never spoke. The troops with whom Tom Harris went away had long since returned. They reported a day's running fight, which was duly mentioned in general orders, but in which they had suffered no losses. If Tom had returned to his place, why did he not come again to Sims's ranch? So she used constantly to ask herself. And then there was his beautiful scrape; he might even come for that. But he did not. The man from Maxwell's came, and so placid was his reception that he straightway went away again. Yet he came again. The pale-faced woman had drooped a little, he thought, and had come to be a blue-veined and frail-looking creature, who seemed to care even less for his distinguished company than ever before. But even while she cooled his ardor with a grand dignity, she seemed listening for some footfall, waiting for some one who never came.

Poor girl; would she never know? Was it to be

like a wilderness poem of somebody waiting, waiting, while the years passed and until death came? There was one woman in all the world to whom she might go, and who knew or could discover where he was for whom she had watched so long, and who never came. Old Sims one day carried this tall frail daughter of his to the post. She was willing to talk with him now, only she said, whenever he came too near the forbidden subject, "You cannot understand, papa," and the old man would again relapse into a sad silence. He could not understand his daughter either. She was of an alien kind to him forever.

The commandant's wife kissed Chicquita, and looked unutterable things. It was come at last,— the task she dreaded, the tale she hoped to lighten as best she might. But the sad face touched her heart, and she wept, and weeping told it all. I do not know what passed between the worldly lady and her *protégée*, as the two sat together holding each other's hands, the one pale and cold, the other crying for sympathy and pity, her dainty shoulder offering a resting-place for a head whose bright coils shone in contrast to the wanness of her cheek. "My husband has always known," she said, "but he hoped you might — forget. We kept it from you, hoping that time would cure all. He was the only man to fall. He was foremost, and the soldiers thought he only went for amusement, and because he hated Indians. They buried him where he fell — they could not do otherwise; and I am sorry we did not tell you long ago. But we did not understand—

did not understand that you were so good and brave as you are. You do not know how much I wish he had never gone. He would have come back if he had lived, and he was very brave. We will all do anything for you that we can. If you will only stay with me for a while, and be petted and nursed, I should so like to have you. It is the saddest thing I have ever known, and you,— you are not like the rest."

Tom was dead. She must have known it before, she changed so slightly at the tidings. Perhaps she had only hoped against hope, having long ago known that the man whose stature she had measured as she lay through that summer night upon the couch he had made for her would have returned had he been alive. The sleeplessness of courage and honor was not for naught. It was the one memory of which she was proud, the one keepsake of him who would never come back. The love of a life in which it was the only glimpse of something brighter and happier was as much a reality as though it had been plighted a thousand times. Perhaps the ancestral courage and hope which had come to her through such degenerate veins helped her to die.

She crept to the bedside, whose topmost cover was a crimson-barred serape; but she never left it again. The bright strong face that had looked back at her in the saddle-leap a few weeks ago, was still hers. What wonder that, since he could not come to her,— to the house that, with a strong woman's fancy she had made for him to protect her in,— she should go to him? The sublimities of life are ever incomplete; the best hopes are hopes only. Her life must have a memory compared to which the realities of most are but tame.

It is but a camp-fire story, and time was when every soldier at the now abandoned post, whose broken walls impress the traveller with a new aspect of desolation as he passes by, knew the place of "Chicquita's Grave." But the years have passed, and now only the legend remains:—the legend and the lonesome mound, that serve at least to recall the almost forgotten truth that there is no land so far and silent that it has not its loves and its graves.

XVII.

ARMY MULES.

THERE is an important personage in military circles who seems not yet to have found a biographer. He has been used as a comparative, has been maligned by having a numerous class likened to him, and honored in the use of a thousand proverbs, maxims, and descriptive epithets. Yet he occupies the unusual position of one who cannot be dispensed with. The army mule has long since become a by-word, and his reputed "cheek" an American synonym. His service with the military is professional, and between him and his drivers there exists a certain well-understood sympathy and kinship. Mule-driving is a passion with a certain class, and the horse takes a place of comparative insignificance, as a creature fit only for the drawing of caissons and the carrying of cavalrymen. The commissary and quartermaster's departments, without which it would be impossible to live, are in charge of the mule. The government of the Republic is the largest mule owner in the world. The two matters of greatest importance in military affairs are, first, the health and efficiency of the men; and second, the condition of the mules.

Nevertheless, he is an outrage upon nature, a monstrosity, a combination of the donkey and the horse, with the qualities of neither and excelling both. He is the puzzle of the brutes, and stands alone in his nature and qualities, unapproachable in devilment, fathomless in cunning, born old in crime, of disreputable paternity and incapable of posterity, stolid, imperturbable, with no love for anything but the perpetration of tricks, no dexterity in aught save the flinging of his heels, no desire for anything but rations — stolen if possible and by preference — and no affection at all. Such is the mule.

Yet he is an animal who deserves a very different biography from any that so far any one has found it in his heart to write of him. There are men whom all mules hate, probably because of the existence of some rivalry between the two; who are ever the victims of one of those lightning blows which are wonders of dexterity and force, considered as coming from so clumsy a limb. These are they who have given our long-eared friend his reputation. The mule is an animal of character, — bad it may be, but still a defined though not a very well understood character. Many men have not that much to recommend them.

Everybody knows this anomaly in animalism, as they fancy very well indeed, unless it should be some far down-eastern young person, who may imagine him to be only a variety of the *genus asinus*. There was a returned soldier once who was accustomed to get himself pitied by enumerating among his hardships the item that he had been more than once obliged to subsist upon mule's milk. But, at least, we all know him by sight in the street. We have marked the queer, knowing, leery, sidelong glance of his eye at us as we passed by. We have seen the furtive agility with which the wisp of hay is stolen from the passing wagon, and the entire stolidity with which he stands asleep in the sun. The yearling mule is undoubtedly the incarnation and sum-total of quadrupedal deviltry. He is the originator of a distinct and uninterrupted series of grotesque diabolisms. With his scant and ungraceful tail tangled with whole acres of heterogeneous burs, and the long and faded hair upon his belly waving in the breeze, his fuzzy mane, scarce grown to any likeness of hair, sits upon him with the same air as do the whiskers of a shaveling country youth. He has in his movements a peculiar jog-trot, which in itself suggests careless and irredeemable depravity. It is the gait of one who steadily goes to the bad, but never quite gets there. At that age, the eyes are foxy and shrewd, and lack the look of deep sadness so often seen in those of his aged relative of the dray and jobbing-wagon. The little black hoofs are hard and polished, and, like those of the goat and chamois, especially fitted for clinging in slippery places. And those ears;—in all his kind they have ever refused to be hidden. Even as he stands thinking, against the sunny side of the barn, they are ever moving,—now backward, now forward, and in opposite ways. You can tell by these tokens almost the moment when an unusually malevolent idea is born within him. When they are laid fairly along his neck, his countenance is a demonstration of the truth of physiognomy. Mischief has then its incarnation. The clumsy limbs astonish you with sudden limberness, and fly high in the air with a rapidity that defies vision. Old, stiff, worn-out, the faculty of acrobatic kicking never leaves him, whatever else may befall his numb faculties.

Men whose labors in this life have taken the strange direction of mule-raising, are supposed to lead short lives and troublous ones. From infancy to age, there is no fence that will hold, no system that will train the creature into staid and respectable barn-yard habits. Place twenty of these youngsters at a long trough, feed them liberally with oats, and it will be more from luck than prudence if he whose duty it is to give them provender succeeds in getting out from among the shaggy conclave with less than twenty out of the forty hoofs having been flung in his face. Ere you can turn to look, the creature has meekly reversed his ears, and is industriously champing his provender, seeming mildly to wonder how you could ever have suspected *him*.

The very existence of the mule argues against the sagacity of his ancestor, the horse. Is there any more pitiful spectacle than a stalwart mare, whose ears are clean-cut and sharp, and whose veins stand out over her glossy skin, looking affectionately over her shoulder at the little dun-colored, fuzzy, impish monstrosity who tugs at her udders? One would think she would run away and abandon it to starve, —if, indeed, a young mule can be starved; or make it convenient to lie down upon it. But she never does, and it goes far to show how poor judges mothers are of their own children.

It has long been known that there is only one way in which a mule can be punished, and, strange to say, that is by imposing a strain upon his sensibilities. A mule by himself is the wretchedest of beasts. He may not be so very particular about its quality, but he must have company; companions to tease and torment, to bite and kick and steal from, and over whose backs he can rest his intelligent head to stare at the passers-by. Place him in a field over whose fence he cannot jump, and which he cannot break. I must be pardoned if I verge upon romance in this supposition,— and he will betake himself to the staid company of the unfrisky cows, or even to the pigs who are there with him, and proceed to bite *their* backs, and otherwise to interfere with their accustomed habits and bodily comfort. But he never forgets his relationship to his more respectable uncles and cousins once removed. He insists upon considering the horse his brother, and, as is well known, can only be coaxed along the high-way to market in peace by being enticed by an elderly gray mare, on whose neck there is a bell, and whom he will follow to the ends of the earth. On the other hand, he disdains his poor relations, the asses, and other mules, maintaining toward them a demeanor which no more becomes him than it does some of his imitators in a higher plane of existence. He will have naught to do with the thistle-eating fraternity, and will scarce recognize them even while undergoing his punishment of solitary confinement.

But all this superficial, and manifestly only one

side of the case. Since it is possible for some reader to say that this chapter is a kind of autobiography, and born of introspection, I will hasten to relate the other side of the story,—part of which is that this curious brute is probably the most useful of the dumb toilers whom man holds in perpetual slavery. His cool philosophy never forsakes him, in labors that no other animal has been found capable of performing. It is on the plains, and in the corrals of the far Southwest, that the mule and his master fully understand each other. These desolate lands, with their long and waterless roads, are the fields of his usefulness. The mule is there a popular and aristocratic beast. The weather-battered wagon-master of a government train knows intimately every animal of the two or three hundred of his herd. The teamster has a pet or characteristic name for each sleek creature of his team of six. He is with them day and night, and enjoys their society, and will steal corn for them much sooner than he would steal it for himself. He will empty his carefully-saved keg, and give each of his companions a hatful of water. A companionship springs up between the man and his mules that is little less than touching. They know him from afar, and he leads them anywhere, merely holding them by the chin.

Under such circumstances, the mule develops wonderfully. He is sedate, patient, tractable, handsome, proud of his bells and his occupation, altogether understanding his business better than any draught animal has done since the Conestoga days. The steady, daily, methodical work suits him. He grows actually fat upon it; and as the years pass, each mule gains for himself a reputation among the knowing ones. I knew a stall in that remote region where for fourteen years stood a sleek and dignified mule known through all the country as "Mole." The old girl had carried the successive commanders of the little post thousands of miles in the numberless scouting expeditions that had gone out thence. She had long been one of the personages of the place, and no one doubted that she knew more than the common run of soldiers, and that if she could have talked her opinions would have been valuable.

I remember another, an ugly little tangle-maned creature who wagged his long ears to a grotesque name that it is not necessary to mention. Too small for ordinary packing purposes, his business from time immemorial had been to carry the officer's mess. His ugly head had known no bridle for years. He was a *gamin* of his tribe. Kettles and pots and long-handled pans were hung and tied to every available projection upon his scrawny person. Countless efforts had been made to make him go hindermost of the long train of his brethren, where, according to rule, he really belonged. Suddenly, always in some particularly narrow place, he would perform that manœuvre known as a "*pasear*." Ducking his head, and whisking his scurvy tail, he would dash through the line from rear to front, and take his place, with all his unsightly appendages, beside the commandant, and in the very place of honor. A thrashing and a sending to the rear only enabled him to perform this pleasing feat the oftener.

Unconscious of personal ugliness, he considered himself the chief ornament to head-quarters. He was always there. He investigated the cookery, and looked after the bedding, and the commandant was usually awakened early in the morning by his fumbling in an investigatory sort of way in his hair. The last exploit of his which I recollect was that of walking in between the officer and the men one morning at guard-mount, two days after having been stolen by the Comanches;— a feat never before performed by man or mule.

It is long since conceded by those who know him that the army mule is the philosopher of the animal kingdom. Heretofore the owl and the raven have shared that reputation, to the unfair exclusion of all others. It is time that mere stupidity should be called by its proper name. The lack of generous spirit which is his notorious fault is the result of a shrewd calculation as to the amount of work he ought to be required to do. A very tired mule will stop in the road, and no amount of persuasion or force will induce him to go further. But his fibres are tough, and his endurance is wonderful, and he performs tasks of which no other animal in the service of man is capable. Ninety miles, a long day and night, he can go without water. Past midnight you will see each long-eared philosopher at his steady jog-trot, wagging his ears backward and forward, and pulling upon his bits. He knows the nature of the emergency as well as his driver does. The nostrils are dilated, the eyes have a distressed look, and the gaunt flanks throb. But there is no dragging, no complaint. On and on in the gloom and silence for you do not know or care how long, and suddenly the whole line sets up that peculiar cry which is not the voice of the horse, or of the ass, neither a mixture of the two. You may know the animal for years in civilization, and not hear it. It means the scent of water, perhaps yet miles away; and soon you can see upon the horizon the stunted trees which stand sparsely upon the banks of the stream which marks the end of the desert.

The carrying capacity of this creature is undoubtedly inherited from the disreputable side of his family, whose flabby sides, thin spines, and cattish hams, indicate anything but a remarkable ability to plod over hill and dale bearing burdens that weigh half as much as themselves. In the usual military operations of the border, wagons are never used. There are no roads, but in their stead steep mountain-sides, narrow passes, rocks, sand, and never so much as a path. It is mostly a country absolutely and irredeemably desolate and barren, and yet all who traverse it must eat. If there were game in any quantity, it could not be killed, for the noise of firearms would render useless all the hard toil of a scouting party.

The train that files out of a frontier post upon one of these scouting expeditions is a very grotesque procession, the whole idea of which is born of necessity in a mountain country, and which is totally unlike anything ever done during the great struggle that was our school of war. Accompanying a limited number of men, is a large number of mules, each one laden with his share of the absolute necessities of life; bread and bacon, coffee and cartridges. There is a master of the mules, whose services are as indispensable as those of the commanding officer. Each solemn beast, impressed with the gravity of his undertaking, follows in the footsteps of the brother who happens to be ahead of him, his huge load swaying from side to side, his long ears wagging, and his countenance taking day by day a deeper solemnity of expression. He does not stumble or wander, and wastes no energy in any kind of deviations; but he often lies down and dies with his load upon his back. His burden is distributed, his saddle thrown away, and he is left where he falls.

A mule's luxury is to roll — not one-sidedly and lazily, but in a regular tumble, accompanied by snorts, groans, and grunts. Every time his pack is removed, he is sure to engage in a general shaking up of his whole corporal system. The whole hundred or two will be at it at once. It comes before eating, drinking, or any other diversion. But the next thing is grass, if there be any, and if not, the nearest approach to it. Then, in the early morning, while yet the stars are shining, comes the reloading and the starting off again. Tired, lame, lean, galled, as he may be, he seldom shows any sign of resentment at the untimely renewal of his toil — a toil that is thankless and cruel, that knows no respite, and that is ended only by death.

There can scarcely be a recollection of a western camp-fire around which the mule is not a figure — sometimes, indeed, too much of one. Dapper Captain Jinks is not then himself—or, rather, he is his true self. It is the scantiest and most cheerless of little fires that is kindled to cook his bacon and boil his coffee. His pillow is a saddle or nothing, his mattress an old blue overcoat, and his covering a gray blanket. His clothes are those of a private, and his hat is the broad-brimmed slouch that is pulled low over his brows by day, worn all night, and used as a universal duster, castigator of insects, fire-persuader, and general *vade mecum*. Sometimes there is that variety of canopy known as a "dog-tent," hoisted upon improvised sticks to keep off the wind, or crawled under by Jinks in case of frost. It is, however, usually eaten by the mules at the beginning of the campaign, and philosophically done without for the remainder.

Here, while the always-thorny ground is covered with recumbent figures pell-mell around him, Jinks props his back against a rock, gazes thoughtfully into the coals, smokes, amuses himself with far-away thoughts, and tells stories. If one were by himself at a little distance, he would be struck by the strange incongruity of the hilarity that occasionally reaches his ears. Ragged sentinels stand sleepily upon the outskirts, not so much as vedettes against the enemy as guardians of the mules. Nevertheless, it would take but little to awake this military repose into great activity and surprising order. Where all was apparent confusion the evening before, at sunrise there is not a vestige left. They were here; they are gone. The long train has wound itself away among voiceless hills, intent upon some dim trail, or has turned suddenly into some unmapped pass, and has left nothing behind but some little heaps of gray ashes.

Sometimes, but in truth not often, the mountain Apache is actually traced to his hiding-place. He has been stalked for three weeks, and has been patiently crept upon while he and his belongings were lying safe in some inaccessible nook of the mountains. It is his hiding-place and storehouse after his last raid, an exploit but for which the military would have let him alone. He has had every advantage over his enemies. He knows the country as a citizen knows the streets of his town. He has made a flying raid upon the settlements, killed, burned, and carried captive. The same band has been in a dozen localities, and has gone here and there, stealing, killing, and waylaying, for the mere love of it. But somebody has gotten upon his trail, and the mules have been packed. It sometimes ends with the complete destruction of his *rancherea*, the destruction of all his winter's provender, the loss of some members of his family, and the great reduction of his fighting force.

It results, therefore, that while the above may seem a digression from the important subject under consideration, the army mule, with all his "cheek," is still the chief factor in all military operations on the frontier. His corral is the most interesting and important appurtenance of a military post, and his care is a thing of solicitude on the part of all concerned in the efficiency of the service. He was adopted in the place of the horse in the beginning, because he had a character, and from it he has never been known to diverge. It is not asserted that anyone quite understands him, or after many years of association with him is able to tell precisely what he might not take it into his long head to do. But he is faithful to his tyrant to the end and death. He will not leave the camp-fire or the wagon, though shelterless and unfed. Once away from his stall, and he persistently stays by his master, carrying him all day and standing beside his bed all night, looking his hunger with all the eloquence of his doleful face, and crying his peculiar note of distress at intervals frequent enough to accomplish his object of keeping his owner awake and sorry. His relative, the horse, has for ages been the especial pet of man, and has deserved to be. Yet there was never a plebeian mule, doomed from colthood to unremitting toil, who was not infinitely his superior in that peculiar knowledge that has never been classified, that "sense" that is neither memory nor mind, which is inadequately described by the term sagacity, which is not instinct, and which is a marked characteristic in all the long-eared and thistle-eating fraternity. He is docile and devilish, tricky and faithful, never requires to be broken and never *is* broken, is always in difficulty and is never injured, is reckless of any and all consequences and yet exceedingly cautious. He is awkward and clumsy in gait and appearance, and slow of foot, yet comes out fresh and vigorous at the end of journeys that wear his rider to illness and lameness. He is, taken all in all, a study in natural history that will never have a definite conclusion, a creature that is a sphinx, and yet a mule.

XVIII.

A LONESOME CHRISTIAN.

GRIMES was his name—"Old Grimes" he was called by the irreverent world that knew him well, and which doubtless he knew too in return, as a man knows something that has not been pleasant to him, and the pain and wickedness and hollowness of which have been forced upon him by a grim experience.

Grimes's name was the only thing about him that offered any poetic suggestion, and was not lightly passed or forgotten by those who saw him every day. The legend of that old man whose dirge has been sung these sixty years — whose coat was old, and gray, and buttoned down before, in every version of that irreverent elegy — is the common inheritance of all the English-speaking race, wherever they wander. The ragged urchins twanged it endlessly in his ears from behind the corners of shanties whenever his bent figure came in sight. Even the grown-up Texans, who lounged, gambled, and traded horses at the sutler's store, repeated it to him as a standing joke that could not be worn out. But he paid no attention or diverted the topic when he could, and hobbled away slowly, ever muttering to himself something that nobody heard or heeded. Had Grimes been a common man, he would have died of the torture of iteration, or have made shift, some fateful day, to have killed some one of his tormentors. It would have been quite to his credit, in the country in which he lived, to have done the latter. But he did neither. In truth, Grimes was not an ordinary person.

The residence of this song-tormented old person was a rough and canvas-covered shanty, situated by a rambling path in the midst of a congregation of such, some better, some worse. The place was known by the denizens of the neighboring post as "Slabtown." The open and unfinished quadrangle, and the square stone houses that had all a homeless and dreary look, were some half-mile away. Fort Concho was confessedly a hard place, all of it. Slabtown was its foster-child, filled with stranded emigrants, cattle-herders, gamblers, and men who had no occupation. Out toward the bleak northwest, Llano Estacado stretched its endless leagues of rock and cactus — the wildest land beneath the flag, governed and owned by the Comanche, and utterly useless and tenantless for all time, save for that Saxon savage almost as wild as he.

But Slabtown, straggling up from the little river's side, sat with its shanties under the lee of the post, fully confiding in its military neighbor. Here were privileged to come and remain through the windy Texas winter, all men, with a due proportion of women, whose tastes or whose occupations led them to the far verge of civilization. Thither came the cattle-man, and watched his wild herds on the neighboring hills, until returning greenness warned him off upon the California trail. Thither returned the man who had accomplished the wonderful journey, laden with fortunate gold. Bearded, broad-brimmed, and belted, here lounged a small army of guides and trailers, playing shrewd games at cards, drinking San Antonio whiskey, and at intervals shooting at each other. The gaunt and long-footed Texas girl, chalky, yellow-haired, and awkward, minced from cabin to cabin with neighborly gossip, and did her calico-and-green-ribbon shopping at the pine counters of the trader's stores. There were urchins many, coatless and shoeless from January to December, who were as the calves of this corral of humanity. Here, too, was that pink of the border, the dashing stage-driver, who, for forty dollars per month, every day ran the gauntlet through sixty miles of Indian-haunted desolation, and who, at the end of his "trick," rewarded himself with two days of dalliance with the belles of Slabtown, to whom, indeed, he was as the apple of their pale eyes.

And among these people lived Father Grimes, and these were they who sang the ancient ditty to him as he passed by. What his occupation was, nobody precisely knew or cared; but they "'lowed" he was "well-heeled," and "had a little tucked away somewhere." In the particular condition of society — or, rather, want of all society — that environed him, the inquiry into Grimes's business would hardly have gone so far as that, had it not been that his daughter occupied a conspicuous position as the prettiest girl at Concho, and was famous alike for the brilliancy of her cheeks and her dresses. She and Father Grimes lived alone, and it was scarcely thought of that at some former period a mother had been necessary in the usual course of nature. "Old Grimes and his gal" filled all the Grimes horizon, and there was no idea or feeling connected with them that had any further association.

It would be entirely in accordance with good taste if it were possible now to describe a dutiful daughter, entirely devoted to her aged father, and resenting the verbal indignities daily heaped upon him. But the facts, as somewhat dimly remembered, altogether forbid. Of all the old man's troubles, his daughter was probably the greatest. She was not gaunt and angular, like the other ladies of Slabtown as a rule; her cheeks were like peonies, and her round figure had a perceptible jellyish shaking as she walked. She disturbed her father's slumbers with hoydenish laughter, while the hours struck small in the night watches, and while her many admirers stayed and would not go. She was a coquette besides, and refused to comfort the paternal heart by assuming the hard duties of a Texan's wife. Sary Grimes was a wild girl, possibly not a bad creature, but, as it might have been expressed in an eastern village, "liable to be talked about"— one of the social punishments not much dreaded, however, in the region of Fort Concho. There was, I fear, a consciousness in her face whenever she passed a man in the road, and it is equally to be feared that her prudent chastity had but little suggestion of snow or crystal in it. But as the belle of Slabtown, she reigned supreme; and, of course, the greater part of her female friends cast aspersions upon her. She kept all her admirers in a state of mind which had in it much torment, with occasional glimpses of beatitude. Charles Hanks, Esq., stage driver, started out upon his trip with a large fortune of happy thoughts, and discussed the object nearest his heart with the box-passenger for twenty miles at once. But when he returned, Sary would no more speak to him than if, as he complained, he "had been a yaller dog." But Mr. Hanks had no special cause of complaint, for he fared as all his contemporaneous rivals did.

Father Grimes's reputation was that he was "allus good to that gal o' his'n." He was never known on any occasion to use a petulant expression to any person or thing. His peculiarity more often remarked than any other was that he did not swear. It was a wonder he did not, for nobody doubted that he had a hard life of it. With regard to Grimes, the half has not been told. We have seen men who had survived some great disaster, some horrible mangling, and went crawling through life thereafter, lame, scarred, deformed, the hideous semblance of a human creature. Such was this poor, rich old man. His limbs were drawn awry. His shapeless hands almost refused to grasp his staff, and every line of his face denoted an experience of pain, happily past for the time, but ever leaving a grim promise to return and wring the distorted limbs anew, until the hour of his relief. Yet Grimes had not been the victim of any sudden accident or great calamity. Fire, nor falling walls, nor the rebellion of man's gigantic servant against his master in rushing steam and falling fragments, were incidents in his hard life. And yet his fate had been little better. His days had been days of pain, and his nights had been spent in torture, and in waiting and praying for daylight or death. It is common enough, but Ariel, bright spirit of enchanted air, suffered and groaned no more in the cloven pine than a strong man may beneath rheumatic torture.

Thus it was that the old man's gentleness was a marvel to those who reviled him daily. Worn and deformed with his battle of years with his enemy, he sat at his cabin door in the sun, and placidly nodded at those who passed by, and whispered to himself, and smiled. Sometimes he had been asked if it had not hurt him while in slow torment his limbs had been twisted and drawn thus. "Oh yes," he said, "it did hurt," but he smiled as he thus answered a question which would have been both superfluous and cruel if the old man had not seemed to possess some panacea that enabled him to almost defy pain.

This distorted figure, this pain-written face, and these strange ways, Father Grimes possessed alone. They were strange in the land, for sturdy, bearded manhood, reckless ways, loud words and a blood-curdling blasphemy were the rule with his associates and near neighbors. While they knew that he had within him something which they neither possesed nor understood, they only said "curus creetur," and passed on. Whatever it was they had no respect for it; they thought him a little crazy. He had done strange things that they knew of. Had he not once tried to interfere with a very promising horse-race on a Sunday? Did he not come down to the trader's store one night last fall, and lift up his quavering voice in a Methodist hymn, and try to get up a prayer-meeting right there among the boys, "and a hundred dollars in the pot, and me with three queens in my hand?" It was Charles Hanks, Esq., who described this scene, and added, "He's a old fool with a stavin' purty gal; 'twas just that wich saved his meat,—a interferin' thataway."

It was not strange that, with these queer ways, Father Grimes was alone in such a place, with only his heart to keep him company. There was a chaplain at the post, but he seemed as yet to have discovered no affinity for this eccentric old man. He preferred soldiers of the cross of more robust tendencies, and in line. If being a Christian was what was the matter with Grimes's dazed head, he had an entire monopoly of the complaint. On bright Sunday mornings there was a formal service on the parade ground, and plumed heads bowed slightly in the etiquette of military devotion. But Father Grimes was as much out of place there as he was at the sutler's, and stood afar off, failing to understand, perhaps, what all this had in common with a camp-meeting in far western Virginia, or with such piety and worship as would have been acceptable to his fellow-believers of the United Brethren in Christ.

Of course he had little control of the hoydenish Sary. That young woman shared somewhat in the current belief regarding her father's mental condition. Living in the same house, they had no companionship; and while she cared for his common wants and daily meals, that was the extent, to all appearance, of her interest in him. He perhaps constituted the sober side of her life; she would have been ready to do battle for him with a ready tongue, but she also claimed the privelege of privately regarding him with as much carelessness and half-contempt as was possible with her knowledge of the fact that he really was her father and she could not help it.

The incident which placed Father Grimes prominently before the public in a new light — an incident all the more remarkable because it was the last in his career — came about in this wise. There came to Concho a long-haired and ambrosial man, who claimed to have been one of those hard riders from the Lone-Star state, who figured so extensively in the cavalry force of the late Confederate army. He was broad-shouldered, tall, swaggering, of a military carriage, and claimed to be "still a rebel and a fighting man, sir." Now Hanks was not just a Yankee, but he and this child of chivalry soon found means of disagreement upon another matter. The Confederate used often to say that he did not care a profane expletive for Miss Grimes, but he made it a point to allow no man to stand before him in the graces of a livin' woman, sir. So, in a few weeks, Hanks and he looked askance at each other, and finally refused to play poker at the same table, and avoided a mutuality in bibulous exercises by common consent. The wicked Sary, gifted with peculiar insight into such matters, flattered the new beau, and smiled upon him with beams particularly bright; albeit, she divided her favors, and gave Hanks enough to keep him alive to the stature and strength of his rival, and the dangers arising from delay and absence. These things did not pass unnoticed by the others, and a keen look-out was kept for the hour when the difficulty should culminate. The patient sitters upon benches and the industrious carvers of deal boxes kept the two men in sight, and watched them with an eye to being present when the time came. They discussed the chances among themselves, much as they discussed the projected race for three hundred yards between Hopkins's bald-face and the spotted pony. They knew Hanks, and generally considered him the better man. There was a slight inclination to prejudice against the Confederate, perhaps. "He's full o' brag," they remarked; "hain't seen his *grit* yet."

One night Father Grimes sat in the inner room of his poor house. The cotton cloth that did duty as glass, puffed in and out in the window frame, and the "grease-dip" burned yellow and dim on the edge of its broken cup. There was the usual chatter and coarse laughter in the outer room, and he knew that the Confederate and Sary were there. This gallant gentleman was in his best mood that night, and the laughter of the girl, and the man's tone of light raillery, reached Grimes's wakeful ears with annoying distinctness. The old man sat in his bent posture near the light, and studied out the words of a big worn volume upon his knee. His grizzled hair lay in tangled confusion upon his neck, and as he stumbled through the sentences he spelled and whispered the words to himself. The night was his enemy and torment. He was passing the dull time of age and affliction, and, withal, gathering comfort from the only book he possessed or needed. It was no common book he pored over and spelled; it is said to have been the Bible.

Presently the outer door opened, and with a gruff salutation Hanks entered. His arrival from his last drive could not have been more than an hour ago. He had not wasted time in paying his respects. He sat down at the rude table, and looked at Sary and her companion. That Hanks was in an ugly humor was quite evident. It was equally evident that he was bent upon the operation known among his kind as "pickin' a fuss." He did not attempt to conceal his feelings, and glowered at his rival, and still sat silent. The dark purpose of the border rowdy was in his eye and the jealousy and anger of all his lawless kind was apparent in the studied deliberateness of all his actions. The other looked at him with a cool grin of defiance. At a meeting of this kind, two such men have little need of tongues.

Presently the late-comer rose slowly, and moved his chair, and sat down almost in front of his rival. The old man in the inner room heard the movement, and started and listened, closing his book. Having thus changed his position, Hanks placed his hands upon his knees, looked his rival obtrusively in the face, and calmly remarked:

"I shouldn't wonder, Mister, ef I thought you was a low down kind of a cuss."

"What?" exclaimed the Confederate.

"I say — are ye list'nin'? — that I shouldn't wonder ef I thought you was a low down sneakin' —"

The Confederate gentleman arose, motioned to Hanks, and moved toward the door. They both went out, moved a little way along the wall toward the old man's flapping window, and stopped.

"I don't do my fightin' in the presence o' wimmen," said the Confederate, "but I'm a fightin' man, an' ye kin hev all ye're spilin' for. There's no use in bein' in a ungentlemanly hurry about this 'ere little diffikilty; to-morrer mornin', — break o' day, sharp, at the sand-bar beyant Stokes's, 'll suit me, ef *you* kin stand it."

"Wot's yer weepins," said the other.

"Navy size — ten paces."

"Seconds?"

"Nary man."

"I'll be thar;" and Old Grimes heard the footsteps die away in opposite directions.

He hobbled into the room where his daughter sat. Her pinky cheeks were a little paler, and there was an unwonted apprehension in her eyes. "Sary," he said, "kin ye do nothin' to keep them two young fellers apart?"

"No, they're two fools, an' it's none of my affair."

"Did ye hear what they said outside?"

"Yes, I heard; I was list'nin'; they kin fight it out. There's better men than either of 'em."

Grimes turned and went back to his little bare room — the little bare and shabby place where the company who came and sat with him were not inhabitants of Slabtown,— and seated himself upon the bed, and communed with himself. It is a strange life, and a wonderful education, that can teach a red-cheeked and hoydenish girl to smile at the passions that lead to the grim revenges of the border. The old man sat and thought, and the hours passed slowly. He lay down upon the rude bed, and perhaps would have slept if he could. Then he rose and occupied himself in reading again, and went out often and looked into the shadows of the still night. Only the far guard-challenge fell upon his ear at intervals, and seemed to announce the passing hours. Finally the ripe stars that glow in the noon of night began to pale in their westward setting. The cocks crew, and the lowing of kine was borne far upon the damp morning air. The day was coming, and even these far fields of solitude and desolation began to be stirred by a feeble pulse of life.

No soul, save these two men, a thoughtless woman, and an old man almost helpless, knew of the meeting on the sands, from which but one, and probably neither, would ever return. Father Grimes got his hat and staff, and hobbled forth. He thought he knew the spot, he would go thither. It was such a journey as he had not made for many a day. He wondered if he would be there in time, and hastened.

The chill air of dawn pierced his frail body, and he shivered. Painfully, and all too slowly, he walked the stepping-stones across the puny torrent, and toiled up the bank upon the other side. He saw the gray streaks in the east, and hastened, groaning, for he remembered the words "at break o' day, sharp." His journey was a pathless one, cactus-grown and tangled with long grass. Finally he reached the crest of the low bluffs, and the little acre of brown sand lay before him in the growing light. Peering with his old eyes, he discovered two figures there. One of them stood listless, while the other paced slowly across a little space; then his companion measured the space likewise, in long and swinging strides. As the old man drew nearer, he saw that the two took opposite places, and that while one leaned forward anxiously, the other's attitude was careless and his weapon hand hung by his side. He shouted with the utmost strength of his old wiry voice, and they seemed to pay no heed. Then, and for the first time in ten years, he tried to run. As he drew closer, he saw that Hanks was nearest to him, and almost between him and the tall Confederate. Then one said "*Ready*," and his adversary answered "Ready." But Grimes noticed that Hanks held his weapon in readiness to fire, while the other brought his slowly up from his side.

The thought must have passed through his mind like a flash; "If I could but push one of them aside, I could save them." But already they had begun to count, slowly and simultaneously: "*one—two—*" and at the word "*two*," Hanks dropped suddenly in his place, and two shots awoke the silence almost together. The tall Confederate stood still a moment, then staggered, and fell backward, while a crimson stream trickled slowly out upon the brown sand, and sank, leaving the stain of murder beside his stark figure, as he lay, with open, staring dead eyes, looking at the glowing sky.

Hanks had dropped suddenly in his place, and had fired before the word. It was the trick that almost disgraces the Comanche from whom he had in a manner acquired it. He now rose up and looked around him furtively. In the sunshine of high noon it was a dreary and silent spot; and now in the purple morning, with the dead man lying as he had fallen, with the brown sand, and the sage, and the gaunt and thorny cactus on every hand, Hanks seemed to shiver, as he buttoned his coat, and looked nervously about him, and stood a moment thinking. Then, by chance or through fear, he cast a glance behind him, and saw Father Grimes sunk down in a heap with his head fallen forward upon his bosom. Perhaps he thought the old man dead; — at least he had caught the bullet meant for himself. He hesitated a moment, looked around the horizon, and then moved by sudden fear, walked rapidly away through the stunted trees beyond the sand. This tale chronicles no further the wanderings of the assassin: he never returned.

Father Grimes slowly raised his head by and by, pressed his hand to his side, and tried to rise. After a while they came and bore him to his cabin, and placed him upon his bed. For ill news travels quickly, and the curiosity of the hard community had quickly hurried a crowd to the spot. While he lay quietly and looked upward through the cabin roof, calm and placid, the post surgeon came, and the commandant, and even the chaplain, and the crowd gathered at the outer door, only parting to permit the passage of another burden that was borne there by chance or a fancied connection with Grimes and his daughter, and laid upon a low bench beside the wall, crying murder through the hush with its white, uncovered face.

They questioned the old man, and brokenly and at intervals he told them all he knew. No, not all; for his mind seemed preoccupied, and at intervals he stopped and lay very quiet, looking at something they could not see, and smiling as he feebly held out his hand. His care-worn and pain-burdened life was passing fast. That they knew, and were awed in the presence of that Death so many of them had courted, so many had pretended to scorn. They watched him, and waited to hear if he had aught else to tell. A little while passed in silence. Suddenly he opened his eyes again, and looked intently toward a corner of the room. It was not a look of scrutiny, doubt, or inquiry, but of happy certainty and surprise. A faint flush stole into the pallor of his old face; his eye brightened, and he stretched forth his hand and tried to lift himself upon his arm. The doctor bent over him (the chaplain was gone home again), and asked him what he would have. The old man turned with a look of surprise, and pointed with his finger.

"Don't you see Him?" he said.

"I see no one;—what is he like?"

"I—I don't know. His face shines, and He

smiles. It is like Him as He walked upon the sea.
. . . . Oh, Master, have you come so far for
me?"

And death sealed upon the scarred and wrinkled face its last beatitude. They went out and left him there, and closed the door. And as they passed through the outer chamber, they saw the girl as she sat by the bench beside the wall, and looked with tearless eyes afar off, and held in her lap her dead lover's cold right hand.

www.ingramcontent.com/pod-product-compliance
Lightning Source LLC
Chambersburg PA
CBHW021206230426
43667CB00006B/578